OECD Studies on Water

Managing the Water-Energy-Land-Food Nexus in Korea

POLICIES AND GOVERNANCE OPTIONS

OECD
BETTER POLICIES FOR BETTER LIVES

Please cite this publication as:
OECD (2018), *Managing the Water-Energy-Land-Food Nexus in Korea: Policies and Governance Options*, OECD Studies on Water, OECD Publishing, Paris.
https://doi.org/10.1787/9789264306523-en

ISBN 978-92-64-30651-6 (print)
ISBN 978-92-64-30652-3 (pdf)

Series: OECD Studies on Water
ISSN 2224-5073 (print)
ISSN 2224-5081 (online)

Photo credits: Cover © JIPEN

Corrigenda to OECD publications may be found on line at: *www.oecd.org/publishing/corrigenda*.

Foreword

The OECD is committed to supporting governments in their efforts to reform policies that influence the availability, use and management of water. OECD National Policy Dialogues on Water, which are demand-driven from OECD member and non-member countries, are designed to help set the water agenda and facilitate ambitious policy reform by:

- Engaging in a constructive and collaborative conversation with stakeholders to identify the key issues and potential ways forward.
- Providing clear options for reform, building on international good practice and a robust analysis of options in the country.
- Establishing a realistic action plan, grounded in policy discussions with a wide range of stakeholders.
- Initiating momentum for change that derives from political buy-in acquired in the consultation process.

OECD National Policy Dialogues on Water have been undertaken in a range of countries focussing on various elements of water policy reform, including financing and pricing, governance, allocation, water security and private sector participation.

This National Policy Dialogue focused on the opportunities and challenges related to managing the water-energy-land-food nexus in Korea. It led to policy recommendations and governance arrangements that can improve the management of the nexus, now and in the future. Water insecurity is often the main bottleneck in the WELF nexus which may limit economic growth across sectors, and impact human wellbeing and ecosystem health. Korea has engaged with the OECD via a national policy dialogue to explore best practices from the wider international community to better manage the WELF nexus at national and basin scales. This dialogue followed a similar effort in 2017 led by the Ministry of Land, Infrastructure and Transport and K-water on economic instruments for water management in Korea.

The process was coordinated by the Korean Ministry of Environment, with engagement from other ministries, including the Ministry of Land, Infrastructure and Transport, Ministry of Agriculture, Food and Rural Affairs, Ministry of Strategy and Finance, Ministry of the Interior, Ministry of Trade, Industry and Energy, Ministry of Public Safety and Security, and the Office for Government Policy Coordination. The process also involved a variety of stakeholders, from other administrations, civil society organisations and academia. The OECD Council Recommendation on Water, unanimously adopted by all member states in December 2016, proved to be a valuable reference to guide discussions and ways forward.

The report is structured into four chapters:

- Chapter 1. *Characterising the Water-Energy-Land-Food Nexus in Korea.* This chapter discusses the key pressures on the nexus – now and in the future – and the capacity of policies and governance arrangements to respond.
- Chapter 2. *Managing water for the Water-Energy-Land-Food nexus in Korea.* This chapter reviews policies and institutional arrangements to manage water quantity and quality in Korea.
- Chapter 3. *Towards policy coherence and sustainable management of the Water-Energy-Land-Food nexus in Korea.* This chapter provides a rationale for improved planning against future water-related risks, independent regulation and other policy instruments to support the sustainable management of the WELF nexus.
- Chapter 4. *Towards effective water governance for the sustainable management of the Water-Energy-Land-Food nexus in Korea.* This chapter reviews current water governance arrangements in Korea and provides ways forward to advance basin-level governance and stakeholder engagement.

The Assessment and Recommendations present the main findings and set out recommendations and an Action Plan to help Korea make further progress towards aligning water policies, practices and governance arrangements for sustainable management of the WELF nexus.

The report takes stock of the insightful dialogue that took place between the OECD Secretariat and Korean stakeholders over 18 months, in particular, during a fact-finding mission (11-15 December 2017) and a policy seminar (9-10 May 2018). The report reflects comments and suggestions received at the meetings and on earlier drafts.

The process illustrates the mutual benefit of OECD National Policy Dialogues on Water, for the country, the OECD Secretariat and all OECD members; we all benefit from sharing international good practices and discussing in detail the practical challenges related to adjustment to national circumstances. This confirms the role of the OECD as a platform that can facilitate national and international initiatives that contribute to sustainable growth.

Acknowledgements

The OECD is indebted to the government of the Republic of Korea, and in particular the Ministry of the Environment, for their co-operation in providing information, for the organisation of the fact-finding mission and the policy seminar, and for facilitating a dialogue with contacts both inside and outside of the government. In particular, Giwon Seo was instrumental in coordinating the process and the contributions from various departments. Dr. Ik-Jae Kim, from the Korean Environmental Institute provided valuable and substantive inputs.

The national policy dialogue was coordinated by Hannah Leckie of the OECD Environment Directorate, under the guidance of Xavier Leflaive, Water Team Leader. The authors of this report were Hannah Leckie, Håkan Tropp of the OECD Centre for Entrepreneurship, SMEs, Regions and Cities, and Ian Barker of Water Policy International. The authors are grateful to Hervé Gilliard of Agence de l'Eau Loire Bretagne, France and Guillaume Gruère of the OECD Trade and Agriculture Directorate, who provided valuable and concrete insights, both in writing and during policy discussions in Korea. Editorial support from Janine Treves and administrative support from Anna Rourke are also gratefully acknowledged.

The OECD Environment Policy Committee and the Working Party on Biodiversity, Water and Ecosystems were consulted and agreed to declassify the report. The government of Korea have approved the Assessment and Recommendations and the Action Plan.

Table of contents

Tables

Figures

Boxes

Acronyms and abbreviations

EIA	Environmental Impact Assessment
GDP	Gross Domestic Product
K-water	Korea Water Resources Corporation
KECO	Korea Environment Corporation
KEI	Korean Environment Institute
KHNP	Korea Hydro & Nuclear Power Corporation
KICT	Korea Institute of civil Engineering
Korea	The Republic of Korea (South Korea)
KRC	Korea Rural Community Corporation
KRIHS	Korea Research Institute for Human Settlements
KRW	Korean Republic Won
KWI	Korea Waterworks Management Institute
LID	Low impact development
MAFRA	Ministry of Agriculture, Food and Rural Affairs
ME	Ministry of Environment
MoI	Ministry of the Interior
MoLIT	Ministry of Land, Infrastructure and Transport
MoSF	Ministry of Strategy and Finance
MoTIE	Ministry of Trade, Industry and Energy
MPSS	Ministry of Public Safety and Security
NDMI	National Disaster Management Research Institute
NGO	Non-Governmental Organisation
NIER	National Institute of Environment Research
PMO	Prime Minister's Office
RBC	River Basin Committee
RMC	River Management Committee
RMF	River Management Fund
Korean TMDL	Korean Total Water Pollution Load Control System
WELF	Water-Energy-Land-Food

Basic Statistics of the Republic of Korea

(2015 or latest available year*; OECD total values in parentheses)[a]

PEOPLE AND SOCIETY					
Population (million)	50.6	(1 274)	Population density per km²	504.7	(35.1)
Share of population by type of region:			Population compound annual growth rate, latest 5 years	0.5	(0.6)
Predominantly urban (%)	69.6	(48.7)	Income inequality (Gini coefficient)	0.31	(0.32)
Intermediate (%)	13.1	(26.0)	Poverty rate (% of population with less than 50% med.income)	14.6	(11.3)
Rural (%)	17.2	(25.3)	Life expectancy	82.2	(80.6)
ECONOMY AND EXTERNAL ACCOUNTS					
Total GDP (billion KRW)	1485 078		Imports of goods and services (% of GDP)	38.9	(29.2)
Total GDP (billion USD current PPPs)	1 749	(51 165)	Main exports (% of total merchandise exports)		
GDP compound annual real growth rate, latest 5 years	3.0	(1.9)	Electrical machinery and equipment and parts thereof	26.3	
GDP per capita (1 000 USD current PPPs)	34.5	(40.1)	Vehicles other than railway or tramway rolling stock, and parts and accessories thereof	13.1	
Value added shares (%)			Nuclear reactors, boilers, machinery and mechanical appliances; parts thereof	11.8	
Agriculture	2.1	(1.7)	Main imports (% of total merchandise imports)		
Industry including construction	34.9	(23.1)	Mineral fuels, mineral oils and products of their distillation; bituminous substances; mineral waxes	23.7	
Services	63.0	(75.2)	Electrical machinery and equipment and parts thereof	17.8	
Exports of goods and services (% of GDP)	45.9	(29.0)	Nuclear reactors, boilers, machinery and mechanical appliances; parts thereof	10.0	
GENERAL GOVERNMENT as percentage of GDP					
Expenditure	32.0	(44.4)	Education expenditure	5.2	(5.4)
Revenue	33.2	(42.4)	Health expenditure	3.9	(6.5)
Gross financial debt	43.7	(86.5)	Environment protection expenditure	0.8	(0.8)
Fiscal balance	1.3	-(2.0)	Environmental taxes: (% of GDP)	2.5	(1.6)
			(% of total tax revenue)	10.3	(5.1)
LABOUR MARKET, SKILLS AND INNOVATION					
Unemployment rate (% of civilian labour force)	3.5	(7.9)	Patent applications in environment-related technologies (% of all technologies, average of latest 3 years)[b]	11.0	(12.0)
Tertiary educational attainment of 25- to 64-year-olds (%)	44.6	(34.5)	Environmental management	2.5	(4.5)
Gross expenditure on R&D (% of GDP)	4.3	(2.4)	Water-related adaptation technologies	0.1	(0.4)
			Climate change mitigation technologies	9.7	(9.8)
ENVIRONMENT					
Energy intensity: TPES per capita (toe/cap.)	5.5	(4.1)	Road vehicle stock (veh./100 inhabitants)	39.9	(58.9)
TPES per GDP (toe/1 000 USD, 2010 PPPs)	0.16	(0.11)	Water stress (abstraction as % of available resources)		(9.7)
Renewables (% of TPES)	1.5	(9.6)	Water abstraction per capita (m³/cap./year)		(819)
Carbon intensity (energy-related CO_2):			Municipal waste per capita (kg/capita)	361	(516)
per capita (t/cap.)	11.2	(9.4)	Material productivity (USD, 2010 PPPs/DMC, kg)	2.2	(1.7)
per GDP (t/1 000 USD, 2010 PPPs)	0.33	(0.26)	Land area (1 000 km²)	97	(34 341)
GHG intensity[c]			% of arable land and permanent crops	17.6	(12.1)
per capita (t/cap.)	13.8	(12.4)	% of permanent meadows and pastures	0.6	(23.2)
per GDP (t/1 000 USD, 2010 PPPs)	0.42	(0.34)	% of forest area	63.6	(31.2)
Mean population exposure to air pollution ($PM_{2.5}$), µg/m³	28.8	(14.0)	% of other land (built-up and other land)	18.2	(33.5)

Notes: * Values earlier than 2010 are not taken into consideration.
a) OECD value = Where the OECD aggregate is not provided in the source database, a simple OECD average of the latest available data is calculated where data exist for a significant number of countries.
b) Higher-value inventions that have sought patent protection in at least two jurisdictions. Average of latest three years.
c) Excluding emissions/removals from land use, land-use change and forestry.
Source: Calculations based on data extracted from databases of the OECD, IEA, Eurostat.

Executive Summary

The Republic of Korea (hereafter simply referred to as Korea) is the eighth-largest OECD economy and has been one of the fastest growing OECD economies over the past decade, driven by a large export-oriented manufacturing sector. However, urbanisation, industrialisation and population growth (at least until 2030) are increasing energy and food demands, which in turn, are exacerbating pressure on Korea's scarce natural resources and ecosystems, including water and land. These pressures and others raise the stakes on how to allocate and re-allocate water and land resource uses across the water-energy-land-food (WELF) nexus for sustainable growth.

Korea faces a number of systemic threats to the water-energy-land-food-nexus, now and in the future

Water insecurity is often the main bottleneck in the WELF nexus which may limit economic growth across sectors, and affect human wellbeing and ecosystem health. Korea's population density and water scarcity are both the highest in the OECD. Climate change, steep topography and increasing urbanisation increase the risk of water scarcity and flooding, and limit opportunities to generate energy from hydropower. An ageing population and recent slow-down in economic growth will limit available public funding for responding to increasing droughts and floods, including investment in climate resilient infrastructure. Furthermore, environmental taxes and charge rates on water abstraction and pollution, and land development are too low to compensate for the environmental and social costs of the mismanagement of water and land, or to encourage pollution reduction and efficient use of water and land resources.

Water resources in river basins are fully, or close to fully, allocated, meaning that new water allocations are not possible without some combination of water use efficiency and supply augmentation. Despite impressive improvement in wastewater treatment, diffuse pollution (predominantly from livestock and urban run-off) increasingly affects scarce water resources.

Korea's advanced water infrastructure network could be made more effective and efficient

Korea has made the transition from an expansionary water economy to a mature water economy. The expansionary phase was characterised by engineering and technological interventions to expand water supplies, often at the expense of the environment. Now in the mature phase, Korea recognises that the interdependencies among water users (cities, industry, agriculture and ecosystems), can be addressed by a combination of water supply augmentation, water use efficiency and water conservation.

Demand-side interventions, options for water reallocations and pollution reductions, and further development of context-specific policy and institutional arrangements need to be developed as competition and pressures on water escalate. The methods for evaluating the choice and implementation of interventions also need to adjust, including anticipating and planning against future risks, reflecting basin-specific issues and institutional contexts, and valuing water and ecosystem services.

A long-term vision is necessary for the transition towards sustainable and resilient management of water within the water-energy-food-nexus

Traditional assumptions about the reliability of a rainy season and the certainty of reservoirs refilling each year, or the magnitude of floods, are likely to be misplaced under a changing climate and increasing development pressures on water and land. Korea would benefit from a long-term vision and plan, to deal with existing problems as well as anticipating and planning against future water risks. Improvements in water quantity and quality monitoring, economic analysis of policy measures, and the incorporation of climate change and socio-economic scenarios would assist in the development of such a plan. A critical element of planning is the assessment of water supplies and cities against a range of shocks, both natural and human. Addressing the nexus sustainably requires Korean policy makers to consider: (i) equity issues related to the allocation of risks and opportunities; (ii) creating more with less, and allocating scarce resources where they add value to society; and (iii) investing to sustain ecosystem services.

Economic instruments would help to manage demand for water, incentivise reductions in water pollution and alleviate pressure on the nexus

Korea has introduced some economic instruments for water management, but there is significant scope for expanding their use. There are ample opportunities for Korea to increase water use efficiency (including reductions in leakage and non-revenue water) and strengthen demand management, to minimise future investment needs in water infrastructure to augment supply and to reallocate water where it creates most value to society. Well-designed water pollution and abstraction charges that reflect the opportunity cost of using water, and which contribute to covering the cost of river basin management, have the potential to help manage demand and restore water quality.

Prioritising investment decisions to achieve water quality objectives is necessary in the context of limited funding. Korea should encourage land use practices that preserve water quality, compensate farmers for required investments or revenue losses, and create demand for added-value food and fibre produced on that land (e.g. through sustainable product labelling schemes). Korea should consider expansion of the Korean Total Water Pollution Load Control System - which has been successful in reducing point source pollution of biochemical oxygen demand and total phosphorus - to include other pollutants (such as nitrogen, heavy metals and pesticides) and to those who contribute to diffuse source pollution.

Korea would benefit from independent water regulation and greater enforcement of environmental compliance

While Korea recognises the importance of using regulation to limit the exploitation or pollution of its rivers and lakes, regulation fails to deliver expected outcomes when compliance is not monitored and enforced. There are opportunities to improve the level of compliance and enforcement of abstraction permits and effluent and discharge standards;

currently, this is limited in Korea and penalties remain rare. In addition, there is a public distrust in the quality of drinking services due to historical pollution events.

Independent regulation in Korea for the protection of the environment, customers' interests and drinking water quality may be an effective response to some of the challenges to regulating water services, including the fragmentation of roles and responsibilities in the sector, public distrust in drinking water services, and the limitations of the tariff setting process. A menu of institutional arrangements can contribute to independent and trusted water regulation.

The long-awaited reform of water governance at national level needs to be swiftly and effectively implemented to foster policy coherence, further engage with stakeholders and manage the WELF nexus at basin level

The recent water governance reform through the adoption of the revised Government Organisation Act, June 2018, merges the vast majority of responsibilities and capacities for water quantity and quality management under the Ministry of Environment. This merge is a step in the right direction for improved policy alignment and coherence. However, improved coordination does not come automatically from a reallocation of responsibilities. The Ministry of Environment will need to develop and implement a water quality and quantity "coordination" strategy for effective merging of responsibilities at national and sub-national levels and achievement of greater coherence between water, energy, land and food policies.

The adoption of the revised Government Organisation Act also provides a unique opportunity for Korea to move towards managing the WELF nexus at the basin scale and to strengthen stakeholder engagement.

Assessment and Recommendations

The Assessment and Recommendations present the main findings of this report and set out recommendations to help Korea make further progress towards aligning water policies, practices and governance arrangements for sustainable management of the Water-Energy-Land-Food Nexus. A draft Action Plan with short-, medium- and long-term steps on how to achieve these recommendations, and suggestions of who may be responsible for them, is presented as Annex 1.A.

Pressures on the Water-Energy-Land-Food Nexus in Korea

Water, energy, land and food are essential for economic growth and development, and there are strong linkages between them (the WELF nexus). Considering these linkages is important for government as policies and investment to manage one dimension of the WELF nexus may have detrimental effects or co-benefits on others. Water insecurity at the regional and local scales is often the main bottleneck in the WELF nexus which may limit economic growth across sectors, and impact human wellbeing and ecosystem health (OECD, 2017a).

The Republic of Korea, the eighth-largest OECD economy, has limited natural resources. Korea is among the few OECD countries both with scarce land and under medium-high water stress (OECD, 2017b,c). Urbanisation, industrialisation, population growth (at least until 2030) and climate change are increasing demands on the WELF nexus. The response to date has been to consume more land and augment the supply of water, at the expense of the environment (OECD, 2017b,c), whilst essentially relying on public funding to finance water infrastructure investments.

An ageing population and recent slow-down in economic growth (OECD, 2016a) will limit available public funding for responding to increasing droughts and floods, including investment in climate resilient infrastructure. Furthermore, environmental tax and charge rates on water abstraction and pollution, and land development are too low to cover observed environmental and social externalities, or to encourage pollution reduction and efficient water and land use (OECD, 2017b,c).

The inability to effectively manage the bottlenecks, trade-offs and synergies within the WELF nexus will generate high costs for the Korean economy and will exacerbate inequalities across regions and social groups, now and in the future. This calls for proactive, co-ordinated and integrated policy and strategic long-term planning to future-proof the WELF nexus and enhance sustainable growth.

Water scarcity

The volume of total water use exceeds the amount of normal water runoff (which is measured during the off-flood season). As such, flood runoff needs to be captured in reservoirs for later use. Korea invests in alternative water resources (e.g. desalination, inter-basin transfers) to supplement dam water supply during periods of drought. These water management options are expensive, energy intensive and have high carbon footprints.

Given the already high water stress and consumption of total available water resources, Korea will need to make substantial efficiency gains in water use and/or water allocation to meet future water demands and maintain economic growth. This is demonstrated by the fact that surface water is already fully allocated in each of the four major river basins – the Han, Geum, Nakdong and Yeongsan/Seomjin River systems – and high rates of leakage by international comparison within some water supply networks (20.6% on average, but up to 41.1% in some areas).

Water supply augmentation can only come at high cost and increasing pressure on public budgets, as the capacity for additional reservoirs in Korea is exhausted (or close to it). Furthermore, recent cases in Brazil (Sao Paulo) and South Africa (Cape Town) confirm that relying on reservoir storage can risk supply failure during severe droughts.

Flooding

Korea's flood risk index is substantially higher than that of other OECD countries. Over 100 regions of Korea have experienced water inundation more than twice in the 2000s. Korea has worked hard to reduce flood risks through investment in infrastructure as well as in forecasting and warning systems. The government has also put in place a plan to improve rainwater drainage capabilities, such as expansion of water control capabilities by 2025 (OECD, 2017c).

Thirty areas have been identified at high-risk of flooding. The government is responding to water-related risks by means of various techniques such as low impact development (LID), groundwater storage, wetland restoration and green infrastructure policies, as well as separating stormwater from the sewerage network. But rates of progress are slow compared with the human and financial costs incurred with each flood event, and the capacity to scale up and replicate pilot projects remains unclear. Mechanisms to coordinate land and water planning, and management upstream within the river basins, are missing.

Water quality

Improvements in point source pollution control in Korea have been admirable. Over 90% of the population of Korea is currently served by wastewater treatment services, compared with 71% in 2000. In addition, 83% of the population benefits from advanced (tertiary) wastewater treatment (OECD, 2017b). Still, there are pending issues related to permitting, compliance, monitoring and enforcement of point source discharges from industry and municipalities (OECD, 2017b). Regulation of water quality focuses on the four major river basins; tributaries and coastal streams, which account for 30% of Korean rivers, largely remain unregulated and unmonitored.

Diffuse pollution (predominantly from livestock and urban stormwater run-off) increasingly affects scarce water resources and will continue to do so with intensive livestock production projected to increase (ME, 2015). The proportion of total pollution attributed to diffuse pollution is projected to reach over 70% by 2020 (ME, 2014a)

Korea currently has the highest nitrogen balance and the second-highest phosphorus balance in the OECD, even though the use of chemical fertilisers has declined (OECD, 2017b; 2018). Episodes of algal blooms are frequent in Korea, triggered by high nutrient levels, warm temperatures, reduced river flow (due to reservoirs) and sunlight.

Progress has been achieved in water quality with the introduction of the Korean Total Water Pollution Load Control System (Korean TMDL, the equivalent of a total maximum daily load programme) in the four main river basins, particularly in the Nakdong River Basin. Since the introduction of the Korean TMDL in 2004, reduction targets in point source pollution control of biochemical oxygen demand and total phosphorus have been achieved. Tributaries and coastal streams are not regulated as part of the Korean TMDL.

There are an array of fragmentised initiatives and pilot projects to increase eco-farming, best management practices, and buy-back of riparian land to improve water quality, but they typically rely on voluntary approaches and come at a high cost in comparison to other potential policy solutions, particularly those that utilise the Polluter Pays Principle. The role of land use planning and management is critical for water quality and resource management.

Historical water pollution incidents (e.g. Nakdong accidents in 1991 and 1994) have resulted in a low public trust in drinking water quality with the majority of citizens using bottled water and home water filters. There is room for improvement in engagement with citizens, industrialists and farmers to raise awareness, increase trust and reach solutions in partnership.

Land use and food production

Built-up, urbanised areas have expanded by 51% between 2002 and 2014; a rate that has far surpassed the population growth (6% over the same period). This reflects rapid industrialisation and urbanisation; 70% of the population lives in urban areas, well above the OECD average of 49% (OECD, 2017b).

Korea's farming model is highly intensive, particularly the livestock sector, which reflects a growing consumer demand for meat products. The intensity of commercial fertiliser and pesticide use is among the highest in the OECD, and livestock density is the second highest after the Netherlands. This has negative ramifications for water and energy use, and land and water pollution. Land acidification is worsening with climate change and agricultural production is expected to decline in both quantity and quality due to climate change and subsequent increase in disease and pests (ME, 2014b).

Currently there are no environmental regulations specifically imposed on agricultural production, with the exception of regulations on livestock manure (OECD, 2018) stipulated under the 2006 Act on the Management and Use of Livestock Excreta. Environmental tax and charge rates on land development are too low to cover environmental and social externalities. The agriculture sector does not pay energy taxes and only partially pays minimal water charges (OECD, 2010). In addition, producer support, as percentage of gross farm receipts (%PSE), is almost three times higher than the OECD average and consists mostly in market price support - a category of support with potentially environmentally harmful effects (OECD, 2018).

Energy supply and use

Korea's economy is among the most energy intensive in the OECD. This is despite the fact that Korea has no oil resources and very limited natural gas reserves. Furthermore, Korea's share of renewables in the energy mix remains the lowest in the OECD. Thus, Korea is highly dependent on external energy sources.

Water and energy supply are intimately connected. While hydropower remains limited in Korea's energy supply mix, water is required to cool thermal and nuclear plants, which are projected to multiply in Korea, thus increasing water needs and minimal flow requirements for future energy production.

Korea has a high energy-water risk relative to other countries in the Asia-Pacific region. One study mapping the water consumption for energy production around the Pacific Rim determined that watersheds at energy-water risk represent 59% of all basins in Korea where water is used in energy production (Tidwell and Moreland, 2016).

The way forward

Korea recognises these challenges and sees the opportunity of improved coordination of policies and institutions in relation to the WELF nexus to better respond to uncertainties and create options for sustainable growth in the short and long term. The recent merging of government organisations responsible for water management is one indication of this. The purpose of the Korea-OECD Water Policy Dialogue is to explore best practices from the wider international community that can inspire such coordination to better manage water resources within the WELF nexus.

Recommendations rest on four priorities for Korea:

1. Anticipate and plan against future water-related risks
2. Better manage water demand and reduce pollution
3. Regulate and enforce compliance
4. Reform institutions and governance.

The rationale for the selection of these priorities are outlined below, followed by recommendations and a draft action plan on how to achieve them.

Anticipate and plan against future water-related risks

Water quality and quantity monitoring and assessment

Managing water and the WELF nexus starts with a good understanding of the state of the resources (water, land), the environment (the ecosystems which the WELF nexus relies upon) and the pressures and demands on them. Robust data and information are necessary to develop effective and proactive water and land policies, to identify priority actions, set the ambition of policies and to monitor compliance and progress.

There are four areas in particular where the current monitoring and assessment regime could be improved in Korea:

1. Monitoring water quality. The breadth of water quality parameters and sampling locations and frequency is limited. The benefit of increasing water quality monitoring capacity and understanding is that pollution loads and 'hotspots' can be identified and targeted, and environmental and health risks can be reduced more cost-effectively (OECD, 2017d,e). To that end: extend the current water quality monitoring programme to tributaries and small streams, and expand monitoring parameters to fully assess human and ecosystem health risks (this should include continuous monitoring of pH, DO, COD, BOD, ammonia, nitrate, phosphate and chlorophyll/blue-green algae (for early warning and control of pollution)); use that data to identify hotspots; target compliance and enforcement of discharge permits in these hotspots; specify land use where it affects water quality most; allocate River Management Funds to improve water quality in hotspots.
2. Groundwater monitoring. While abstraction of water from aquifers is monitored to a limited extent in Korea, information on groundwater quality and surface water-groundwater connections is lacking. This is an issue, as droughts and sea level rise are projected to increase pressure on groundwater resources. More specifically: ensure a sufficient network of groundwater monitoring boreholes that

enable robust understanding across each aquifer and their interactions with surface water; use field and satellite data to routinely monitor groundwater levels and depletion; document groundwater quality on at least a quarterly basis, and more frequently where pollution risks are high; use data to tailor compliance monitoring of water abstraction and pollution permits and regulate land use changes; consider groundwater recharge to replenish aquifers and mitigate saline intrusions.

3. Ecological monitoring. In practice: routinely monitor aquatic invertebrates, macrophytes (aquatic plants) and fish to understand ecosystem health. Adjust water and land management and the controls on abstraction and pollution accordingly.
4. River flow monitoring. Develop naturalised flow sequences for each major river, where the effect of artificial influences can be accounted for. Use the natural baseline as the basis for decisions to determine ecological flows and sustainable volumes of abstraction and discharge.

Korea would benefit from more systematically monitoring the costs of action and inaction, the impact on economic and social development, and in particular, how these costs are distributed across regions or social groups. Such economic monitoring or appraisal would support informed discussion on how risks (of water scarcity, floods, or pollution) and opportunities (for economic development) are allocated across regions and groups, and how the distinctive capacities of such groups to respond to these risks or opportunities are taken into account.

For instance, economic monitoring or appraisal could document how senior water rights holders (i.e. water users who benefit from the most secure entitlements to use water) benefit from a privileged situation: they may only use a portion of their water entitlement, while new comers may be denied access to river water. As such, senior water rights holders may be protected against risks of drought while more valuable water uses are at risk. Whilst the customary rights of senior water rights holders are recognised in civil law, they can be socially inequitable and economically inefficient.

Economic analyses should document the privileged position of senior water rights holders and monetise the opportunity costs of preventing other uses of water. Analyses should document the social costs of the current allocation of water-related risks and the potential economic benefits of allocating risks to those best equipped to address them (for instance distinguishing between rice farmers, livestock farmers and farmers who grow perennial crops). Such data is essential to develop cost-effective and equitable responses to nexus-related challenges.

Anticipating and planning

While Korea has robust experience with planning for water, land use and infrastructure developments, planning would benefit from four major developments:

1. Planning should be forward-looking. In Korea, water and infrastructure plans are routinely based on meeting the impact of the worst drought in the historic record, however, the past climate record is not necessarily representative of the future. Planning would be more resilient when a long-term, forward-looking, intergenerational perspective is taken, which considers the potential for extreme, unprecedented events from climate change.

2. Plans should reflect uncertainties. Relying upon a single set of forecasts as the basis for policy decisions and investment – whether for water or energy security, flood risk planning, or land use - is likely to lead to poor decisions. Each plan should explore different socio-economic and climate change scenarios under a range of plausible visions of the future. It should test strategic decisions for their strengths, weaknesses and resilience.
3. Fragmented, single-issue planning should move towards coordinated planning across features of the WELF nexus. Planning should be coordinated across all water uses, including agriculture. Planning should also be coordinated across water, land use, agriculture development and energy supply. Inconsistencies or tensions should be systematically identified. Synergies and opportunities should be explored. Synergies can result in allocation of land and water to its most beneficial use for society, reduced reliance on additional infrastructure, and greater security in terms of water, food or energy at least cost for the community.
4. Coordinated planning is more readily achieved at the scale of river basins, where synergies, trade-offs and options to manage them are more apparent than at the national scale. In particular, options to manage trade-offs benefit from local knowledge, which is difficult to replicate or capture at national level. It benefits from stakeholder engagement, to reflect a range of perspectives and build on diverse expertise. Therefore, plans that relate to water, agriculture and food, land use or energy should preferably be developed at basin scale; national plans should reflect basin specificities.
5. Plans should drive decisions on a range of issues. Plans should clearly establish the overall purpose, objectives and priorities for sustainable management of the WELF nexus. They should define acceptable levels of water security (risk of scarcity, floods or pollution) for the communities involved, and the actions and costs required to achieve such levels. Plans should form the basis of regulations (for instance on land use, water abstraction or discharge permits) and the reference for infrastructure development and public investment. They should be backed by a robust financing strategy. Without such attributes, plans remain an ambition only and a lost opportunity.

Better manage water demand and reduce pollution

Increase water use efficiency and demand management efforts

The 2016 OECD Council Recommendation on Water – endorsed by the Korean Government – claims that demand management is the first best option to manage water scarcity. Supply augmentation is just postponing problems to a future date, as recent drought episodes in Brazil and South Africa suggest.

There are ample opportunities for Korea to increase water use efficiency (including reductions in leakage and non-revenue water) and strengthen demand management, to minimise future investment needs in water infrastructure to augment supply and to reallocate water where it creates most value to society. Well-designed water abstraction charges that reflect the opportunity cost of using water have the potential to help manage demand. The OECD report on *Enhancing Water Use Efficiency in Korea: Policy Issues and Recommendations* (OECD, 2017c) explores how Korea can transition towards such a system.

Water charges should be set so that they incentivise the adoption of water saving practices and technologies in agriculture, industry and households to reduce unsustainable use of water in the face of climate change. For example, the uptake of more efficient irrigation technologies, such as drip irrigation, could significantly reduce agricultural water consumption - if water saved is returned to the water system - and would also reduce pumping and energy costs and diffuse pollution risks. While improving water use efficiency is necessary to move forward a green growth strategy in agriculture, caution is required to avoid perverse effects such as: a reduction in water availability for other users and the environment, expansion of irrigated land areas with water saved, and an increased dependence on water resources and the risks associated with climate change (OECD, 2016b). Mitigating these unintended consequences of water use efficiency gains requires appropriate water accounting at the basin scale that considers not just withdrawals but also water returning to the system. Accounting for return flows should be studied more systemically to assess their relative importance in Korea's watersheds. In a second step, return flows should be accounted for in water allocation systems to better reflect overall water supply and demand, and thus improve the efficiency of water allocation (OECD, 2015a). Thirdly, water efficiency gains should be accompanied by regulation to appropriately direct the use of saved water and prevent the perverse effects described above.

Decisions on how to operate dams and how to share water amongst agriculture, energy, industry, municipalities and the environment should be improved in Korea in order to generate more value from water. The use of reclaimed water under the Korean Construction Code and water quality "fit for purpose" should be expanded beyond greenfield projects to reduce reliance on raw water resources and provide a dependable, locally-controlled water supply. Water reuse also has the added advantage of reducing water treatment and energy costs, diverting pollution to sensitive ecosystems, returning nutrients to the land, and can be used to augment groundwater supplies.

Strengthen water quality management

Water quality is a distinctive part of the WELF nexus in Korea. Water pollution contributes to water scarcity, and affects land and energy resources. Pressures from a range of policies and developments can affect water quality, such as water allocation, flood management, urban development, alterations to the natural morphology of water bodies, land and soil management practices, agricultural support and climate change.

There are opportunities to improve the level of compliance and enforcement of effluent and discharge standards; currently, this is limited in Korea and penalties remain rare. Korea should set Environmental Quality Standards at the upper limit of acceptability to protect human health or the ecosystem and extend coverage to all streams (beyond the four major rivers). The permissible pollution load should take into account the river flow regime, the breadth of polluting substances that might adversely affect ecosystem health, and the sensitivity of the ecosystem at different places down the river, from small tributaries down to the estuary. Discharge permits should be adjusted accordingly.

Korea should expand the Korean TMDL to include a broader range of pollutants, including nitrogen and other pollutants that are of concern to human and ecosystem health in each river basin (e.g. heavy metals and pesticides), polluters (including diffuse pollution from agriculture), and tributary streams so that the Korean TMDL reaches its full potential. As a second step, Korea should consider establishing a water quality trading scheme amongst polluters within the Korean TMDL system to cost-effectively meet water quality goals whilst limiting restrictions on future economic development.

Improving the policy framework to manage livestock manure is a priority considering the future growth potential of the livestock sector. In addition to current efforts from ME and MAFRA to subsidise manure treatment and convert manure into reusable compost and fertilisers, a comprehensive policy approach beyond regulation is necessary – combining regulatory and economic incentives with capacity-building of producers and building partnerships between stakeholders. For example, Korea should: set regulations requiring good farming practices nationwide; increase education campaigns and advisory services in the farming community; establish targeted risk-based agri-environmental support payments in exchange for best farming practices (beyond mandatory good farming practices) in ecologically sensitive areas and drinking water sources; and enhance partnerships between livestock and cropping farms and industry to recycle and re-use livestock manure through on-farm application, biogas production and composting into organic fertilisers.

The River Management Fund (RMF) has significant potential to better leverage available funds to support upstream water quality projects and improve overall water quality. For example, requests to sell and retire land are oversubscribed suggesting that water quality objectives could be achieved at a lower cost. Prioritising investment decisions to achieve water quality objectives is necessary in the context of limited funding. For instance, Korea should: carefully select land that can most effectively contribute to improvements in water quality; encourage land use practices that conserve water and preserve water quality; compensate farmers for required investments or revenue losses; create demand for added-value food and fibre produced on that land (e.g. through sustainable product labelling schemes). As a final resort, land may be purchased for retirement or contractual use under strict environmental requirements if the above options have not produced intended results.

Regulate and enforce compliance

While Korea recognises the importance of using regulation to limit the exploitation or pollution of its rivers and lakes, regulation fails to deliver expected outcomes when compliance is not monitored and enforced. In Korea, regulation for agricultural water use is not systematic and with lax enforcement, and monitoring and control of groundwater abstractions is limited. In addition, the level of compliance and enforcement of effluent standards is limited and penalties remain rare; in 2013, only 35% of wastewater discharge infringements required corrective measures (ME, 2014c).

The efficiency of inspection for compliance of permits for the most polluting discharges depends on continuous monitoring of key parameters and at least daily analysis monitoring of all permitted substances. It also depends on how process failures are reported and dealt with. Smaller discharges with less risk of causing serious pollution would be subject to a less rigorous compliance monitoring regime.

To align with best international practices, and to deploy resources most effectively, Korea would be wise to adopt a risk-based approach to environmental regulation and compliance monitoring. More specifically, Korea should target compliance monitoring where the risks of non-compliance are highest, or where their consequences on human and ecosystems' health are most severe. Ideally, such an approach would be underpinned by a process of independent regulation with powers and authority to take action where necessary. This would significantly enhance citizens' trust in the institutions involved in managing water and the WELF nexus.

Independent regulation in Korea for the protection of the environment, customers' interests and drinking water quality may be an effective response to some of the challenges to regulating water services, including the fragmentation of roles and responsibilities in the sector, the public distrust in drinking water services, and the limitations of the tariff setting process. International best practices clearly demonstrate the multiple benefits of a clear separation between regulatory, policy making and project implementation functions. When it comes to water supply and sanitation services, regulatory functions include: i) setting and reporting on performance targets for water service providers, and ii) setting tariffs at the appropriate level to cover operational expenditures and capital investment to improve the level and standard of water supply and sanitation services. These functions can be discharged in several ways, within or outside ME, as long as they are shielded from third party interference.

Reform institutions and governance

Korea's water security challenges are increasingly complex: they do not fit into a single ministerial portfolio; they cut across several policy areas, and spread across administrative boundaries and jurisdictions; and their resolution depends on expertise from both government and non-government actors at multiple levels.

Reform institutional coordination

Korea lacks effective vertical and horizontal coordination mechanisms across scales and stakeholders, leading to inefficiencies of both financial and physical resources and non-optimal water services provisions to citizens and private sector.

Korea should reflect basin issues in national policies as a priority. It should give increased priority to policy alignment and inter-ministerial coordination so that national and sub-national ministries and agencies are capacitated and incentivised to make co-ordination work effectively for sustainable long-term management of the WELF nexus.

The recent water governance reform through the adoption of the revised Government Organisation Act, June 2018, merges responsibilities of water quantity and quality management under one ministry (ME). This merge is a step in the right direction for improved policy alignment and coherency. However, improved coordination does not come automatically; ME will need to develop and implement a water quality and quantity "coordination" strategy for effective merging of responsibilities at national and sub-national levels.

As part of a staged institutional development approach towards strengthened cross sector coordination for the WELF nexus, ME, MoLIT and MAFRA, together with stakeholder organisations at basin level, should develop a national level inter-ministerial coordination platform to coordinate policies that affect water quality, quantity and ecology, land use planning and economic uses of water such as food and energy production. Such a platform should operate routinely without prejudice to future institutional arrangements. The objective of the platform should be to propose long-term institutional set ups for managing the WELF nexus. The platform should also open up to other government and non-government stakeholders, including from the basin level. Steps towards such a platform should include: 1) assessment and analysis of current water related responsibilities and institutional set-up at national level to identify institutional gaps and over-laps; 2) assessment of capacity development needs among both government and non-government stakeholders and financing gaps and; 3) assessment of the available skills for the delivery of policy objectives, and an action plan to address skills and resources gaps; and 4) ME to take initiative and lead national stakeholder workshop for collection of government and non-government stakeholders views and ideas on improving coordination of WELF nexus.

Under the new Framework Act on Water Management, most basin level organisations (with the exception of the five regional Construction Management Offices) have been transferred to ME responsibility. There are several coordination gains to be made by also transferring responsibilities of long-term planning under the ME at national level to organisations at the basin level.

Coordination is essentially about various stakeholders inter-acting, exchanging views and making common decisions. It is therefore important to incentivise and capacitate government officials through staff exchanges between and within ministries and basin-level organisations to encourage peer-to-peer learning for coherent approaches to WELF nexus coordination. It is proposed that ME puts in place staff capacity development programmes that encourage staff exchanges between national and basin level institutions.

Manage water and the nexus at basin level

The river basin scale is considered an appropriate level for long term water quantity and quality planning, data collection, conflict mediation and policy coordination and engagement across sectors and stakeholders. The very essence of managing water at the basin level is that the unique characteristics of each basin (varying hydrological, ecological and socio-economic opportunities and challenges) can be taken into account in the planning and implementation of river basin management plans, water use charges and investment priorities.

Stakeholder organisations at basin level should set and implement objectives, targets and priorities as part of developing river basin management plans for Korea's four major river basins - Han, Geum, Nakdong and Yeongsan/Seomjin River systems. National water priorities should be taken into account as part of the planning process. Korea should also give special attention to the remaining 30% of medium and smaller rivers that do not fall under the current system of four river major basin areas, and to integrating surface and groundwater management policies and processes.

As part of establishing and implementing viable river basin plans, the setting of water use charges should be done at the basin level to better reflect investment needs for improved water management in the WELF nexus.

The adoption of the revised Government Organisation Act, June 2018, provides a unique opportunity for Korea to move towards managing the WELF nexus at the basin scale. The ME should undertake the following:

- The proposed national coordination platform on WELF nexus (see above) should develop options for improved coordination between national and basin levels. Basin management plans need to be based on national water priorities and policies, and hence the coordination between these levels will be key for effective policy implementation.
- In support of the increased emphasis on river basin delivery, ME should develop policy and process guidance (with the involvement of the basin organisations) to

support consistent and coherent operational delivery, and to help maintain focus on national policy objectives.

- ME should assess and analyse the existing water-related basin organisations with regard to their current capacities and future needs to effectively perform a set of proposed management functions at the basin level, such as: long-term river basin management plans, setting and managing water use charges and the River Management Fund, conflict mediation and data collection. In addition, ME should assess and analyse the entire institutional structure at basin level to identify gaps, overlaps and coordination opportunities. To be included in the assessment of the basin-level institutional structure are the River Basin Committees, River Management Committees, River Basin Environmental Offices, Regional Environmental Offices, Flood Control Offices, and River Adjustment Councils.
- ME should initiate a dialogue with government and non-government stakeholders as part of developing establishing a coordination platform at basin scale that cuts across sectors and stakeholders for effective planning and implementation. For example, MoLIT retains responsibility for river bank maintenance for flood protection, land use planning and river planning, and MAFRA is responsible for water in agriculture. It is important to include non-government interest such as from water users, environmental NGOs and farmers associations. The stakeholder platforms can be under the jurisdiction of a basin organisation. ME can also look at international experiences, such as in France and/or other countries, in their development and implementation of stakeholder platforms.

Strengthen stakeholder engagement

Stakeholder engagement through inclusive national, basin or local water governance is increasingly recognised as critical to secure support for reforms, draw upon stakeholder water knowledge, raise awareness about water risks and costs, increase users' willingness to pay, and to manage and mediate conflicts (OECD, 2015b and 2015c). Legal and policy provisions for stakeholder engagement in water management in Korea do exist, but implementation in practice remains limited. Continued development and implementation of policies and laws that assure decentralisation and wider inclusion of society into policy and planning processes is considered important for improved outcomes of water management.

For any stakeholder platform or mechanism, it is important that the design relates to its intended purposes of improving coordination of water quality and quantity management and WELF nexus. To get started, pilot stakeholder engagement initiatives should be considered and scaled up, until stakeholder coordination platforms with government and non-government actors is put in place in each of the four river basins as well as at national level.

The ME, in collaboration with MAFRA, MoLIT and the basin organisations, should undertake the following at national level, as well as in each of the four major river basins:

- Promote inclusiveness and equity: Map all stakeholders who have a stake in the outcome or that are likely to be affected, as well as their core interests and capacities;
- Make processes transparent and accountable: Define the objectives of stakeholder engagement and the expected use of their inputs;

- Level the playing field between stakeholders: Allocate sufficient financial and human resources and share the same information with all stakeholders. Capacity development should target weaker stakeholders;
- Be adaptive: Customise the type and level of stakeholder engagement depending on the objectives and characteristics of stakeholders;
- Promote efficiency: Assess the outcomes of stakeholder processes on a regular basis to learn, adjust and improve; and
- Institutionalise stakeholder processes: Stakeholder engagement processes should be embedded in clear policy and legal frameworks and in organisational structures and modalities with responsible government authorities.

Recommendations

With the ultimate goal of achieving sustainable management of the WELF nexus in Korea, recommendations build on four priorities: 1) Anticipate and plan against future water-related risks; 2) Manage water quantity and quality; 3) Regulate and enforce compliance; and 4) Reform institutions and governance. Recommendations for each of these priorities are outlined below and in Figure 1. An Action Plan detailing how to achieve these recommendations, and suggestions of who may be responsible for them, is presented as Annex 1.A.

1. Anticipate and plan against future water-related risks

Implement a robust water quantity and quality monitoring and assessment framework

- Invest in water quantity and quality monitoring and assessment.
- Collect data on key issues at basin and sub-basin levels for both surface and groundwater bodies. Extend coverage of monitoring to streams not covered by the four major rivers. Routinely monitor groundwater levels and quality. Monitor water quality on a larger range of substances on a daily basis.
- Identify where water scarcity, floods or pollution pose a risk to ecosystem degradation, damage to assets, or systemic risks to the WELF nexus and human well-being. Tailor the following accordingly to reduce risks: i) water abstraction and discharge permits, ii) compliance monitoring and enforcement, and iii) land use regulation.
- Assess the economic and social costs and the social distribution impacts of policies, regulations and practices that relate to the WELF nexus.

Coordinate plans across sectors, and increase resilience of policies that affect the WELF nexus

- Develop plans based upon plausible socio-economic and climate change scenarios to assess the strengths and weaknesses of different policy options. England and Wales offer valuable experience.

- Join up land and water planning and management, preferably at basin scale, with the aim of reducing flood runoff, increasing infiltration and improving water quality.
- Ensure plans drive policies and investments that contribute to the WELF nexus. Review existing water, agricultural, energy and land policy instruments to improve their coherence with policy objectives and reduce conflicting incentives.
- Use resilience thinking to assess the vulnerability of systems to shocks such as extreme droughts. England and Wales offer valuable experience.
- Put in place a long-term strategy to deliver drought and flood resilience with funding for drought and flood risk management matching increasing risk over the coming decades.
- Ensure that water supply planning is based upon a 'portfolio' approach, with a range of options with different risk profiles and resilience. Lessons from Australia, and England and Wales may be useful to Korea.

Scale-up investment and innovation to improve effectiveness

- Scale up the current initiatives on Low Impact Development and green infrastructure to reduce urban flood risk.

2. Better manage water demand and reduce pollution

Increase water use efficiency and demand management efforts

- Implement programmes of water efficiency savings and demand management – targeted at agricultural, industrial and household users. Increase water charges to reflect the scarcity of water in basins and to incentivise water conservation. Australia, the United States and other OECD countries provide examples of good practice. Scale up efforts to reduce leakage and non-revenue water within water supply networks.
- Develop a water use efficiency strategy for agriculture that explicitly prevents increases in irrigated areas and dependence on water resources where water is scarce, and ensures sufficient groundwater recharge, environmental flows, water availability for downstream users and effluent dilution. This will require: i) establishment of water accounting at the basin scale that considers not just withdrawals but also water returning to the system; ii) accounting for return flows in water allocation systems to better reflect overall water supply and demand, and thus improve the efficiency of water allocation; and iii) regulation to appropriately direct the use of water saved through efficiency gains, in order to prevent perverse outcomes.

Improve water allocation for ecological flows

- Provide guidance on how introducing revised environmental flows will be carried out in practice, including reallocation of existing water rights if necessary whilst minimising tensions between users.

Strengthen water quality management

- Expand the Korean TMDL to include the whole basin (including small/medium tributary rivers) and other water quality parameters linked to local ecological limits and social values on water quality.

- In the longer-term, include all diffuse source polluters (including agriculture) in the Korean TMDL programme. Experience from the United States and New Zealand can guide Korea.
- In the longer-term, consider replacing the water use charge with economic instruments that incentivise reductions in water pollution at lowest cost to society. Charges in France and water quality trading schemes in the United States are examples of good practice.
- Use targeted, risk-based regulations to reduce diffuse source pollution of rivers, lakes and groundwater, such as mandating livestock units' manure management and good management practices. Experience from the EU Nitrate pollution prevention regulations is relevant.

Harness voluntary action and improve education

- Use agri-environmental support payments or payment for ecosystem services in exchange for the uptake of best farming practices in ecologically-sensitive or drinking water catchment areas. Germany and the United Kingdom offer examples of good practice.
- Increase education campaigns and advisory services in the farming community as a precursor to introducing regulations.

3. Regulate and enforce compliance

Strengthen compliance monitoring and enforcement capacity

- Adopt a risk-based approach to regulation and compliance monitoring.
- Establish independent monitoring, auditing and reporting of drinking water quality.
- Introduce permit controls on all abstractions as part of a reformed water allocation regime. Commence groundwater permitting on a risk basis, including an assessment of interference between boreholes and their impact on surface waters, the risk of saline intrusion, and to ensure that total groundwater abstraction is kept within sustainable limits (i.e. doesn't exceed recharge).
- Ensure compliance monitoring assesses and manages the total pollution load, and accounts for the river flow regime and the sensitivity of the ecosystem at different places down the river. The European Union Water Framework Directive is an example of good practice.

Establish independent regulation with strong regulating powers

- Consider the benefits of independent regulation for the protection of the environment, customers' interests and drinking water quality with powers to take action where necessary against breaches of permits and standards, and to set tariffs at the appropriate level to cover operational expenditures and capital investment to improve the level and standard of water supply and sanitation services.

4. Reform institutions and governance

Reform institutional coordination

- Reflect basin issues in national policies as a priority. Give increased priority to policy alignment and inter-ministerial coordination so that national and sub-national ministries and agencies are capacitated and incentivised to make co-ordination work effectively along the management of WELF-nexus.
- Develop and implement a water quality and quantity "coordination" strategy for effective merging of the issues at national and sub-national levels.
- Put in place an inter-ministerial stakeholder platform at national level to coordinate policies within ME, MoLIT and MAFRA that affect river management, including water quality, quantity and ecology, land use planning and economic uses of water such as food and energy production. Other government and non-government stakeholders should be invited to be part of such a platform.
- Incentivise and capacitate government officials to interact between and within ministries and government departments, exchange views and make common decisions on the WELF nexus. This could be facilitated through staff exchanges and peer-to-peer learning.

Create a stakeholder engagement framework

- ME should engage with stakeholders, government and non-government, to strengthen the basin level management of WELF nexus and to reflect basin issues in national policies and priorities. International experiences (such as France, the Netherlands and Canada) offer examples of good practices.
- Establish stakeholder coordination platforms in each of the four river basins as well as at national level with government representatives and non-government actors. This will require: 1) define the objectives of stakeholder engagement and the expected use of inputs; 2) customise the type and level of stakeholder engagement depending on objectives and characteristics of stakeholders and; 3) map stakeholders and their core interests and capacities. Stakeholder platforms should as a minimum fulfil basic criteria of inclusiveness, transparency and that all stakeholders have access to the same information. In the transition to the establishment of formal stakeholder coordination platforms, ME should scale up pilot stakeholder engagement processes.
- Invest in stakeholder processes and provide financial and capacity development support, especially to weaker stakeholder groups.

Transition to basin-level governance

- Assess and analyse the River Management Committees (RMCs) with regard to their current capacities and future needs to effectively perform a set of proposed management functions at the basin level. In addition, assess and analyse the entire institutional landscape at basin level to identify gaps, overlaps and coordination opportunities. Consider merging RMCs with the River Basin Committees (RBCs) to form a combined basin organisation for water management in each of the four major river basins of Korea.

- Devolve water management functions to the basin level. RBCs should set and implement objectives, targets and priorities as part of developing and implementing river basin management plans for Korea's four major river basins. Transferred responsibilities should include the development and implementation of river basin management plans, financing and investment strategies, setting of water and pollution charges, data collection and mediation of basin water-related conflicts. National water priorities should be taken into account as part of the planning process.
- Develop policy and process guidance (with the involvement of the RBCs) to support consistent and coherent operational delivery, and to help maintain focus on national policy objectives. Oversee delivery in order to promote the sharing of good practice.
- Establish coordination platforms at basin scale that cuts across sectors and stakeholders for effective planning and implementation.

Figure 1. Achieving sustainable management of the WELF nexus in Korea

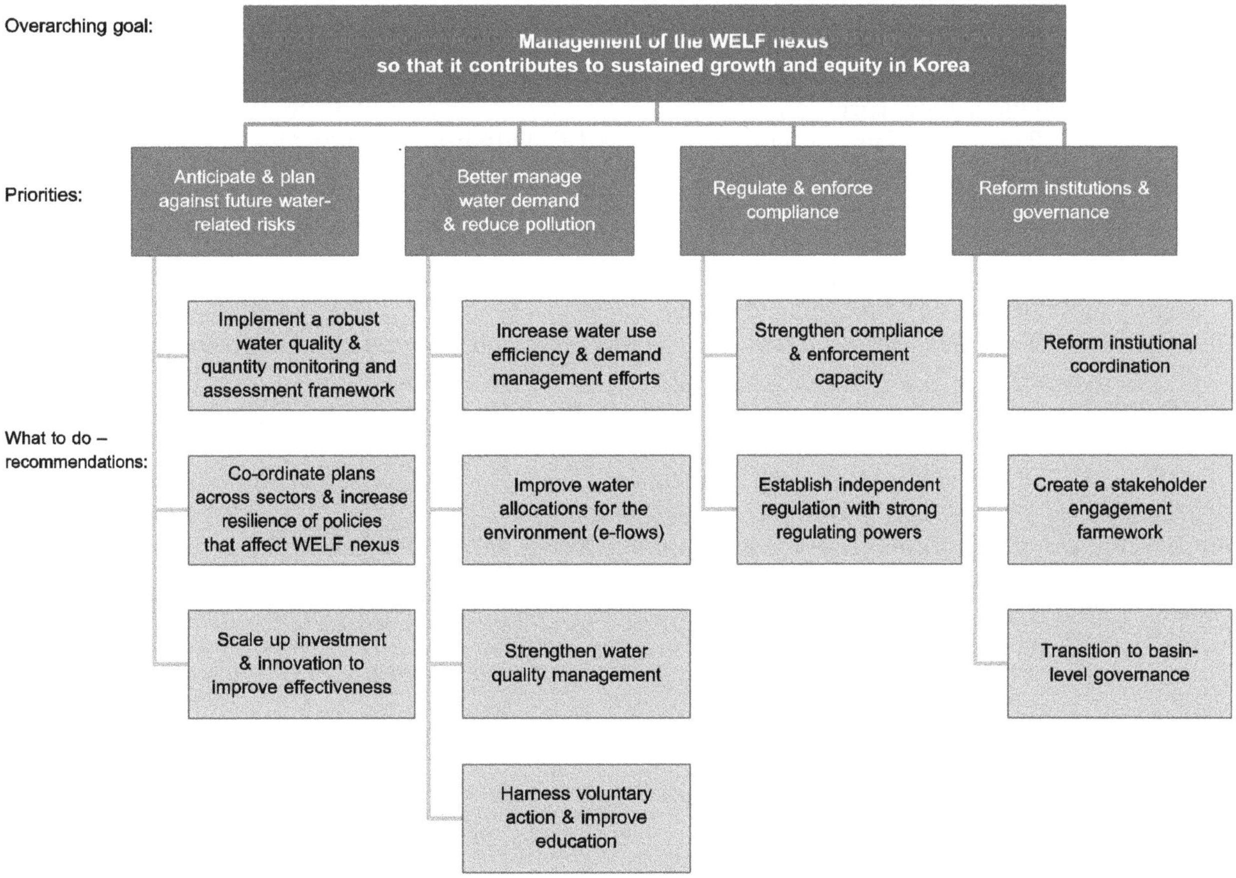

References

ME (2015), Ecorea: Environmental Review 2015: Korea, Ministry of Environment, Sejong. http://eng.me.go.kr/eng/web/board/read.do?pagerOffset=0&maxPageItems=10&maxIndexPages=10&searchKey=&searchValue=&menuId=30&orgCd=&boardId=565930&boardMasterId=547&boardCategoryId=&decorator=.

ME (2014a), Introduction to NPS pollution management in Korea. In: Presented at the International Symposium for the 22nd Anniversary of World Water Day. National Institute of Environment Research, Incheon, South Korea.

ME (2014b), "The Fifth National Report to the Convention on Biological Diversity", Ministry of Environment, Sejong. www.cbd.int/doc/world/kr/kr-nr-05-en.pdf.

ME (2014c), Environment Statistics Yearbook, Ministry of Environment, Sejong, http://webbook.me.go.kr/DLi-File/091/020/003/5588561.pdf.

OECD (2018, forthcoming), *Innovation, Agricultural Productivity and Sustainability in Korea,* OECD Publishing, Paris.

OECD (2017a), *The Land-Water-Energy Nexus: Biophysical and Economic Consequences*, OECD Publishing, Paris. http://dx.doi.org/10.1787/9789264279360-en.

OECD (2017b), *OECD Environmental Performance Reviews: Korea 2017*, OECD Publishing, Paris. http://dx.doi.org/10.1787/9789264268265-en.

OECD (2017c), *Enhancing Water Use Efficiency in Korea: Policy Issues and Recommendations*, OECD Studies on Water, OECD Publishing, Paris. http://dx.doi.org/10.1787/9789264281707-en.

OECD (2017d), *Diffuse Pollution, Degraded Waters: Emerging Policy Solutions*, OECD Studies on Water, OECD Publishing, Paris. http://dx.doi.org/10.1787/9789264269064-en.

OECD (2017e), *Water Risk Hotspots for Agriculture*, OECD Studies on Water, OECD Publishing, Paris. http://dx.doi.org/10.1787/9789264279551-en.

OECD (2016a), *OECD Economic Surveys: Korea 2016*, OECD Publishing, Paris, http://dx.doi.org/10.1787/eco_surveys-kor-2016-en.

OECD (2016b), *Mitigating Droughts and Floods in Agriculture: Policy Lessons and Approaches*, OECD Studies on Water, OECD Publishing, Paris. http://dx.doi.org/10.1787/9789264246744-en.

OECD (2015a), *Water Resources Allocation: Sharing Risks and Opportunities*, OECD Publishing, Paris. http://dx.doi.org/10.1787/9789264229631-en.

OECD (2015b), *Stakeholder Engagement for Inclusive Water Governance*, OECD Studies on Water, OECD Publishing, Paris. http://dx.doi.org/10.1787/9789264231122-en.

OECD (2015c), OECD Water Governance Principles, www.oecd.org/gov/regional-policy/OECD-Principles-on-Water-Governance-brochure.pdf.

OECD (2010), *Agricultural Water Pricing: Japan and Korea*, OECD Publishing, Paris. http://dx.doi.org/10.1787/9789264083578-13-en.

Tidwell, V. and B. Moreland (2016), Mapping water consumption for energy production around the Pacific Rim, Environmental Research Letters (2016) 094008.

Annex 1.A. Recommended Action Plan

This Action Plan identifies key steps for the implementation of the main policy recommendations and ways forward set out in this report. The ultimate goal is to create the conditions for the effective design and efficient implementation of water and WELF-related policies in a shared responsibility across levels of government, but also across public, private and non-profit sectors.

In practice, all of these measures will not materialise at once. The Action Plan suggests champions or institutions that can lead implementation over the short-, medium- and long-terms. The critical issue is whether the momentum created by the policy dialogue can continue, and an iterative and incremental process leads to improved management of the WELF nexus to deliver expected benefits for Korea. The process will facilitate reviews and revisions so that the system improves over time as more information about water resources, their use and the consequences of policies becomes available.

Annex Table 1.A.1. Action Plan for achieving sustainable management of the WELF nexus in Korea

Objective	Action	Possible champions/partners	Timeline
Anticipate and plan against future water-related risks			
Implement a robust water quantity and quality monitoring and assessment framework	Review location (e.g. downstream of effluent discharges, tributaries and coastal rivers), frequency (to understand daily and seasonal variability and total load) and parameters (e.g. metals, organics, pharmaceuticals) in water quality monitoring.	ME	Short-medium
	Review location (e.g. downstream of major effluent discharges, tributaries, and coastal rivers), frequency and comprehensiveness of ecological monitoring. Aim to understand current state of ecology in entire basin and progress towards target ecological status.	ME	Short-medium
	Review river flow monitoring, together with abstraction and discharge volumes, in order to generate a naturalised flow sequence to support development of environmental flow targets.	ME, with MAFRA, MoTIE, MoLIT	Short-medium
	Review groundwater level and quality monitoring network and data collection from pumping to better understand impact of abstraction and surface water-groundwater interaction and adjust regulation and entitlements accordingly.	ME, with MAFRA	Short-medium
	Use monitoring information on the state of the environment, and the pressures on it, to establish an integrated plan with costed measures for its protection and improvement	ME	Medium
Coordinate plans across sectors, and increase resilience of policies that affect the WELF nexus	Develop balanced twin-track long-term plans (at least 25 years ahead) for water supply for each river basin, with demand management integral to the strategy, to deliver agreed levels of service across all sectors. Plans should: i) be tested on a range of socio-economic and climate scenarios, incorporating unprecedented events, ii) consider a menu of options with different risk profiles and resilience, and iii) coordinate initiatives across the WELF nexus.	ME, with MoLIT, MAFRA, MoTIE, MPSS	Short-medium
	Assess the impact on water users from the introduction of e-flows, and appraise options for maintaining supply security without compromising environmental standards.	ME, with MoLIT, MAFRA, MoTIE	Medium
	For each river basin, develop a drought plan, which would set out an agreed series of actions to be escalated as a drought worsens, supported by EIAs to understand and mitigate impacts, in order to ensure a proactive approach to drought risk management.	RBCs, with ME, MoLIT, MAFRA, MoTIE, MPSS, MoI,	Short-medium
	For each water supply and urban area, use international good practice to assess resilience against shocks (e.g. droughts, floods, cyber-attacks, human error, natural disasters), and take action to minimise the duration and impact from such events.	RBCs, with ME, MoLIT, MAFRA, MoTIE, MPSS	Medium
	Aim to consolidate plans where possible into a single integrated process, in order to exploit synergies and opportunities, and reduce conflicting incentives. Join up land and water planning and management, preferably at basin scale, with the aim of reducing flood runoff, increasing infiltration and improving water quality.	RBCs, with ME, MoLIT, MAFRA, MoTIE, MoI, Prime Minister's Office	Medium
	Carry out *ex post* assessments of all major water-related developments and ensure that lessons are incorporated into future planning and investment.	ME	Short-medium
Scale up investment and innovation to improve effectiveness	Adopt international good practice on green-blue cities in order to accelerate the pace of introduction of Low Impact Development, Working with Natural Processes principles, and more effective controls on land use.	ME and MoLIT	Medium-long
Better manage water demand and reduce pollution			
Better manage water demand	Manage groundwater proactively, and introduce abstraction controls on wells and boreholes.	ME, with MAFRA	Medium
	Introduce abstraction permitting for all surface water abstractions (perhaps above a certain volume threshold) and set permits to ensure compliance with e-flows and to drive water efficient behaviour.	ME, with MAFRA	Medium
	Proactively monitor and enforce compliance with abstraction permits, taking a risk-based approach.	ME, with MAFRA	Short-medium
	Aim to reduce leakage to international good practice. Establish benchmarking and target setting to help drive leakage reduction and provide a focus on asset condition and repair.	ME	Medium-long
	Introduce water charges for abstraction and water pollution, at the basin scale,	RBCs, with ME, MoSF,	Medium-

Objective	Action	Possible champions/partners	Timeline
	reflecting environmental externalities and the opportunity cost of using water.	MoI	long
	Develop a water use efficiency strategy for agriculture that explicitly prevents increases in irrigated areas and dependence on water resources where water is scarce, and ensures sufficient groundwater recharge, environmental flows, water availability for downstream users and effluent dilution. This will require: i) establishment of water accounting at the basin scale that considers not just withdrawals but also water returning to the system; ii) accounting for return flows in water allocation systems to better reflect overall water supply and demand, and thus improve the efficiency of water allocation; and iii) regulation to appropriately direct the use of water saved through efficiency gains, in order to prevent perverse outcomes.	MAFRA, ME, RBCs	Short-medium
Improve water allocations for the environment (e-flows)	Develop a strategy on how introducing revised environmental flows will be carried out in practice, including reallocation of existing water rights if necessary whilst minimising tensions between users.	ME, with MoLIT, MAFRA, MoTIE, RBCs	Short-medium
Strengthen water quality management	Use improved water quality monitoring data to model current state of catchments, identify hotspots, and to then control all inputs of a pollutant (using permits for point sources, alternative mechanisms for diffuse sources) so that total load does not exceed environmental capacity (dilution and ecological sensitivity) at any location.	ME, with MAFRA, RBCs	Medium
	Proactively monitor and enforce compliance with discharge permits, taking a risk-based approach.	ME	Short-medium
	Step up efforts with the farming sector to reduce fertiliser and pesticide use, and to improve manure management, specifically on land that affects water quality most (e.g. riparian land, permeable land above shallow aquifers, land in close proximity to drinking water sources and sensitive ecosystems). Consider different policy options to deliver reductions in pollutant load (e.g. expanding Korean TMDL, pollution charges, water quality trading, payments for ecosystem services).	MAFRA, with ME, RBCs	Medium
	Determine an official list of good and best farm management practices to reduce diffuse pollution risks to surface and groundwater, with the aim of making good practices mandatory and best practice voluntary.	MAFRA, with ME	Short-medium
	Phase out the water use charge, which does not reflect the amount of pollution, nor the polluter-pays principle, and exempts agriculture.	ME	Medium
Harness voluntary action and improve education	Actively promote more efficient use of water (and the reasons why this is necessary) and reductions in water pollution to householders, industry and farmers, setting targets if necessary.	RBCs, with ME, MAFRA	Medium
	Set up payments in exchange for the voluntary uptake of best farm management practices to improve water quality.	ME, with MAFRA and RBCs	Medium-long
Regulate and enforce compliance			
Strengthen compliance and enforcement capacity	Adopt a risk-based approach to regulation and compliance monitoring to focus on where there is greatest risk to the environment, public health, the economy, other water users, or of non-compliance by the operator.	ME, with MAFRA and RBCs	Medium
	Review the need to commence groundwater permitting on a risk basis, including an assessment of interference between boreholes and their impact on surface waters, the risk of saline intrusion, and the overall sustainability of abstraction in each aquifer unit. Consider the use of test pumping and numerical models as aids to decision making.	ME, with MAFRA and RBCs	Short-medium
	Introduce permit controls on all abstractions as part of a reformed water allocation regime. Establish a mechanism to ensure that permitting policy can adapt as rainfall, river flows, groundwater yields and human demands change over time, so that it becomes flexible and adaptive, and able to maintain sustainable exploitation of natural resources.	ME, with MAFRA and RBCs	Medium
	Ensure compliance monitoring assesses and manages the total pollution load, and accounts for the river flow regime and the sensitivity of the ecosystem at different places down the river. The European Union Water Framework Directive is an example of good practice.	ME, with MAFRA and RBCs	Short-medium
	Ensure inspection and control mechanisms as well as sanctions and penalties in case of non-enforcement and compliance. Depending on the severity of the breach, and the attitude of the permit holder, this could range from a verbal warning, to a written warning, to sanctions or a fine, or criminal prosecution. If necessary, use enforcement mechanisms to set an example of persistent poor compliance, and	ME, with MAFRA and RBCs	Short-medium

Objective	Action	Possible champions/partners	Timeline
	publicise the action taken as a warning to others.		
	Carry out inspections and audits of reported water abstraction when water charges are set on self-reported water abstraction. Ensure that the inspection visit raises awareness of the consequences of non-compliance.	MAFRA, with ME	Short-medium
	Promote regular monitoring and evaluation of the adequacy, implementation and results of water policies to assess to what extent they fulfil the intended outcomes and adapt where needed.	ME, with MAFRA and RBCs	Short-medium
Establish independent regulation with strong regulating powers	Ensure that environmental regulation is independent and coordinated across all basins, and that it operates consistently and fairly so that poor performers are targeted and permit standards enforced.	ME, with RBCs	Medium
	Look after customers' interests by establishing independent regulation to ensure that all aspects of water supply are operating efficiently, are delivering to agreed levels of service, and are responding to complaints.	ME, with RBCs	Medium
	Establish independent regulation of drinking water quality compliance, and publish information on the performance of each supply, and details of enforcement action taken against any breaches of standards.	ME, with RBCs	Medium
	The establishment of independent and trusted water regulation for the protection of the environment, customers' interests and drinking water quality can be discharged in several ways, within or outside of ME - as long as they are shielded from third party interference. This includes ensuring a clear separation between regulatory, policy making and project implementation functions.	ME	Medium
Reform institutions and governance			
Reform institutional coordination	Establish inter-ministerial stakeholder platform at national level for improved coordination of WELF nexus and river management, including water quality and quantity management. Steps towards such a platform should include to: 1) Assess and analyse current water related organisational mandates and responsibilities, policy gaps and overlaps at national level; 2) Review national water policy and organisational frameworks in relation to shifting managerial responsibilities (e.g. planning, conflict mediation, data collection, etc.) to basin level organisations (e.g. RBCs); 3) Assess capacity development and financing needs and opportunities among both government and non-government stakeholders and; 4) Organise a series of national stakeholder workshops and dialogues for trust-building and to collect government and non-government stakeholder views and ideas on the design of a stakeholder platform to improve coordination of WELF nexus. OECD Principles on Water Governance and related indicator framework can be used as a voluntary tool to facilitate stakeholder dialogues. Expected outcomes of activities 1-4 are: Establish national joint vision, objectives and strategies for improved WELF nexus coordination across sectors and stakeholders; proposal developed on the design (roles and responsibilities, composition, and financing) of national stakeholder platform.	PMO, ME, MoLIT, MAFRA, MoTIE, RBCs, local and regional governments local community representatives, academia, water user groups, NGOs, private sector, etc.	Short-medium
	Initiate and promote government staff exchange programmes between national and basin levels to promote coordination of the WELF nexus.	ME, RBCs	Short-medium
	Assign clear divisions of roles and responsibilities between ME and MoLIT for effective implementation of coordinated management of water quantity and water quality at both national and basin levels.	PMO, ME, MoLIT, RBCs	Short-Medium
Create a stakeholder engagement framework	To establish stakeholder coordination platforms (at both national and basin levels), ME should in broad consultations with government and non-government stakeholders: 1) Map and assess stakeholders (ministries, local and regional government, NGOs, private sector, academia, community representatives, etc.) and their core interests and capacities; 2) Define the objectives of stakeholder engagement and the expected use of inputs and; 3) Customise the type and level of stakeholder engagement depending on objectives and characteristics of stakeholders. Stakeholder platforms should as a minimum fulfil basic criteria of inclusiveness, transparency and that all stakeholders have access to the same information.	ME, with MoLIT, MAFRA, MoTIE, RBCs, local and regional governments local community representatives, academia, water user groups, NGOs, private sector, etc.	Short-medium
	Develop and design capacity-development programmes targeting different	ME, with MoLIT,	Short-

Objective	Action	Possible champions/partners	Timeline
	constituencies for more effective participation in stakeholder engagement processes. Provide incentives in the form of small grants (travel grants, grants for holding local stakeholder meetings, etc.) for which stakeholders (non-government in particular) can apply to improve their capacities to take part in stakeholder processes. Stakeholders with weaker capacities should be prioritised.	MAFRA, MoTIE, RBCs, local and regional governments local community representatives, academia, water user groups, NGOs, private sector, etc.	medium
	Formalise stakeholder engagement in law and organisation rules and procedures to shift from an *ad-hoc* based to a structured process at 1) national level and: 2) river basin level.	PMO, ME, MoLIT, MAFRA, MoTIE, RBCs	Long
Transition to basin-level governance	Devolve water management responsibilities at the basin level to RBCs. Steps towards such an ambition should include: 1) Consider merging River Management Committees (RMCs, formerly under the remit of MoLIT) with the River Basin Committees (RBCs, under the remit of ME) to form a combined basin organisation for water management in each of the four major river basins of Korea. 2) Establish a vision, objectives and implementation strategies for managing water at basin scale by: Reviewing the functions, mandate, composition and capacity of RMCs and RBCs, and assessing capabilities for data collection, river basin management planning, conflict mediation, setting and managing water user charges, stakeholder engagement and financial viability. 3) Assess and identify institutional overlaps, and management and economic efficiency opportunities at the basin scale for improved coordination among: the RBCs, River Basin Environmental Offices, Regional Environmental Offices, Flood Control Offices and River Adjustment Councils. 4) Review mandates, stakeholder processes and compositions of river basin organisations in other OECD countries to consider which elements may benefit Korea. Undertake study tours (to France and/or other countries) for peer-learning on establishing responsibilities and functions of river basin organisations. Expected outcomes of activities 1-4 are: Establish mandate for and design of joint vision, objectives and strategies for improved WELF nexus coordination across sectors and stakeholders; and proposal developed on the design (roles and responsibilities, composition, and financing) of basin level stakeholder platform and the role of central government to support RBCs.	ME, with MoLIT, MAFRA, MoTIE, RBCs, local and regional governments local community representatives, academia, water user groups, NGOs, private sector, etc.	Short-medium
	Formalise devolvement of water management responsibilities at the basin level to RBCs in law and organisational rules and procedures to shift from an *ad-hoc* based to a structured process of stakeholder engagement.	PMO, ME, MoLIT, MAFRA, MoTIE, RBCs	Long
	Develop and oversee the implementation of policy and process guidance to ensure a consistent and coherent approach to river basin planning and the delivery of actions in support of policy objectives.	ME, with RBCs, MAFRA and MOLIT	Long
	Assign clear divisions of roles and responsibilities between ME and MoLIT for effective implementation of coordinated management of water quantity and water quality at basin level (See above for similar recommendation. These actions should be combined).	PMO, ME, MoLIT, MAFRA, MoTIE, RBCs	Short-medium

Chapter 1. Characterising the Water-Energy-Land-Food Nexus in Korea

This chapter outlines the trends of, and pressures on, Korea's water, land and energy resources in the context of economic and social development. Distinctive pressures in each of the four main river basins are documented. The chapter concludes with an assessment of the capacity of Korea to respond to pressures and tensions, and the need for future-proofing the water-energy-land-food (WELF) nexus.

1.1. Pressures on the water-energy-land-food nexus in Korea

The water, energy, land and food (WELF) nexus concept is an ideal vehicle for improving understanding of the linkages across these sectors (Figure 1.1). It is useful to identify measures to reduce the pressures and trade-offs, and enhance synergies among the sectors (Ringler et al., 2013).

Figure 1.1. Conceptual framework of the WELF nexus and its drivers of change

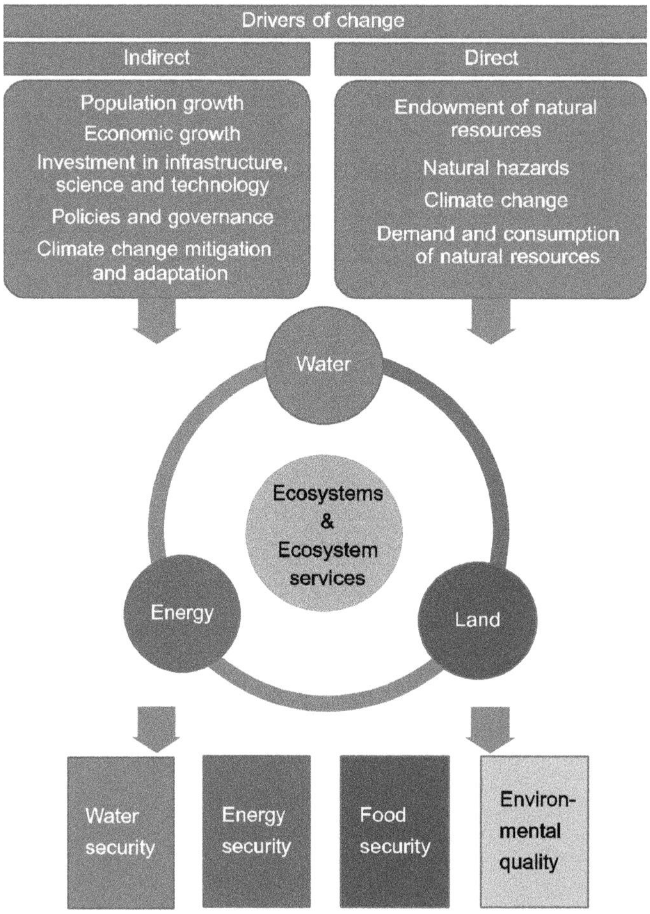

Source: Adapted from Ringler, C., Bhaduri, A. and R. Lawford (2013), The nexus across water, energy, land and food (WELF): potential for improved resource use efficiency? *Current Opinion in Environmental Sustainability 2013*, 5:617–624.

This section outlines the main pressures on water, land and energy resources in Korea. However, it is important to note that heterogeneity between and within river basins is large, with each river basin facing a unique portfolio of water- and nexus-related risks.

1.1.1. Water resources

Korea is among the few OECD countries under medium-high water stress. However, information on freshwater resources and abstractions is fragmented and could be improved, particularly regarding groundwater resources.

In Korea, precipitation is concentrated over the period from June to September, with large variations by year and in each of the four major river basins - the Han, Geum, Nakdong and Yeongsan/Seomjin River systems (Figure 1.2). This poses a major challenge for water management. Steep topography and rapid urbanisation exacerbate the consequences of frequent drought and flooding caused by rainfall patterns (OECD, 2017 a, b).

Figure 1.2. The four major river basins of Korea and the quantity of water resources in each

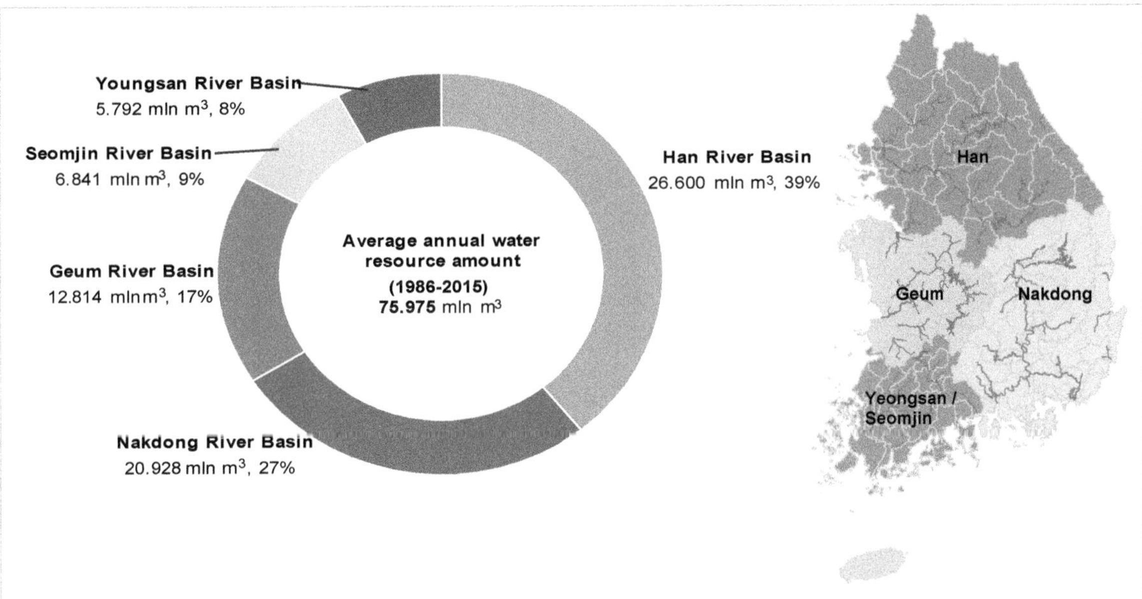

Source: (MOLIT, 2017), The 4th Long-term Comprehensive Plan of Water Resources (2001-2020) 3rd revision plan.

Water scarcity

As of 2014, the amount of water abstraction reached 33% of total available water in Korea (MoLIT, 2017), significantly higher than all other OECD countries (OECD, 2017b). Hotspots at high risk for water scarcity are present in each of the four major river basins. Scarcity is particularly acute in coastal areas of the mainland and the islands of Korea (Figure 1.3). The volume of total water use exceeds the amount of normal water runoff (which is measured during the off-flood season). As such, flood runoff needs to be captured in reservoirs for later use, desalination is necessary to supplement dam water supply and inter-basin transfers are required during periods of drought. These water management options are expensive, energy intensive and have high carbon footprints.

Figure 1.3. Water scarcity risk evaluation 2020, Korea

Note: High water scarcity (demand exceeds supply >20 million m^3); Medium water scarcity (demand exceeds supply >0-20 million m^3).
Source: MoLIT (2017), The 4th Long-term Comprehensive Plan of Water Resources (2001-2020), 3rd revision.

Surface water use in Korea amounted to 25.1 billion m^3 in 2014 (MoLIT, 2017). Agriculture is the dominant user of water, accounting for 61% of water use in 2014, a decrease from 80% in 1980 (Figure 1.4). Water for domestic purposes accounted for 30% and industrial usage for 9%, in 2014 (MoLIT, 2017). Household per capita consumption in Korea is high compared with most European countries. At 282 l/head/day it is twice that of England and Wales, and more than double (UK Environment Agency, 2008) that in the Netherlands (131 l/h/d), Germany (115 l/h/d) or Belgium (107 l/h/d). Ten percent of available water is designated as river maintenance water and is considered part of total water use, although it is not abstracted from rivers for intentional use (OECD, 2017a).

Recorded groundwater use and the number of groundwater wells have increased significantly (by 140% and 200% respectively) from 1996 to 2013. Groundwater consumption in 2013 was 4071 M m^3 (Lee and Kwon, 2016). Agriculture has led the increase in total groundwater use. This has been largely due to: i) recent multiple and prolonged droughts leading to groundwater exploitation in an effort to secure water resources; and ii) the fact that groundwater use for agriculture is exempted from water charges under the current policy to improve agricultural productivity and farmers' welfare (Lee and Kwon, 2016). As groundwater use has increased, related problems such as overexploitation and pollution has also increased, resulting in groundwater-level decline and abandoned wells susceptible to contamination (Lee and Kwon, 2015; Jung et al., 2012). Furthermore, increasing rainfall variability and periods of drought caused by a changing climate have reduced groundwater recharge conditions. Thus, effective investigation of groundwater levels and quality, and a holistic approach to secure sustainable groundwater resources are important issues for Korea.

Figure 1.4. Water use by sector

Hundred million cubic metres, 1965-2014

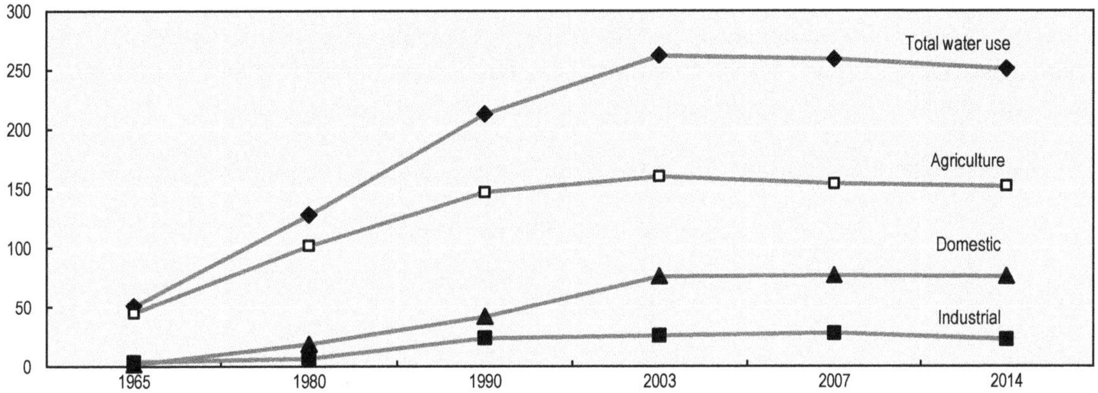

Source: MoLIT (2017), The 4th Long-term Comprehensive Plan of Water Resources (2001-2020), 3rd revision.

The total volume of freshwater abstraction is expected to increase by 4% by 2020 compared to 2007. The greatest increase in water use by 2020 is expected from industry (52%). A modest increase is expected in domestic consumption (4%), together with a modest decrease in agricultural water use (3%), by 2020 (OECD, 2017a).

Droughts have become routine in the spring, putting supply systems under stress. Climate change is likely to increase the frequency and severity of droughts, making Korea more vulnerable to water shortages. Furthermore, the Ministry of Environment (ME) is requesting additional water for environmental flows in river basins, which implies trade-offs will need to be made. It is not clear how this will be achieved given current societal demands for water, or how future water demand will be met.

There appears to be a general perception that droughts are manageable; a risky complacency given the almost total reliance on reservoir storage and recent experience in Australia, Brazil and South Africa. Responses to drought are *ad hoc*, on a case-by-case basis. K-water can obtain water from KRC reservoirs and streams, at a cost and if physically possible. Municipalities can charge special tariffs and penalties for overuse in times of a drought but they are rarely implemented. In December, 2017, MOI announced the introduction a of tariff system that allows for the flexibility of water rates to be reduced or increased based on the water consumption in the event of a drought. Drought action plans are currently being drafted. Inter-basin transfers and desalination are additional responses to drought, but cannot quickly be brought into production during a drought; they are part of a broader suite of options which robust resilience planning would identify.

Given the already high water stress and consumption of total available water resources, Korea will need to make substantial gains in water use efficiency to meet these future water demands and maintain economic growth; water supply augmentation alone will not be sufficient. Without more sustainable management and long-term planning of land and water resources, there will not be sufficient water supply for demand in the future which will potentially limit economic growth. This is already the case with surface water being fully allocated and the capacity for additional reservoirs exhausted in each of the four major river basins.

Flooding

Korea's vulnerability to flooding is higher than that of other countries (Figure 1.5), at 6.85 casualties per million people exposed, and in recent years there has been significant financial impact and numbers of people affected. Over the last decade (2006-15), flood damages totalled KRW 4 899.5 billion (Han River basin: KRW 2 047.7 billion) and affected almost 200,000 people (Han River basin: 135 900) (OECD, 2017b).

Figure 1.5. Human vulnerability to flooding, Korea and other selected OECD countries

Number killed per million exposed, 2004

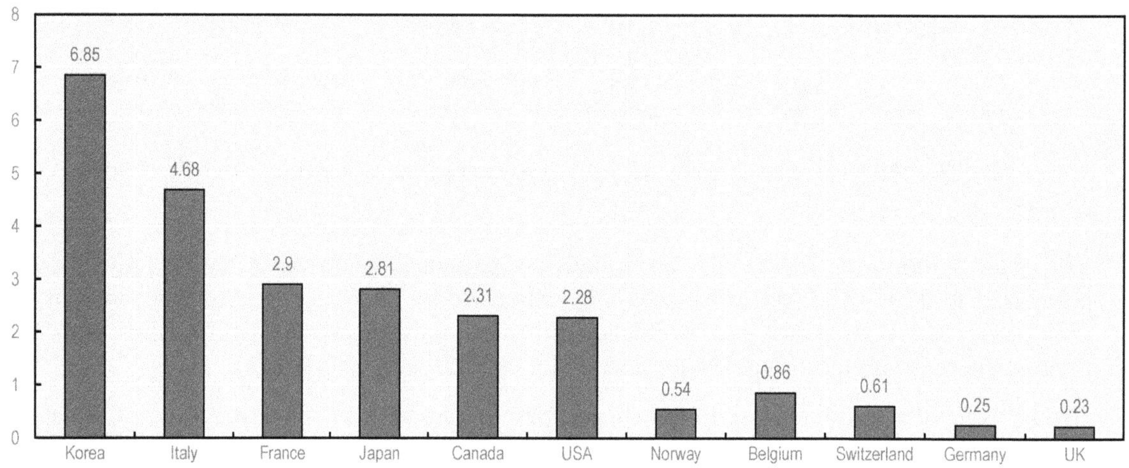

Source: UNDP (2004), Reducing Disaster Risk: A Challenge for Development. United Nations Development Programme, New York, USA.

Over 100 regions of Korea experienced water inundation more than twice in the 2000s. Since then, the government has put in place a plan to refine rainwater exclusion capabilities, such as expansion of water control capabilities by 2025 (OECD, 2017b).

The Korea Meteorological Administration projects higher precipitation and more frequent and intense rainfall events, exposing particularly densely-populated cities to a greater risk of flooding from overloading of sewerage and drainage networks and from over-topping of river flood defences. Thirty areas have been identified as high-risk of flooding. MoLIT is setting up a comprehensive plan for flood protection measures in downtown areas which have a high risk of flooding.

Smart water management is a speciality of Korea. It is a real-time water management information system which aims to help secure the stability, safety, and effectiveness of water by combining various devices and ICT technology. There are a number of low impact development (LID) pilot projects that are being tested and applied through diffuse source pollution reduction support projects. Together with green infrastructures, groundwater storage, wetland restoration and land use planning, LID can reduce building more liabilities exposed to increased flood risks. The question remains on the capacity to disseminate and scale-up these innovative projects and solutions.

Water pollution

Korea recognises the importance of water quality for sustained growth and healthy freshwater ecosystems. Improvements in biochemical oxygen demand and total phosphorus have been achieved in the four river basins with the introduction of the Korean Total Water Pollution Load Control System (Korean TMDL, Korean TMDL, the equivalent of a total maximum daily load programme) in 2004 to control point source pollution (Figure 1.6).

Figure 1.6. Changes in water quality in Korea's four major river basins

Left: Biochemical Oxygen Demand (BOD); Right: Total phosphorus (TP), 2006-2015

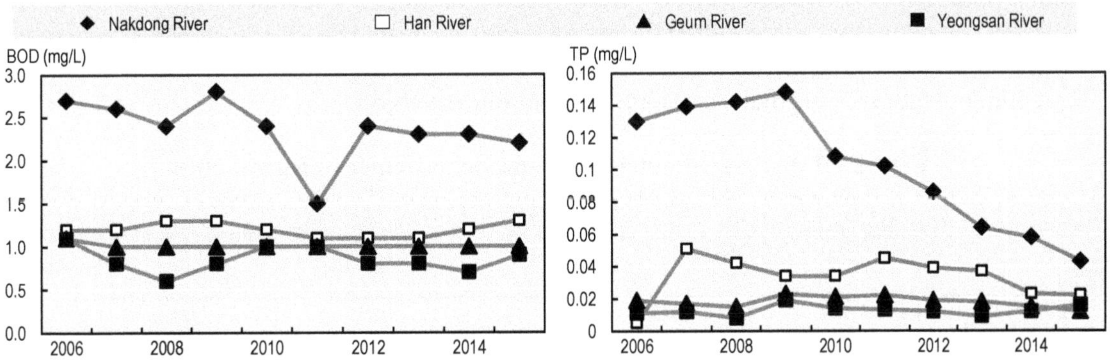

Source: ME and KEI (2016), River Management Funds for the Four Major River Systems, Korea Environmental Policy Bulletin, No. 44, Vol. XIV, Issue 4, 2016.

However, some challenges remain in water quality management:

- Diffuse pollution from agriculture is now the predominant source of water pollution, given the significant advances made in municipal wastewater treatment and an increase in livestock production (ME, 2015). In 2014, 93% of the population was served by wastewater treatment services, compared with 71% in 2000. In addition, 83% of the population benefits from advanced (tertiary) treatment - a remarkable increase from almost nothing (1%) in 2000 (OECD, 2017a). Livestock production increased from 15% to 43% between 1970 and 2015, mostly at the expense of rice production (OECD, 2018).
- Korea has the highest nitrogen balance and the second highest phosphorus balance in the OECD, even though the use of chemical fertilisers has declined (OECD, 2017a; 2018). Whereas most countries have succeeded in reducing their nitrogen balance, it has increased in Korea from 213.1 kg/ha in 1990-92 to 249 kg/ha in 2012-14. Over the same period in the Netherlands it fell from 309 kg/ha to 148 kg/ha as a result of manure quotas and manure application limits. Both nitrogen and phosphorus balances are the highest in Gyeonggi province which has the largest dairy industry and the second largest swine industry in Korea (Figure 1.7). The main sources of pollutants affecting nutrient loading include livestock manure and fertilisers.

- Nutrients in lakes, rivers and coastal waters are a significant problem, leading to eutrophication, algal blooms and increasing water treatment costs.
- Diffuse pollution is also a concern in urban areas where localised flooding results in sewer overflows from combined sewer systems.
- Historical water pollution incidents and contamination of tap water (e.g. Nakdong accidents 1991 and 1994) have resulted in a low public trust in drinking water quality with the majority of citizens using bottled water and home water filters.
- There remain issues related to permitting, compliance, monitoring and enforcement of point source discharges from industry and municipalities.

Other polluting substances (e.g. organics, metals, and emerging pollutants) do not appear to be routinely monitored in such a way as to drive action, so the true pollution picture is not known. Each of the four major river basins has damaged aquatic ecosystems due to water pollution, loss of connectivity from reservoirs and low residual flows. Degraded surface water quality has resulted in an increase in groundwater use as an alternative water source. As groundwater use increased, related problems such as overexploitation and contamination of groundwater has drawn public attention.

Figure 1.7. Estimated nutrient balance by province in Korea, 2014

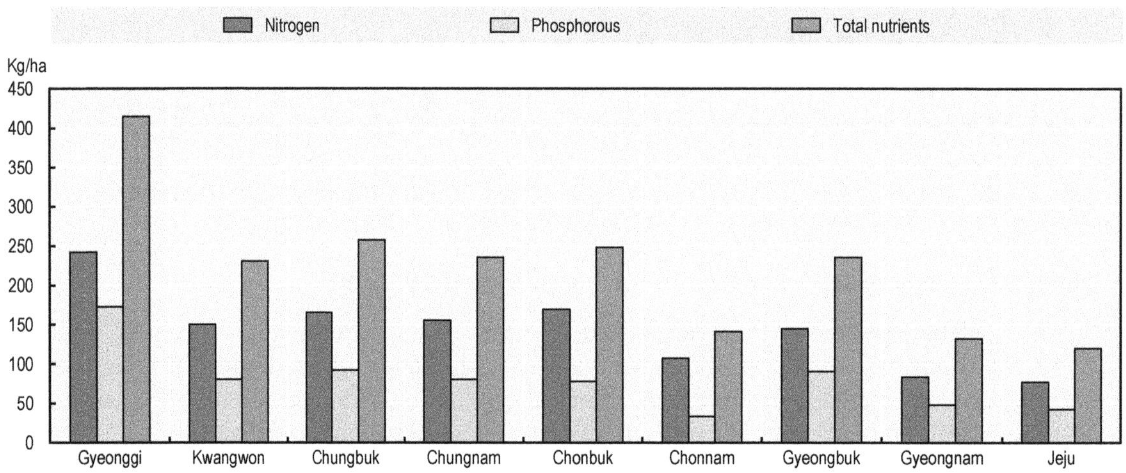

Source: Kim et al. (2015a), *Directions for Introducing Total Maximum Nutrient Loading System of Cultivated Land*, p. 91, Korean Rural Economic Institute Research Report.

There are an array of fragmentised initiatives and pilot projects to increase eco-farming, best management practices, and buy-back riparian land to improve water quality but they typically rely on voluntary approaches (i.e. are not regulatory) and come at a high cost in comparison to other potential policy solutions, particularly those that utilise the Polluter-Pays Principle. The government is also striving to improve its nutrient balance and reduce land acidity by increasing reuse of manure and effluent, and reducing chemical use of fertilisers. The role of land use planning and management will be critical for water quality and resource management. There is room for improvement in engagement with citizens, industrialists and farmers to raise awareness, increase trust and reach solutions in partnership.

Korea has plans to rearrange sewerage infrastructure by 2025 by having full separation of foul sewage and rainwater runoff, enabling it to better cope with 30-year flood risks.

Thirty priority areas have been identified. Options include low impact development (LID) in new cities, underground storage, constructed wetlands and other green infrastructure solutions in existing built environments.

1.1.2. Land resources and food production

Korea is a relatively small, mountainous peninsula with over 3 200 islands and a total land area of about 100 000 km². Forests accounted for 64% of the land area in 2013, a much higher share than the OECD average of 31%. The area of agricultural land is reducing, even though there are regulatory restrictions on the conversion of high quality farm land. The area of agricultural land decreased from 22% to 18% of total land area between 1990 and 2014 as the demand for development land and public reclamation projects increased (OECD, 2017a).

Korea faces rapid urbanisation and deterioration of natural ecosystems (Figure 1.8). Over 70% of the population lives in urban areas, well above the OECD average of 49% (Basic Statistics). Built-up, urbanised areas have expanded by 51% between 2002 and 2014; a rate that has far surpassed the population growth (6% over the same period). This reflects rapid industrialisation and urbanisation; 70% of the population lives in urban areas, well above the OECD average of 49% (OECD, 2017a). Over the same period, the area of grasslands decreased by 24% and of wetlands by 61% (OECD, 2017a). Lost agricultural and forest land was mainly converted to artificial surfaces, leading to habitat fragmentation and biodiversity loss, in particular in rice paddies, which host various ecosystems and about 527 species, and whose area has shrunk by 17% since 2003 (MOLIT, 2016, 2015; ME, 2014; MAFRA, 2015).

Figure 1.8. Urbanisation in Korea is inducing land use change

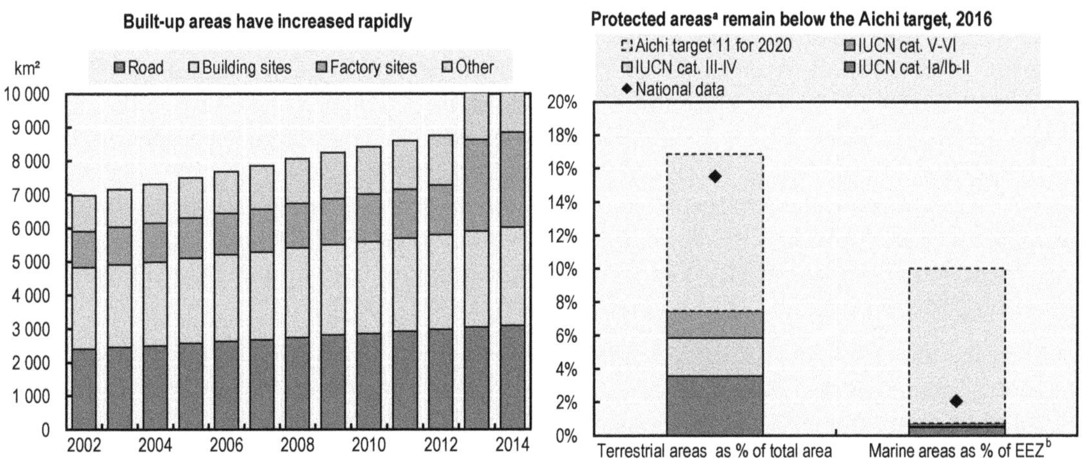

Note: a) International protected areas (UNESCO biosphere reserves, Ramsar wetlands and World Natural Heritage sites) are included in the IUCN categories. b) The exclusive economic zone (EEZ) stretches from the baseline out to 200 nautical miles from the coast.

Source: OECD (2017a), *OECD Environmental Performance Reviews: Korea 2017*, OECD Publishing, Paris. http://dx.doi.org/10.1787/9789264268265-en.

Land use for agriculture is dominated by rice; paddies accounted for 55% of the cultivated area in 2014, although down from 61% in 2003 (MAFRA, 2014, 2015). Livestock production rose by 18% from 2006 to 2016 (FAO, 2016). Organic farming represented 1.5% of agricultural land in 2012, compared with the OECD average of 2.2%

(OECD, 2017a). The observed gradual shift in the production of paddy rice to more value-added livestock and greenhouse products reflects Korean consumers' preferences. Aging farmers could perpetuate this land use change as they retire from small scale rice farming. Changes in agricultural production from rice to upland livestock and greenhouse crops may impact the timing, seasonality and volume of water consumption as well as water pollution and energy consumption. Such changes may lead to an increased reliance on groundwater. A trend towards more intensive livestock production and associated diffuse water pollution will pose a risk to surface and groundwater quality, despite efforts at managing domestic and industrial wastewater discharges.

Korea's farming model is highly intensive, with negative ramifications for water and energy use, and land and water pollution. Land acidification is worsening with climate change and agricultural production is expected to decline in both quantity and quality due to climate change and subsequent increase in disease and pests (ME, 2014). The intensity of commercial fertiliser and pesticide use is among the highest in the OECD, and livestock density is the second highest after the Netherlands. Nevertheless, apparent consumption of nitrogen and phosphate fertilisers and pesticides decreased more than crop production, resulting in a relative decoupling. However, livestock-related surpluses of nitrogen and phosphorus have risen with increased livestock production (FAO, 2016; OECD, 2013; MAFRA, 2015) and the management of diffuse source water pollution is a challenge for Korea.

More than 65% of Korean farms are less than one hectare in size, and 59% of farmers are over 65. This fragmentation of land occupation and the farming demographic increases the difficulty and complexity of raising awareness of the need to improve agricultural practice to reduce environmental impacts.

Korea remains one of the largest providers of producer support for agriculture in the OECD (OECD, 2018; 2016). Producer support, as percentage of gross farm receipts (%PSE), is almost three times higher than the OECD average and consists mostly in market price support, a category of support with potentially environmentally harmful effects (OECD, 2018). The agriculture sector does not pay energy taxes and only partially pays water charges (OECD, 2010). The 60% of rice lands in larger schemes under the management of the Korea Rural Community Corporation (KRC) have been exempted from agricultural water charges (excluding mandatory labour levies) since 2000. The smaller schemes outside KRC domain, managed under the oversight of local governments by Irrigation Associations (IAs) or by individual farmers, remain largely responsible for covering all their capital, O&M and labour costs (OECD, 2010).

Given the above trends, effective land use planning will be critical for water quality and quantity management. Potential tensions over water allocation volumes for agriculture compared with municipal and industrial use will need to be identified and resolved through rigorous supply-demand planning. A key challenge will be to increase farmers' willingness and ability to adjust to best environmental practices as the nature of food production changes.

1.1.3. Energy resources

Korea's economy is among the most energy intensive in the OECD. This is despite that Korea has no oil resources and limited natural gas reserves; it produces small amounts of anthracite (high quality coal). Thus, Korea is highly dependent on external energy sources. Net imports account for 87% of total primary energy supply, more than triple the OECD average of 25% (IEA, 2016). Fostering energy supply autonomy and reducing greenhouse gas emissions from the sector is a driver of energy policies and an element of Korea's green growth strategy.

Korea's share of renewables in the energy mix remains the lowest in the OECD and the country has fallen short of its intermediate renewables targets (OECD, 2017a) (Figure 1.9). With its mountainous topography, contested and militarised waters and high population density, it may face greater challenges to renewable energy development than other countries, particularly with regard to hydropower generation; hydroelectric power generation accounts for less than 1% of total power generation in Korea.

Figure 1.9. Korea's current and future planned energy mix

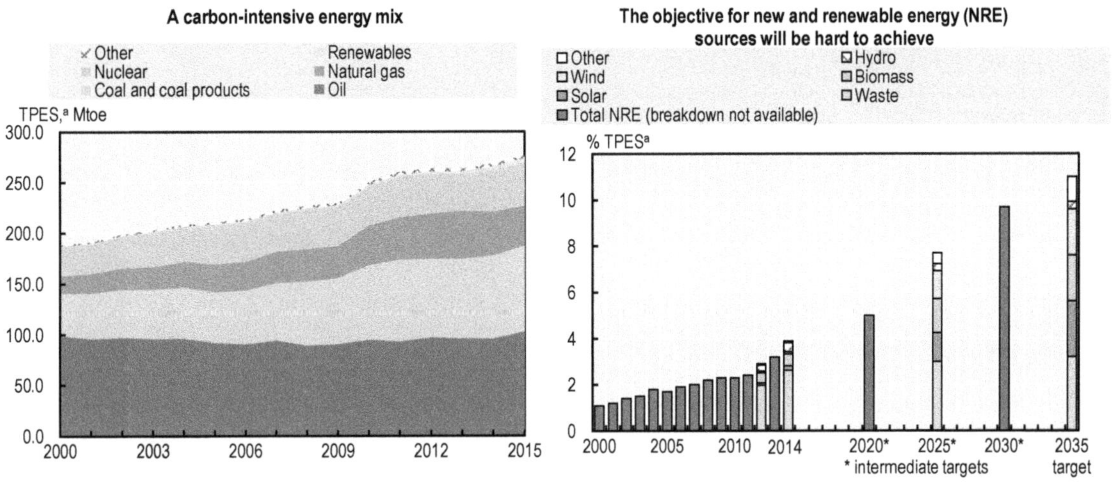

Note: a) TPES: Total primary energy supply. Breakdown excludes electricity trade.
Source: OECD (2017a), *OECD Environmental Performance Reviews: Korea 2017*, OECD Publishing, Paris. http://dx.doi.org/10.1787/9789264268265-en

The electricity consumption of Korea increased from 76.7 TWh in 1990 to 423.2 TWh in 2013 (Kim and Cho, 2017) (Figure 1.10). This was associated with an increase in industrial production and electrification of the industrial sector, and in response to low electricity prices and a distorted energy price system (Kim et al., 2015b; Kim and Shin, 2016). The industrial sector is the highest electricity consumer group (87%; 2013 figures), and is expected to remain so as the economy grows (Kim and Cho, 2017). The energy use intensity of the Korean industry remains high due to the lack of a price signal and incentives to improve energy efficiency (ibid). The agriculture sector does not pay energy taxes, and energy-intensive industries such as cement and steel are exempt from the bituminous coal tax (OECD, 2017a).

The power reserve ratio reaches dangerously low levels (<5%) during summer heat waves when power consumption increases for air conditioning (Kim and Cho, 2017). The sudden blackout in 2011 caused major inconvenience and costs to the industrial sectors (ibid).

Figure 1.10. Energy use and intensity of use by sector, 1990-2013

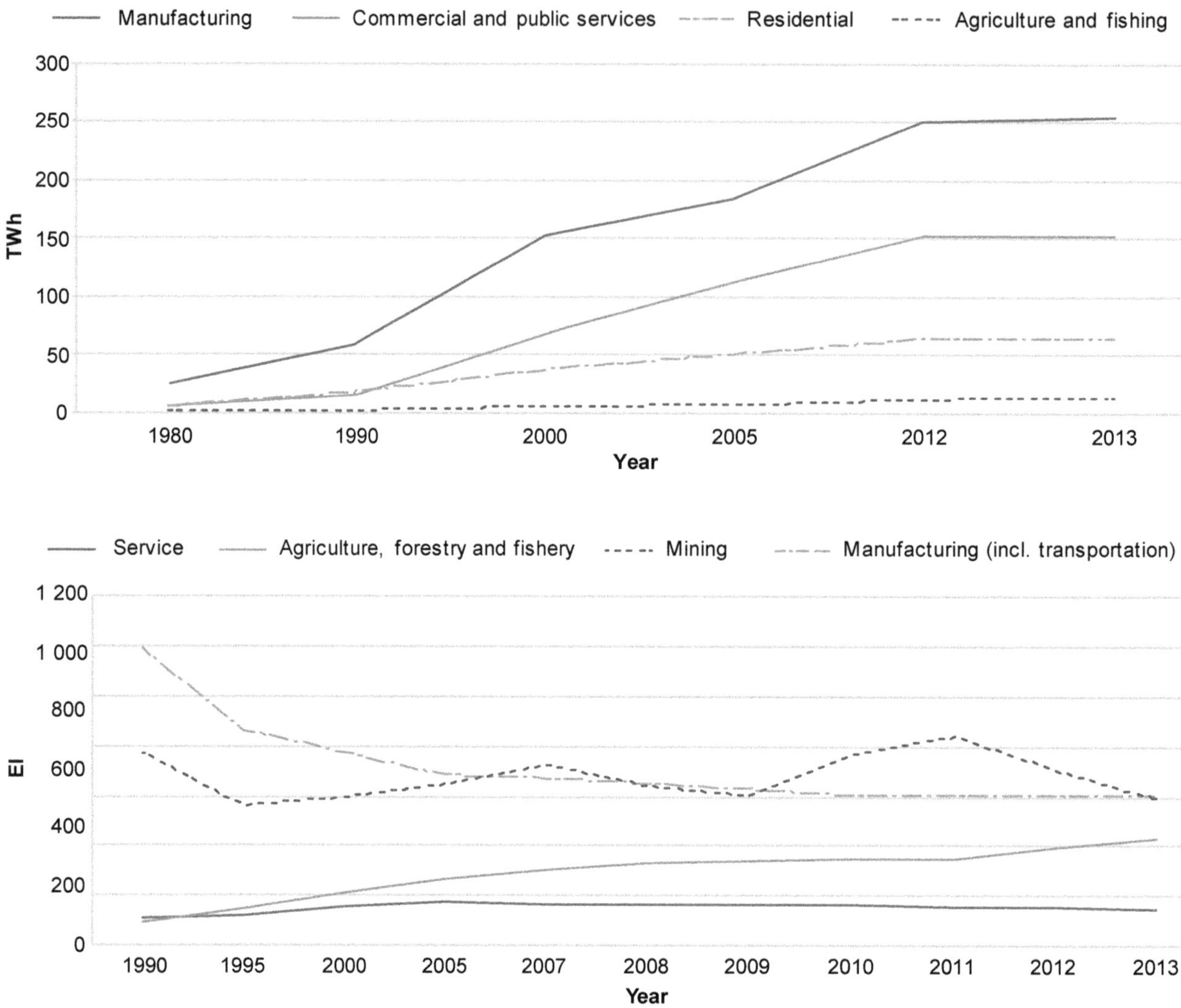

Source: Kim, K. and Y. Cho (2017), Estimation of power outage costs in the industrial sector of South Korea, Energy Policy, Vol. 101, Feb 2017, pp. 236-24.

There remain opportunities to exploit. The government is pushing for wind and solar photovoltaic power to become core pillars of Korea's new and renewable energy mix, and is also promoting strong growth in solar thermal and geothermal energy (Invest Korea, 2015). Efforts in both support for renewables and energy demand management need to be significantly scaled up if the country is to meet its long-term target of 11% renewables in total primary energy supply by 2035, already pushed back from 2030 (Figure 1.9) (OECD, 2017a).

Whilst water consumption by the energy sector is small in comparison to other sectors, water efficiency in the energy sector can still make a significant difference. There are opportunities for water recycling for cooling power plants, advanced cooling systems that use less water, and there is potential to partner with other sectors to increase water use efficiency and lower water stress. Although limited land area in Korea means that the scope for biofuels is restricted, any biofuels production will need to be managed carefully to reduce trade-offs associated with increased water and land use, water pollution and reduced food production.

There are also opportunities to reduce energy consumption in the water sector. For example through energy capture from wastewater treatment plants, energy-efficient pumping systems, decentralised water services and improvements in water leakages, which improve water supply and reduce energy demand. Designing water infrastructure to the right size for future needs will also increase efficiencies. Desalination is a particularly energy-intensive and costly way of augmenting water supply and will need to be managed carefully. There may be opportunities to unify hydropower dams and multi-purpose dams to improve water resource management. For example, when the hydropower dam in the Han River is converted into a multi-purpose dam and operated in real-time, it can secure a flood control capacity of about 240 million cubic metres and an additional water supply capacity of 540 to 880 million cubic metres.

Korea has a high energy-water risk relative to other countries in the Asia-Pacific region. One study mapping the water consumption for energy production around the Pacific Rim determined that watersheds at energy-water risk represent 59% of all basins in Korea where water is used in energy production (Tidwell and Moreland, 2016). Energy policy must consider land and water impacts, and trade-offs must be understood and explicit water demand from the energy sector needs to be accounted for in water allocation regimes. Drought planning is necessary to ensure water for cooling in order to prevent black-outs. Thermal pollution from water used for cooling needs to be considered in water quality and aquatic ecosystem management. Once built, power plants have a very limited ability to shift between different sources of water supply, so their location with respect to the availability of water is a critical consideration. The water resource must be reliable and the flow must be sufficient to provide the thermal capacity to receive the cooling water discharge without adverse impact on the ecology after use and discharge. Droughts can result in a number of simultaneous problems: river flows reduce so water may not be available for abstraction, the flow may not be sufficient to safely absorb the heating effect of the warm discharge water, and electricity demand can surge because of air conditioning demands.

In a water-stressed country such as Korea, with numerous competing pressures on its water resources, the water-energy nexus is an important consideration. Thermal generation technologies which involve significant water loss through evaporation will increasingly become less viable during droughts, either because of lack of water for effective cooling or because the lost resource is unsustainable. Similarly, the operation of hydropower plants may become increasingly contentious where unacceptable impacts on users and communities, river flow regimes and the river environment (in particular on fish passage) may occur. These tensions within the nexus will require clear policy thinking to establish priorities and an energy strategy which considers water impacts. Renewable energy options – in particular wind and solar – may become more attractive as a result.

1.1.4. Upstream versus downstream disparities

Population and industrial growth in Korea have placed increased pressures on limited available water resources, creating water use conflicts between stakeholders. A legacy of absent land and water use planning and restrictions at the basin level has created tensions between land development for economic growth and environmental impacts. This has typically manifested as water pollution with subsequent tensions between upstream and downstream users. Conflicts have also taken place over the environmental suitability of dam construction sites and over the decision-making process for national water resources plans. A lack of public consultation and stakeholder engagement on water resource planning, infrastructure development, and policies related to water rights and pollution management has not helped the situation (Choi et al. 2017). Examples of conflicts over water quantity and quality in Korea are presented in Table 1.1.

Table 1.1. Examples of conflicts over water quantity and quality, Korea

Type of conflict	Description
Water quantity	Opposition of Imsil County (Imsil-gun) to using Owon stream for non-agricultural water supply to Jeonju-city
	Conflicts among local people (Gochang), golf field owners (Anseong), and KRCC (Korea Rural Community Corporation) over supplying agricultural water to golf fields
	Opposition from the local people of Gamsu-ri, Danjang-myeon and Milyang-city to construction of a bottled water factory due to concerns over groundwater depletion and potential impacts on water availability for farming and domestic use.
	Conflicts between farmers and government over water rights in the Seomjingang Dam and Seongdeok Dam, and the conversion of agricultural water supply to multiple-purpose water supply
	Disputes with K-water over water use rights, for example with Gyeonggi providence over the water use right of the Paldang Dam, with Chuncheon city over the water use right of the Soyanggang Dam, and with Seoul city over the recognition of vested water use rights.
	Regional conflicts between the downstream region of the Geum River and the Jun-Ju region receiving trans-basin water from Yongdam reservoir.
	Conflicts over the environmental suitability of the Yeongwol Dam and Hantan River Dam projects due to impacts on landscape and ecological resources, as well as the threat of water pollution.
Water quality	Frequent conflicts between local governments over water quality deterioration in the early 1990s, which led to a new measure for environment-friendly river basin restoration.
	Frequent conflicts over the responsibility for water quality management among up-, mid-, and downstream stakeholders along the Han River basin.
	Requests from local people for the closure of fishing sites in the upper flood stage area of the Chodang reservoir due to water contamination.

Sources: Choi, I-C, et al. (2017), Water Policy Reforms in South Korea: A Historical Review and Ongoing Challenges for Sustainable Water Governance and Management, *Water*, Vol. 9, 717; Labadie, J.W. et al. (2007), Decision Support System for Adaptive River Basin Management: Application to the Geum River Basin, Korea, *Water International*, Vol. 32:3, 397-415; Moon et al. (2012), A Study on Advancement Policy of Water Usage Recognition, Korean Environment Institute (KEI); Song, Y-I. et al. (2010), Strategic environmental assessment for dam planning: a case study of South Korea's experience, *Water International*, Vol. 35:4, 397-408.

There are also disparities between urban and rural communities in Korea. Rapid industrialisation in urban areas, and the migration of young generations from rural to urban areas, have led to rural areas being economically left behind and an expanding income gap between farms and urban households[1]. Off-farm employment opportunities are limited in rural areas, in particular for the aged population (almost 60% of farmers are more than 65 years old) (OECD, 2017a). Diffuse source pollution, particularly from livestock farming has become the main source of water pollution and has caused conflicts over water rights between local governments in upstream versus downstream regions and urban versus rural communities (Choi et al., 2017).

Promoting sustainable use of land and water resources, and increasing preparedness to climate change, is an important policy agenda to assure long-term growth in agriculture and in cities. For example, opportunities exist to optimise land use and value-added food production, and to re-orient agriculture production subsidies away from direct producer and price support towards support encouraging, or conditional on, the provision of environmental services (e.g. water management, flood buffering, biodiversity protection), and spatially targeted and tailored agri-environmental payments. Such an approach may be agreeable with Korean consumers who are increasingly interested in environmentally-friendly agriculture and products. Broader stakeholder engagement is required in planning and decision-making of policies related to water resource planning, infrastructure development and policies related to water rights and pollution management.

1.2. Distinctive WELF issues in the four river basins

There are distinct tensions within the WELF nexus at different scales in Korea, which reflect local economic, social and environment conditions. This suggests that the nexus needs to be addressed in different – although coordinated – ways in each basin (for a map of the basins, see Figure 1.2). Key characteristics of each of the four major river basins in Korea are outlined below. This information was received as part of the OECD background report provided by ME for this project.

The Han River – the most northern basin – serves over half of the population of Korea. It has a higher level of protection of water sources to secure safe household and industrial water supply for Seoul city. Despite this, water pollution, high water demands and ageing water infrastructure remain key issues for the basin. Diffuse pollution and toxic effluent discharges, including from abandoned mines, have increased. The frequency of algal blooms has also increased. There is demand for community involvement, environmental awareness and water-related recreation.

The Geum River – the smallest and most western basin - serves 12% of Korea's population and has the largest proportion of land use dedicated for agriculture (28% of the basin area). Key issues in the basin include water scarcity, algal blooms, high rates of water pollution incidents and degraded aquatic ecosystems in comparison with other basins. Measures of securing alternative water resources in preparation for droughts are inadequate. The Geum River Basin has slightly lower Water Use Charges (KRW 160/m^3) than the other three river basins (KRW 170/m^3).

The Nakdong River – the largest and most eastern basin – serves about one-quarter of the population of Korea. Key issues include an increase in algal blooms and toxic water pollution from inadequate management of diffuse agricultural pollution and point source pollution from industry, and ageing water infrastructure and associated costs for improvement. It is estimated that 70% of water pollution in the Nakdong River comes from diffuse pollution, of which livestock emissions are the largest source. There are concerns about lack of compliance, monitoring and enforcement of industrial discharge permits and a lack of restrictions on land use in the Nakdong basin. There are tensions between upstream and downstream water users and polluters, particularly over the quality of surface water available for, and flooding of, downstream cities. Effective water management, policy coherence and stakeholder engagement will be critical for reducing water conflicts, and improving water quality, ecosystem functioning and resilience to climate change in the Nakdong basin.

The Yeongsan/Seomjin River – the most southern and water scarce basin – serves 8% of Korea's population and has over one-quarter of its land dedicated to agriculture. Key issues in the basin include water scarcity, an increase in algal blooms, diffuse urban and agricultural pollution and toxic point source discharges, and declining aquatic ecosystem health. Water transfers from other basins and desalination is necessary to meet water demands in the Yeongsan/Seomjin basin. There is also concern that the ability of ageing infrastructure to deliver quality water services and respond to heavy rainfall and flooding is inadequate.

In each of the four major river basins, there is limited management of water in tributaries, despite tributaries accounting for approximately 30% of rivers. Discharge standards and emission permits apply but these are not routinely monitored or enforced. Tributaries are excluded from the Korean TMDL. Small coastal catchments are also excluded from monitoring and regulation at central level. Municipalities are supposed to manage the tributaries and small coastal catchments but with no upstream and downstream coordination among them, and with no or limited links to other levels of water governance (basin, region, national).

The National Groundwater Information Centre collects information on groundwater quantity, quality and abstraction in Korea. Under the 1994 Groundwater Act, a database is being developed to gather groundwater quantity and quality data. Some artificial aquifer recharge has occurred by municipalities as a drought risk reduction measure but there is little evidence of robust data and appropriate comprehensive policy to manage abstraction and pollution of groundwater at the national or aquifer levels. The two main issues for groundwater are improving understanding of groundwater quality and implementing management strategies (i.e. allocation regimes reinforced by permitting and monitoring) for each groundwater unit.

1.3. Capacity to respond to pressures and tensions

1.3.1. Coordination across institutions

Korea's institutional framework for water management is multi-layered and multi-faceted to accommodate the different water uses in the country: drinking water, irrigation, industrial supply, hydropower and cooling, and environmental needs. However, the number of government institutions, agencies and other bodies (Table 1.2) involved in water management at central, basin and local levels attests to a fragmented institutional landscape that has high inefficiencies. While these institutions may allow for fast policy making and response to crises, they raise important coordination challenges for the development and implementation of integrated, coherent and inclusive water policy and the sustainable management of the WELF nexus.

The fragmentation of responsibilities for water amongst different ministries has also resulted in a multitude of water management plans. The main water plans and programmes are presented in Table 1.3. The ME has created 35 water-related plans, and is trying to streamline the four main ones into the Water Environment Management Master Plan for water quality and ecosystem health and the National Waterworks Master Plan, which includes tap (drinking) water policy.

The recent water governance reform through the adoption of the revised Government Organisation Act, June 2018, merges responsibilities of water quantity and quality management under one ministry (ME). This merge is a step in the right direction for improved policy alignment and coherency. However, improved coordination does not come automatically; ME will need to develop and implement a water quality and quantity "coordination" strategy for effective merging of responsibilities at national and sub-national levels (see 0).

Table 1.2. Overview of government roles and responsibilities for water in Korea

Institution	Responsibilities
Government ministries	
Ministry of Environment (ME)	Local waterworks management, drinking water management, sewage policy, water quality management, aquatic ecosystem health. Development and coordination of plans for the conservation, use, allocation and development of water resources, multi-regional water supply and river basin management. Long-term water resource planning and water control planning for river basins. Water infrastructure development, and coastal and river reclamation.
Ministry of Land, Infrastructure and Transport (MoLIT)	Land management, river maintenance, and planning related to construction of cities, roads, etc.
Ministry of Agriculture, Food and Rural Affairs (MAFRA)	Securing stable food production, agricultural water development and management, including irrigation dam management.
The Ministry of Strategy and Finance (MoSF)	Economic and fiscal policies, public expenditures, taxes, tariffs and public fund management, including for the water sector.
Ministry of the Interior (MoI)	Oversees decentralisation and the interactions between central and local authorities. Contributes to planning the tariff strategy for drinking water and sanitation service provision.
Ministry of Trade, Industry and Energy (MoTIE)	National power development, including hydropower.
Ministry of Public Safety and Security (MPSS)	Public safety and disaster prevention.
Office for Government Policy Coordination	Directing, adjusting and overseeing central administrative authorities underneath the Prime Minister's Office (PMO). Managing, analysing and assessing policies in regard to social risks, conflicts and pending problems, including water-related conflicts.
Government institutes and committees	
National Disaster Management Research Institute (NDMI)	Practical disaster management capacity building, including guidance, information, analysis and technology. Works under the Ministry of Public Safety and Security.
National Institute of Environmental Research (NIER)	Research on total water pollution load control, water quality standards, water-environmental engineering, aquatic ecosystems and integrated water quality management and evaluation processes (e.g. water quality predictions, etc.). Works under the ME.
National Water Resource Management Committee	Co-ordination of water-related stakeholders and agencies across levels of government.
River Management Committees (RMCs)	Deliberation on, and mediation of, important issues and disputes on river management. There are two types of RMCs: 1) Central RMCs, which exist under the ME (until recently, they were under the responsibility of MoLIT); and 2) Local RMCs, which operate at the basin level and sit under local governments.
River Basin Committees (RBCs)	Deliberating bodies that unite all stakeholders from each river basin district. Under the remit of ME. RBCs manage the River Management Funds which support upstream water quality projects.
Water Tariff Committee	Deliberation on water charges (for dam water and multi-regional water).
State-owned corporations	
Korea Water Resources Corporation (K-water)	Operation and management of water resources facilities, including bulk water supply to municipalities and industries through dams and multi-regional water supply systems. Acts under the authority of ME.
Korea Environment Corporation (KECO)	Operation and management of local waterworks through consignment contracts with local governments. Supports policy making and implementation for water, sewage and water quality management. Acts under the authority of ME.
Korea Rural Community Corporation (KRC)	Implementation of development projects in farming and fishing villages, and operating agricultural water and agricultural irrigation facilities. Acts under the auspices of MAFRA.
Korea Hydro- and Nuclear Power (KHNP)	Operation of ten hydropower plants under the authority of MoTIE.
Research institutes	
Korea Environment Institute (KEI)	Science-based policy advice for government, public sector and civil society, including on water quality. Review of environmental impact assessments for major development projects.
Korea Institute of Civil Engineering and Building Technology (KICT)	R&D to improve public safety and the quality of life, including advice on government policies and strategic plans regarding water resources, flood damage, drought control, waterway surveys, subterranean water mapping and climate change.
Korea Research Institute for Human Settlements (KRIHS)	Research on spatial policy, territorial development and competitiveness, and green growth, including water resources and river basin management.

Source: Summary from OECD (2017b), *Enhancing Water Use Efficiency in Korea: Policy Issues and Recommendations*, OECD Studies on Water, OECD Publishing, Paris. http://dx.doi.org/10.1787/9789264281707-en.

Table 1.3. Main water plans and programmes

Ministry in charge	Plans and programmes	Mandate	Timeline and purpose
ME	The Framework Act on Water Management		This new Act establishes a master plan for water management at the national level and for the four major river basins based on the concept of integrated water management. A national management committee and basin committees will promote sustainable and integrated water management. To be enacted in June 2019
	The Water Management Technology and Industry Act		This new Act aims to enhance quality of life through the development of water management technology and promoting the water industry. To be enacted in December 2018.
	River Act		Operation of river facilities, such as dams, reservoirs and floodgates. Water allocation including use, management and adjustment in use of river water
	Water Environment Management Master Plan	Water Environment Conservation Act (Art. 24 of 234)	Ten-year plan to achieve water quality targets and create an ecologically healthy water environment 2006-15, 2016-25
	Long-term Comprehensive Plan for Water Resources	Act on the Investigation, Planning, and Management of Water Resources (Art.17)	Twenty-year plan for stable security and effective use, development and preservation of water resources 2001-20, 2006-20, 2011-20 (revision)
	Comprehensive Water Control Plans for River Basin	Act on the Investigation, Planning, and Management of Water Resources (Art.18)	Ten-year plan for development and appropriate use of river basin water resources, river environment improvement, river basin flood prevention and flood damage minimisation National rivers: 2005-15 (established by the MOLIT) Local rivers: varies (established by local governments)
	Comprehensive Mid-term Plan on the Ecological Stream Restoration Project	Water Environment Management Master Plan	Restoration of damaged rivers by removing artificial disturbances, maintaining integrity of ecosystem 2011-15, 2016-20
	National Sewage Master Plan	Sewerage Act (Art. 4)	Ten-year plan for development and implementation of national sewerage policy 2006-15, 2016-25
	National Waterworks Master Plan	Water Supply and Waterworks Installation Act (Art. 5)	Ten-year plan for development of national waterworks policy, effective water use and stable tap water supply 2006-15, 2016-25
	National Water Reuse Plan	Promotion of and Support for Water Reuse Act (Art.5)	Ten-year plan for promotion of water reuse and facilitation of related technology development 2011-20
	Basic Plan for Soil Conservation	Soil Environment Conversation Act (Art. 4)	Ten-year plan for prevention of soil contamination, restoration and purification of contaminated soil and provision of soil-groundwater nexus 2010-19
	Water Demand Management Plan		Tap water saving through effective water demand management 2000-06, 2007-16
	Long-term Dam Construction Plans	Act on Construction of Dams and Assistance, etc. to their Environs (Art. 4)	Ten-year plan to develop water resources in an efficient and environment-friendly manner 2012-21
	Groundwater Management Master Plan	Groundwater Act (Art. 6)	Ten-Year plan for appropriate development and use, and the efficient preservation and management of groundwater 2012-21
	Basic Plan for Waterworks Installation and Management (Multiregional and industrial)	Water Supply and Waterworks Installation Act (Art. 4)	Ten-year plan to install and manage general and industrial waterworks in a proper and reasonable manner 2012-25, 2015-25 (revision)
MOLIT	River Act		Construction and maintenance of flood control, construction of river facilities (e.g. dams, reservoirs, floodgates). River Information Management System.
	Special Act on the Compensation of Land		Compensation to property owners for loss of transferred land for river management

Ministry in charge	Plans and programmes	Mandate	Timeline and purpose
	Incorporated into River		
	Natural River improvement programme	River Act	Restoration of river channels to near-natural state to improve aquatic habitat and amenity services
	Special Act on the Eco-friendly Conservation and Utilisation of the Area around Dams		To conserve and manage the environment, and develop economy around the dam is for balanced and sustainable development of country
PMO, MAFRA, ME, MOLIT, etc.	Comprehensive measures on diffuse source pollution		Control of diffuse pollution sources (agricultural fields, livestock facilities, urban areas, roads, etc.) 2004-11, 2012-20
MAFRA	Rural Water use Rationalisation Plan	Rearrangement of Agricultural and Fishing Village Act (Art. 15)	Ten-year plan for efficient development, use and preservation of rural water 1999
	Comprehensive measures to combat drought in the agricultural sector		Effective management of agriculture water use to minimise the impact of drought December 2015

Source: OECD (2017a), *OECD Environmental Performance Reviews: Korea 2017*, OECD Publishing, Paris. http://dx.doi.org/10.1787/9789264268265-en.

The following points outline the main water governance issues identified from the OECD fact-finding mission:

- Five ministries, several director generals, multiple directorates and divisional units each manage certain aspects of water, and commonly in silos. There are additional costs from such a silo approach. A staged approach towards policy integration is being considered, first merging water quantity, quality and ecosystems; and then combining with disaster management for floods and droughts, urban planning, and agriculture. Even with the recent institutional merging of water responsibilities to ME, integration of water quality and quantity management calls for structural changes within ME, as well as motivated, incentivised and capacitated staff to make integration successful.
- There appears to be a dislocation between centrally formulated policies and their implementation at a local scale.
- Korea has a largely reactive (as opposed to preventive) response to water crises, which comes at a high cost. The increasing frequency and severity of droughts in particular are exposing system failures and a lack of resilience planning to water-related shocks. Preventive river maintenance and the installation of emergency spillways and spillway expansions are helping to reduce flood risks in high-risk areas of Korea.
- There are 77 laws that deal with water which are not necessarily consistent with one another nor factor in unintended consequences from implementation. For example, in 2017, the ME decided to introduce ecological flows without a clear vision of how they affect the rights of other users, and without guidance on how to implement them in practice. While e-flows are an essential constituent of sustainable water management in the Korean context, this way of proceeding may potentially expose and increase tensions between water users.
- As heard during the fact-finding mission "There is a plan for every thing, but not *A* plan for *Everything*". ME has a 20-year Water Resources Plan (previously

under the responsibility of MoLIT), revised every 5 years, and a 10-year Water Environment Strategy. With the transfer of water resources responsibilities from MoLIT to ME, it is envisaged that these plans will be coordinated in the short term, but at their next iteration they should be merged. MAFRA has a 10-year Water Use Rationalisation Plan for the efficient development and management of agricultural water, and there are multiple 10-year plans by government research organisations under MoTIE. However, there is little link or coordination between each of the plans and only about 10% of plans actually translate into action.

1.3.2. Capacities to adjust policies to local situations and coordinate across sectors

Korea's capacity to adjust policies to local circumstances is limited. As investigated in the OECD (2017b) report *Enhancing Water Use Efficiency in Korea: Policy Issues and Recommendations*, three economic instruments formerly under the remit of MoLIT contribute to water quantity management and could potentially promote water use efficiency in Korea:

1. A **river water use fee** is levied on water users (energy generators, industry, and domestic users) who abstract water from a river;
2. A **dam water tariff** is a uniform volumetric tariff levied on water users who abstract water secured in a dam via a contract with K-water; and
3. **Multi-regional water tariffs** are two-part tariffs set nationwide to partially recover the costs of supplying water through multi-regional systems; different tariffs apply to different water quality grades (raw water, settled water, purified water).

In addition, a **water use charge** under the remit of ME partially overlaps with the river use fee. The water use charge is paid by downstream urban residents and industries based on consumption of water and used for River Management Funds (RMFs) which support projects for managing and improving water quality upstream. Charges are similar in each basin and based on previous years financing demand from local governments, and not future needs. The various water charges and who is responsible, pays and exempt are outlined in Table 1.4.

Table 1.4. Charges on water abstraction in Korea

Water Charge	Charge, 2016 (KRW/ m³)	Who collects	Who pays	Who is exempted
River water use fee	52.7	Provinces and metropolitan cities	Municipalities, industries	Irrigators, etc.
Dam water tariff	52.7	K-water	Municipalities, industries	Irrigators (they seldom use K-water reservoirs), etc.
Multi-regional water tariff		K-water	Municipalities, industries	
Raw water	233.7			
Settled water	328.0			
Purified water	432.8			
Water use charge		Downstream municipalities, under remit of ME	Downstream municipalities, industries (end-users)	Irrigators, upstream water users
Han, Nakdong and Yeongsan/ Seomjin River Basins	170			
Geum River Basin	160			

Source: Adapted from OECD (2017b), *Enhancing Water Use Efficiency in Korea: Policy Issues and Recommendations*, OECD Studies on Water, OECD Publishing, Paris. http://dx.doi.org/10.1787/9789264281707-en.

None of the above economic instruments are designed to promote water use efficiency or address increasing scarcity (already the highest amongst OECD countries). Charges are not differentiated by basin and therefore do not reflect local water security issues and financing requirements. Furthermore, they do not generate sufficient revenue required to maintain and extend existing water infrastructure at the basin level. Irrigators are largely exempt from water abstraction charges (OECD, 2017a), despite the agriculture sector being the greatest user of water.

Low cost-recovery of water supply and sanitation services reduces the funding available for effective operation, maintenance and upgrades/replacements of infrastructure: a significant risk given that national infrastructure assets are ageing, with all components of a similar age. Infrastructure in multi-regional supply systems over 20 years are expected to reach 49.6% by 2020 and 79.6% by 2025 out of total facility capacity (Table 1.5). Furthermore, the working age population (aged between 15 and 64 years old) is expected to decline by 15% between 2010 and 2040. Together with slowing economic growth, this will result in a reduced ability to publically fund water infrastructure.

Table 1.5. The proportion of aging water infrastructure over 20 years

Water infrastructure	2014	2020	2025
Multi-regional water supply system	26.3%	49.6%	79.6%
Local water supply system	30.6%	37.7%	45.9%

Source: OECD (2017b), *Enhancing Water Use Efficiency in Korea: Policy Issues and Recommendations*, OECD Studies on Water, OECD Publishing, Paris. http://dx.doi.org/10.1787/9789264281707-en.

Ineffective water management policies in Korea manifest in the following ways:

- **The prevailing water allocation regime fails to allocate water where it is most useful**. The capacity of water allocation regimes in Korea to deliver sustainable water management and allocate water where is creates most value is hampered by the coexistence of water entitlements acquired before and after the construction of dams. It is not clear whether water is over allocated or overused; abstraction limits are not routinely monitored for compliance or enforced (OECD, 2017b).

- **Leakage and non-revenue water are high** (average 20.6%) in water supply networks to households and industry. The target is to reduce leakage to 15%. Some areas are being prioritised because of the scale of this nationwide challenge (some areas have leakage as high as 50%).
- **There is low public awareness of the degree of water scarcity** in Korea. Industrial water use is geared towards economic production rather than water efficiency. Low water charges provide little incentive to reduce water consumption, in particular where water is scarce, the opportunity cost of using it is high or augmenting supply is expensive. Per capita household use is among the highest in the world, at 282 litres per person per day (l/p/d).
- KREI recognises **water use inefficiency within the agriculture sector**. It has a research project on how to increase water use efficiency and demand-side management. The question remaining is how any saved water will be reallocated and used.
- **Dams that have lost their function** have been under the spotlight, particularly those that have led to deterioration in water quality and aggravated conflict between upstream and downstream communities. MOSF are planning for two additional hydropower dams.
- **Groundwater resources could be faced with problems caused by over-abstraction and pollution**. In coastal areas, there is concern about saline intrusion. Groundwater - primarily used for irrigation and greenhouse farming because of its superior water quality in comparison to river water - is neither properly monitored nor regulated, and is at risk from agricultural and industrial pollution.

With limited freshwater resources to harness, and with droughts and floods becoming more frequent and severe, the focus of the future is turning towards improvements in water use efficiency and demand management, or the reuse of wastewater[2]. There are opportunities to manage water resources and existing infrastructure in a coordinated way (OECD, 2017b). Decisions on how to operate dams and how to share water amongst agriculture, energy, industry, municipalities and the environment can be improved in Korea in generate more value from water. It will be critical to address the public's lack of awareness of water scarcity risk; their focus is on water quality despite repeated droughts. A popular saying in Korea is that when something is wasted "you use it like water".

1.4. A need for future-proofing the WELF nexus in Korea

The WELF nexus faces dramatic changes in Korea, and the past is a poor predictor of future risks, uncertainties and opportunities. Recent droughts across the world have highlighted the fact that historic weather records are no guide to today's rainfall patterns. Even where climate change predictions suggest that, on average, rainfall in the future may not be very different to that experienced in the historic record, they ignore the risk of more frequent, longer duration and more extreme events. It is extreme events which test water supply systems to their limits.

Traditional assumptions about the reliability of a rainy season, and the certainty of reservoirs refilling each year, are likely to be misplaced. Since the turn of the Millennium, prolonged droughts in Australia, California, Brazil (Sao Paulo) and South Africa (Cape Town) have exposed the vulnerability of supply systems which rely heavily on reservoir storage and the flawed thinking that storage capacity equates to water supply security. It does, but only when the reservoirs are full. The lessons learned from these recent droughts elsewhere are particularly relevant in the Korean context, for four reasons:

1. They demonstrate that it is essential to have drought plans in place before a drought develops, so that the triggers for actions are agreed in advance, negotiations over compromises and trade-offs have already been settled, and roles and responsibilities are clear.
2. They show that a structured approach to water resource supply planning can reduce the likelihood of emergency measures being required during a drought. All but the most extreme events will have been considered as part of day-to-day management, and investment and operational processes will be in place to manage drought on a routine basis.
3. They all impacted supply systems which relied heavily on reservoir storage, with very few alternative sources; very similar to the Korean situation.
4. They all exposed the dangers of relying on an approach to water supply planning and underlying assumptions about the reliability of sources based upon historic norms and a continuation or extension of business as usual.

Korea is not immune to droughts. A recent series of spring droughts has mainly impacted agricultural production, but each has brought the risk of wider disruption to water supplies. In early 2018, in South Gyeongsang Province, emergency measures were needed to maintain supplies. Municipalities in South Jeolla Province have also been impacted: reservoirs supplying Sinan-gun were at only 18 percent of capacity, and they sought 87 billion won (USD 76 million) in emergency funds from the central government and provided 16 billion won from their own reserves to divert water from flowing to the ocean (Ko Dong-hwan, 2017).

The government recognises the risk from drought, and have prepared a comprehensive countermeasure against drought at the committee under the direction of the Office for Government Policy Coordination (drought is a cross-departmental issue). It seeks greater resilience through more connectivity across water supply systems, the use of treated effluent for irrigation and industrial water supply, and better demand management. However, Korea relies heavily on a disaster response mechanism, including drought warning systems and compensatory payments issued by the interagency Drought Task Force. Disaster prevention, through scenario planning for land use and investment does not receive similar attention.

Future scenario and investment planning will be essential to assess: the potential range of climate change impacts and costs related to water availability and water supply security; the effect of demographic changes on water demand; different economic scenarios for water demand and water quality; and land use, food and energy production scenarios for water demand and quality. Future scenarios will need to look further ahead than 20 years, to drive land use, urban and infrastructure development, as well as non-infrastructure options such as demand management and behaviour change. Responses need to be prioritised, reflecting effectiveness and cost-efficiency, now and in the future.

Notes

[1] The relative level of average farm household income declined to 65% of average urban household income, which is low when compared to almost all other OECD countries.

[2] The Korean Construction Code now requires the use of reclaimed water for large greenfield projects.

References

Choi, I-C, et al. (2017), Water Policy Reforms in South Korea: A Historical Review and Ongoing Challenges for Sustainable Water Governance and Management, *Water*, 9, pp 717.

IEA (2016), "World Indicators", *IEA World Energy Statistics and Balances* (database), http://dx.doi.org/10.1787/data-00514-en (accessed in July 2016).

Invest Korea (2015), *New and Renewable Energy,* Invest Korea, Seoul, www.investkorea.org/en/published/publications.do?mode=download&articleNo=71367&attachNo=10696.

FAO (2016), *FAOSTAT* (database), http://faostat3.fao.org/home/E (accessed in July 2016).

Jung, C.D. et al. (2012), Efficient management method of groundwater in farming and fishing villages, *Journal of Soil and Groundwater Environment*, 17,pp 81–90.

Kim, K. and Y. Cho (2017), Estimation of power outage costs in the industrial sector of South Korea, *Energy Policy*, 101, pp. 236-24.

Kim, C. and J. Shin (2016), Electricity pricing policy alternatives to control rapid electrification in. Korea J. *Electr. Eng. Technol.* 11 (2), pp 285–299.

Kim, C. G. et al. (2015a), "Directions for Introducing Total Maximum Nutrient Loading System of Cultivated Land", *Korean Rural Economic Institute Research Report.*

Kim, K., Nam, H., Cho, Y. (2015b). Estimation of the inconvenience cost of a rolling blackout in the residential sector: the case of South Korea. Energy Policy, 76, pp 76–86.

Ko Dong-hwan (2017), Drought causes water shortage crisis in southern Korea. Korea Times, 20 June 2017. http://www.koreatimes.co.kr/www/nation/2017/06/371_231587.html.

Labadie, J.W. et al. (2007), Decision Support System for Adaptive River Basin Management: Application to the Geum River Basin, Korea, *Water International*, 32:3,pp 397-415.

Lee, J.Y. and K. Kwon (2016), Current Status of Groundwater Monitoring Networks in Korea, *Water*, 8, pp 168.

Lee, J.Y. and K. Kwon (2015), Groundwater resources in Gangwon Province: Tasks and perspectives responding to droughts, *Journal of the Geological Society of Korea*, 51, pp 585–595.

MAFRA (2015), *Agriculture, food and rural affairs statistics yearbook 2015*, Ministry of Agriculture, Food and Rural Affairs, Sejong.

MAFRA (2014), *Agriculture, food and rural affairs statistics yearbook 2014*, Ministry of Agriculture, Food and Rural Affairs, Sejong.

ME and KEI (2016), River Management Funds for the Four Major River Systems, Korea Environmental Policy Bulletin, No. 44, Vol. XIV, Issue 4.

ME (2015), *Ecorea: Environmental Review 2015, Korea*, Ministry of Environment, Sejong, http://eng.me.go.kr/eng/web/board/read.do?pagerOffset=0&maxPageItems=10&maxIndexPages=10&searchKey=&searchValue=&menuId=30&orgCd=&boardId=565930&boardMasterId=547&boardCategoryId=&decorator=.

ME (2014), "The Fifth National Report to the Convention on Biological Diversity", Ministry of Environment, Sejong. www.cbd.int/doc/world/kr/kr-nr-05-en.pdf.

Moon et al. (2012), *A Study on Advancement Policy of Water Usage Recognition*, Korean Environment Institute (KEI).

MoLIT (2017), The 4th Long-term Comprehensive Plan of Water Resources (2001-2020), 3rd revision plan.

MOLIT (2016), *Statistical Yearbook 2015,* Ministry of Land, Infrastructure and Transport, Sejong.

MOLIT (2015), *Statistical Yearbook 2014,* Ministry of Land, Infrastructure and Transport, Sejong.

OECD (2018, forthcoming), Innovation, Agricultural Productivity and Sustainability in Korea.

OECD (2017a), *OECD Environmental Performance Reviews: Korea 2017*, OECD Publishing, Paris. http://dx.doi.org/10.1787/9789264268265-en.

OECD (2017b), E*nhancing Water Use Efficiency in Korea: Policy Issues and Recommendations*, OECD Studies on Water, OECD Publishing, Paris. http://dx.doi.org/10.1787/9789264281707-en.

OECD (2016), Agricultural Policy Monitoring and Evaluation 2016, OECD Publishing, Paris, http://dx.doi.org/10.1787/agr_pol-2016-en.

OECD (2013), "Environmental Performance of Agriculture (Edition 2013)", *OECD Agriculture Statistics* (database), http://dx.doi.org/10.1787/data-00660-en, (accessed in July 2016).

OECD (2010), *Agricultural Water Pricing: Japan and Korea*, OECD Publishing, Paris. http://dx.doi.org/10.1787/9789264083578-13-en.

Ringler, C., Bhaduri, A. and R. Lawford (2013), The nexus across water, energy, land and food (WELF): potential for improved resource use efficiency?, *Current Opinion in Environmental Sustainability 2013*, 5:617–624.

Song, Y-I. et al. (2010), Strategic environmental assessment for dam planning: a case study of South Korea's experience, *Water International*, 35(4), pp 397-408.

Tidwell, V. and B. Moreland (2016), Mapping water consumption for energy production around the Pacific Rim, Environmental Research Letters (2016) 094008.

UNDP (2004), Reducing Disaster Risk: A Challenge for Development. United Nations Development Programme, New York, USA

UK Environment Agency (2008), *International Comparisons of Domestic Per Capita Consumption.* Report by Aquaterra for Environment Agency, England and Wales.

Chapter 2. Managing water for the Water-Energy-Land-Food nexus in Korea

This chapter provides practical water policy guidance to improve water management for the WELF nexus in Korea. It reviews the water quantity and quality monitoring framework in Korea, and focuses on policies to strengthen the management of water demand and water quality.

2.1. Water quality and quantity monitoring

Managing land and water resources well starts with a good understanding of the state and trends of the environment and the pressures on it. All elements of monitoring, data retrieval, archiving and analysis must integrate and work efficiently together.

There are four areas in particular where the Korean monitoring and assessment regime appears to be in need of review.

1. *The range of parameters in the water quality monitoring programme is limited.*

Experience from the USA and across Europe shows that in catchments where there are discharges of sewage and industrial effluents, or widespread agriculture, then there are many other pollutants, such as metals, hydrocarbons, pesticides, organics and pharmaceuticals which need to be monitored because of their impact on the environment and risk to human health (OECD, 2017a). Only once these parameters are monitored, and their concentrations understood, can pollution loads be managed so as to reduce environmental and health risks. In particular, this means understanding where the pollution 'hot spots' are so that permits and enforcement can be tightened up as necessary, and for river water quality monitoring to reflect the range of pollutants which pose a risk to ecosystems. Over time, as a clearer picture emerges of the most degraded water bodies and aquifers, measures can be better targeted through planning processes. As illustrated in Table 2.1, the range of parameters in Korea's water quality monitoring programme is limited.

Table 2.1. List of parameters monitoring in surface and groundwater bodies

Water resource	Water quality parameter
River water	pH, DO,SS, COD, BOD, cd, As, CN, Hg, Pb, Cr^{+6}, ABS, PCB, T-P, T-N etc.
Groundwater	pH, colon bacillus, NO3-N, chloride ion , bacteria, cd, As, CN, Hg, organophosphorus, Pb, phenol, Cr^{+6}, trichloroethylene, tetrachloroethylene, benzene, toluene, ethylbenzene, xylene etc.

Source: Water Resources Management Information System; WAMIS, *In*: OECD Background report provided by ME.

Where and how water quality is monitored is also important. Critical locations will be downstream of major discharges of household or industrial effluent, or of potentially polluting activities such as mining, both at active sites and abandoned mines. Whether these are monitored routinely, or as part of the permit compliance process, will be a matter of judgement.

The frequency at which samples are taken matters, in terms of the level of confidence in the reliability of the data. Two or four samples a year may not be representative of the water quality for the rest of the year – or even of the day on which the samples were taken. The frequency of water quality monitoring therefore needs to reflect the likelihood of variability, which will be different in each water body. Once there is confidence that there is little variation, then the frequency of sampling may be scaled back to surveillance monitoring. Where more variability exists, then sufficient samples need to be taken in order to have statistical confidence in the results. In some critical locations, continuous real-time monitoring will be appropriate. This is particularly the case for compliance monitoring of effluent discharges and drinking water intakes, and is dealt with in more detail below.

2. *Efforts to routinely monitor aquatic invertebrates, macrophytes (aquatic plants) and fish need to increase.*

Without an understanding of ecosystem health it is impossible to know whether water and land management and the controls on abstraction and pollution are effective and sustainable. For example, the ecology downstream of a major discharge can provide indications as to whether permit limits are being regularly breached, in a way which occasional effluent samples might not be able to. In order to understand the pollution pressures on ecosystems, water quality monitoring and ecological monitoring should be harmonised. The National Aquatic Ecological Monitoring Programme monitors ecosystems in the four main rivers. Habitat conditions in all rivers have declined between 2008 and 2014 (OECD, 2017b), and the Geum and Yeongsan rivers have also deteriorated based on their scores for fish and diatoms. The ecosystem health of tributaries and small rivers is not reported. If the introduction of ecological flows is to be successful they will need to reflect not just the needs of the current ecology but also targets for more diverse and abundant ecosystems, in all rivers.

3. *River flow data and trends are limited.*

River flows will be affected by abstractions and discharges and so could be higher, or lower, than they would be if there were no human influences. It is important to use measured flow data to then develop naturalised flow sequences, where the effect of the artificial influences can be accounted for and the natural baseline then used as the basis for a policy decision to determine safe volumes of abstraction and volumes to be allocated for ecological flows. Modelling naturalised flows downstream of reservoirs will also help to establish an appropriate pattern of releases for environmental purposes. In addition, the trends over time in naturalised flow sequences can help to indicate the effect on runoff from changes in land use, and potentially be an early indication of climate change.

4. *More information on surface water-groundwater interactions, are needed.*

The distribution of groundwater monitoring boreholes provides a picture of the overall aquifer behaviour, and the Integrated Groundwater Information Service supports maps of groundwater level data across Korea. However, in locations where there are concentrations of abstraction boreholes, it is important to understand whether these are operating sustainably, or whether groundwater levels are declining because abstraction is exceeding recharge. This information, together with an understanding of groundwater-surface water interaction is essential to developing abstraction policy and water allocation regimes. Similarly, the existing comprehensive groundwater quality monitoring regime needs not only to consider risk but also to improve knowledge of the impact of other sources of diffuse pollution from agriculture and industry, and the policy decisions to reduce it.

Therefore, points to consider for any review of internal processes in monitoring include:

1. Review the location, frequency and parameters in water quality monitoring
2. Ensure that ecological monitoring is representative of the entire river basin and the range of ecosystems
3. Use naturalised river flows as the basis for water allocation regimes
4. Ensure that groundwater–surface water interactions are understood and managed to prevent over-abstraction and contamination.

2.2. Water demand management for the WELF nexus

2.2.1. The need to move away from 'predict and provide'

The traditional, engineered approach to securing water supplies in most countries, including Korea, has been 'predict and provide' – an expanding water economy. This resulted in storage infrastructure being developed to meet whatever forecasts of demand were produced, leading to an unsustainable spiral where more and more water was taken from the environment to meet the ever-increasing needs of economic and population growth, and creating a false impression that water is readily available.

Over time, most nations face the tension of how to maintain supplies to a growing population and economy, when the most economically viable building sites for reservoirs have been exploited and water scarcity becomes a growing challenge. As illustrated in Chapter 1. , this is the case for Korea.

The OECD report on water use efficiency in Korea (OECD, 2017c) has established that such a supply augmentation strategy to managing water quantity has performed extremely well over the last four decades, supporting rapid demographic and economic growth in Korea. However, this strategy has now reached a limit and Korea is exploring a shift towards a combined approach that pays more attention to managing demand for water.

Managing demand for water will be essential for future water security in Korea, but will require a different perspective on water management. For demand-side measures to be effective, water users should recognise that they are part of the solution. In England and Wales, the economic regulator Ofwat has challenged water companies to work with their customers to transform them from passive recipients of a service to active participants in water management. Users need to understand that it is their (excessive) use of water which threatens water security, and that they need to value water as a scarce and valuable resource. A number of factors mean that this is not the case in Korea:

- Water and sanitation charges are the lowest in the OECD (OECD, 2017c). Generally low and declining cost recovery rates do little to incentivise water efficiency and threaten the financial sustainability of the sector.
- Cultural norms reinforce water as a commodity which can be wasted: 'using it like water' is an expression which highlights its lack of value.
- Water in the natural environment (environmental flows), and the ecosystems it supports, is not valued as a service for society.
- Abstraction licences are poorly enforced, if at all, and there are no meaningful charges.
- There is a perception that water resources scarcity is not an issue in Korea – even recent droughts appear not to have shaken the apparent complacency – and so saving water is not viewed as important.

By contrast, water quality *is* of concern, as a result of high-profile pollution incidents and drinking water contamination. However, the response has been for citizens to buy bottled water and use water filters, rather than clamour for tighter controls on industrial and agricultural pollution. These ambivalent perspectives on sustainable water management are at the heart of many of Korea's challenges with the WELF nexus.

Korea needs to consider how it can move towards better management of water demand, and to raise awareness across all sectors about the risks of profligate use. The OECD report on water use efficiency in Korea (OECD, 2017c) explores this issue in some depth. It stresses the benefits - and the challenges - of designing a water abstraction charge that reflects the opportunity costs of using water. That charge should be higher where water is scarce and users compete to access the resource.

The following sections address related aspects of demand management and water efficiency, including leakage control and water efficiency programmes. They would deliver best if a well-designed abstraction charge is in place.

It is important that cultural attitudes related to the inefficient household use of water – one of the highest in the OECD – are addressed. Maintained engagement, education and awareness campaigns - not just during droughts – are required to promote behaviour change.

2.2.2. Leakage control

Droughts highlight leakage as an emotive issue. At a time when householders, farmers and industry are being asked to use less water, the volumes lost through leakage come under the political and media spotlight. Leakage rates are often seen as an indicator of the performance of a water company and can make a significant difference to the willingness of customers to cooperate with water restrictions.

Urban leakage rates across the world vary significantly. Displaying leakage rates as a percentage is criticised by professionals, since it may not be clear what it is a percentage of (total water into supply, water delivered etc.) and the percentage leakage number can appear to reduce if consumption goes up and leakage remains static. Other metrics, such as cubic metres lost per kilometre of mains length or by number of connections, can provide better comparators, as can the Infrastructure Leakage Index (ILI) (Winarni, 2009). The ILI is a water losses performance indicator which provides a rational basis for comparisons for water losses. It is not clear why leakage rates in some parts of Korea are so high (up to 35% in some areas), although the following issues are fundamental to leakage in any supply system and some or all may need attention:

- Quality and speed of repairs
- Extent of active leakage control measures
- Pressure management
- Pipeline and asset management, including the choice of materials, design, installation, maintenance, renewal/refurbishment, replacement.

For non-specialists, leakage as a percentage of the water put into supply is an accessible and meaningful statistic. At 16.3% as a national average, Korea compares moderately well with other nations, but at a regional and municipal level (e.g. Gwangju at 56.8%), leakage rates are extremely high. Excessive leakage rates cost money. The water has to be pumped and treated, and represents a lost revenue opportunity. In addition, low pressure from bursts can risk contamination from polluted groundwater and sewers entering the distribution network, jeopardising human health. Australia learned that demand management and leakage control was a cost-effective measure during its 10-year Millennium Drought. Building new dams would have cost USD1,370 per Megalitre (Ml) of water delivered (Alliance for Water Efficiency, 2017). By contrast, the same volume could be added by plugging leaks in the network at a cost of only USD365/Ml. Replacing high flow plumbing fixtures cost just USD454/Ml, less than a third of the cost of developing new supply.

Basic leak detection measures on a reactive basis, and proactive find and fix techniques, can be cost effective for tackling large bursts and unseen leaks. Improved pressure management can immediately reduce total losses since pressure is a major driver of leakage and background losses. For example, achieving the low leakage rates in Copenhagen (7%) and Amsterdam (5%) is helped by relatively low network pressures, but the low leakage rates do also require active network monitoring and leakage control. Increasingly, new technology including the use of remote sensing is proving effective in active leakage identification and control.

A leakage control strategy needs to operate in parallel with a water resources plan, so that progress in leakage reduction is made systematically to contribute towards maintaining the supply-demand balance, and is more aggressive where and when water is most scarce. Data on leakage 'hotspots' and burst frequency can help to identify those parts of the network where mains refurbishment or replacement is a priority. Benchmarking and target setting can help to drive leakage reduction and provide a focus on asset condition and repair.

2.2.3. The value of managing demand through water efficiency programmes

Efficient water use in homes, industry, businesses and energy and agriculture production has an important part to play within the Twin Track approach to water resources planning and management, as a long-term and scalable investment driven by strategic planning.

The restrictions and trade-offs required during droughts between agricultural and urban use expose the need for a more equitable and efficient approach to water use and allocation in Korea. Agricultural water use in Korea, which accounts for 62% of abstracted water, incurs only low or no charges (OECD, 2017b), and is not subject to the same abstraction controls as other uses, such as a requirement to measure abstracted volumes. The costs – whether from the consequences of excessive and unsustainable abstraction, or of diffuse pollution from nutrient or sediment runoff – are externalised, and any attempt to have them internalised is resisted. The lack of regulation and enforcement, weak or absent policies to link water use and land use, and no sustainable baseline for abstraction, mean that other water users and the environment bear the consequences of inefficient water use by agriculture.

Due to the high water stress in Korea, there is an urgent need for more efficient irrigation processes, such as drip irrigation (SAI Platform, 2012), and for water to be used more beneficially ('for higher value use'). Better agronomic practices and improved crop varieties are other options to reduce impacts on the water system.

Given the volumes of freshwater used directly and indirectly by agriculture, the sector has a responsibility to use it wisely, recognising that other needs, including the environment, may not have access to the water they need. This would mean that there would be an increased output per unit input of water – a principle which would expected in any other sector – with incentives (abstraction charges) that signal the scarcity of water. It would also bring other benefits such as reducing pumping costs and fertiliser application, and reducing diffuse pollution risks. However, it is essential to understand that caution is required to avoid unintended impacts from water use efficiency, such as: a reduction in water availability for other users and the environment, expansion of irrigated land areas with water saved, and an increased dependence on water resources and the risks associated with climate change (OECD, 2016a). Inefficient irrigation systems may be benefitting groundwater recharge, ecosystems and effluent dilution, particularly in areas growing paddy rice. For example, in Japan, it was estimated that irrigated rice cultivation contributes over 23% of total groundwater recharge (Mitsubishi Research Institute, 2001; OECD, 2015a).

Mitigating the unintended consequences of water use efficiency gains implies appropriate water accounting at the basin scale that considers not just withdrawals but also water returning to the system. Moving from hydrological science to the inclusion of such return flows in water right systems is, however, a complex task. The allocation regime must take account of and manage these issues; it should not allow farmers to continue to abstract as much as they did before unless the volumes are sustainable. Firstly, accounting for return flows should be studied systemically to assess their relative importance in basins and aquifers. In a second step, return flows would need to be accounted for in water allocation systems to better reflect overall water supply and demand, and thus improve the efficiency of water allocation (OECD, 2015b). Thirdly, water efficiency gains should be accompanied by a regulation to appropriately direct the use of saved water and prevent the perverse effects described above (OECD, 2016a). This will require a dialogue with farmers to ensure that they do not simply increase the irrigated area because they think that they have more water to do so.

Improved water efficiency and water conservation is also required for the Korean industry sector. A major driver towards water efficiency in industry can be the charges levied on water abstraction and wastewater discharges to sewer. Many industries abstract directly from rivers and groundwater, rather than relying on treated mains water. The charges for doing so provide little incentive to minimise abstraction rates or use water efficiently. Discharges of effluent have few controls and compliance monitoring and enforcement is weak or non-existent. There are a number of policy options to address these shortcomings outlined below (additional regulatory mechanisms are dealt with in Chapter 3.):

- Set permitted abstraction and discharge charges at levels which incentivise sustainable behaviour.
- Use permits to control abstraction volumes so that they are within sustainable limits.
- Use permits to control a comprehensive and relevant (to the process being regulated) range of pollutants, and total pollution load (toxicity and volume).
- When abstraction permits are applied for or reviewed, set volumes in line with international benchmark data for water-efficient processes for the relevant industry, for example as cubic metres per tonne of output or unit produced. Challenge existing permit holders to adopt best practice so that their water use is in the upper quartile internationally for their industry.
- Monitor compliance with abstraction and discharge permit conditions and take enforcement action where breaches are observed. Charges for abstractions and discharges can be linked to operator performance so that consistently good performers have a lower regulatory burden (fewer inspection visits and less frequent provision of data) and a lower charge compared with poor performers.
- Where enforcement action is necessary to address permit infringements, fines and other sanctions should reflect the environmental and social impacts.

- In those river basins where water is scarce, and during time of drought, target high water-using industries for action on water efficiency.

Smart meters can provide information that will aid network optimisation and customer-facing information to drive water conservation. Low-cost IoT-based sensing devices (e.g. of flow, pressure, quality) monitoring, analysing and transmitting data throughout the water network (from a well to a household) can have a significant benefit on the entire water value chain. The Smart Water Initiative in Korea (OECD, 2017c) pursued by K-water has the potential to significantly improve the efficiency of water use in the urban environment. Pilot projects to advise consumers about drinking water quality and water consumption would, if rolled out more widely, help raise awareness about water and volumes used. However, the low level of water charges provide little or no incentive towards behaviour change.

2.3. Managing water quality for the WELF nexus

Rapid expansion of the Korean economy has resulted in serious degradation of water supplies and freshwater ecosystems from municipal, industrial and agricultural pollution. Water quality is a distinctive part of the WELF nexus in Korea. Water pollution contributes to water scarcity; impacts land and food, energy and industrial production; effects drinking water and human health; reduces biodiversity and ecosystems services; and generates conflicts between upstream and downstream users. The agriculture sector, in particular livestock farming, is a major contributor to water pollution in Korea (OECD, 2018, 2017a). Despite the introduction of an additional water use charge in 1999 for downstream water users to pay for upstream farmers to reduce agricultural intensification, and that vast investments in water pollution treatment facilities have been made, water pollution problems are still encountered (Choi et al., 2017).

This section of the report assesses Korea's current water quality management regime and suggests a hierarchy of water quality principles for action. It highlights the importance of environmental regulation and linking water quality management with water quantity and land management at the basin scale. Options for water quality policy reform in Korea are recommended for the short- and longer-terms. International case studies are cited as examples of what Korea may aim to achieve.

2.3.1. Water quality management in Korea

The Environmental Standard of Water Quality of Aquatic Ecosystem, as a part of Korea's Environmental Standard, lays out the Korean government's water quality goals that are required to secure human and ecosystem health. It also provides a framework for policy instruments used to manage water quality.

Four main policy instruments are used to manage water quality in Korea:

- *The total pollution load control programme*, which aims to reduce point source pollution of total phosphorus and biochemical oxygen demand.
- *Regulations for the control of wastewater discharges from industry and municipal wastewater treatment plants* to protect human and ecosystem health.
- *Regulations on livestock manure*, stipulated under the Act on the Management and Use of Livestock Excreta.

- *Water use charges*, which are collected as River Management Funds (RMF) to support upstream water quality projects selected by River Basin Committees at the basin-level.

Despite the above policy instruments to control water pollution, improvements in water quality remain limited. It is recognised that diffuse source pollution, particularly from livestock farming, is now the main source of pollution; the proportion of total pollution attributed to diffuse pollution is projected to reach over 70% by 2020 (ME, 2014a). Each of the above policy instruments are assessed in the following sections.

The Total Pollution Load Control Programme

The Korean total pollution load control (Korean TMDL) programme currently focuses on the regulation of total phosphorus (TP) and biochemical oxygen demand (BOD) from point sources of pollution only. Targets are set in each of the four major river basins according to development plans provided by local authorities. Since the introduction of the Korean TMDL in 2004, reduction targets in point source pollution have been achieved. With the aim of meeting water quality targets, government subsidies (through the RMF) have supported investments in wastewater treatment plants and land purchases to retire sensitive areas from intensive land use (such as riparian buffer strips). A summary of the Korean TMDL programme is provided in Box 2.1.

Box 2.1. The Total Pollution Load Control Management System, Korea

In 2004, the Korean Total Water Pollution Load Control programme (Korean TMDL, the equivalent of a total maximum daily load programme) was introduced to improve water quality management policy in Korea. The TMDL allocates pollution load reductions necessary to reduce the sources of pollution and achieve desired water quality. It is aimed at water quality improvement and economic growth simultaneously.

Water quality targets are set periodically for each of the four main river basins - the Nakdong, Geum, Youngsan-Seomjin and Han. Local water quality targets and implementation plans are then established to achieve the overarching target for the watershed. Biochemical oxygen demand (BOD) was selected as the first target parameter in 2004, followed by total phosphorus (TP) in 2011. Targets near the boundaries between provinces and cities are required to be notified so that water quality targets can be attained in co-operation.

Permissible total maximum daily pollutant loads are calculated using scientific water quality modelling at the watershed, local and individual property levels. Economic development, population growth, pollutant reduction and local development planning are considered together. The Korean TMDL management system clarifies the responsibility of each relevant entity by identifying each pollution load by local government, sub-local government and individual polluter, with a view to meeting and staying on the water quality target.

Once the water quality targets are set, governors and mayors develop detailed local development plans and annual plans for pollution reduction, with a view to meeting the load allocation of each watershed. In co-operation with stakeholders, governors and mayors then decide how to allocate pollution load permits to individuals in order to attain and maintain the overarching target for the watershed. It is up to each local government and the stakeholder how to allocate these pollution loads. Technical Guidelines for Korean TMDL Management provided by the National Institute of Environmental Research require pollution load permits be set through water quality modelling, considering equity, efficiency and effectiveness of reducing pollution loads. Voluntary allocation through stakeholder co-operation and engagement is also encouraged in the Technical Guidelines (NIER, 2014).

Implementation and performance of the Korean TMDL system is evaluated every year by central government. When improvements are required, central government may ask a governor or mayor to establish and take necessary measures: for example, putting further restrictions on urban and industrial development projects, suspension or cutbacks of financial support, or restriction on installation or modification of facilities where discharging wastewater. River Management Funds (RMFs) also offer support for implementing the TMDL system. Since 2004, RMFs have supported investments in wastewater treatment plants and land purchases to retire sensitive areas from intensive land use to riparian buffer strips. In addition, new pollution reduction technologies and approaches through R&D projects is a factor attributable to the success of the TMDL system.

In 2013, water quality targets were achieved for 81% of rivers. Figure 2.1 is a demonstration of the success of the Korean TMDL system in the Nakdong, Geum and Yeongsan Rivers. However, water quality targets were achieved in only 12% of lakes; Korea's lakes and reservoirs are particularly vulnerable due to the high residence time in comparison to rivers (as are most lakes around the world). Strict management is considered necessary to achieve continuous water quality improvements in in later stages of TMDL implementation (Kim et al., 2016).

Figure 2.1. Water quality improvements under the Total Pollution Load Control Management System Korea

BOD, 2004-2010

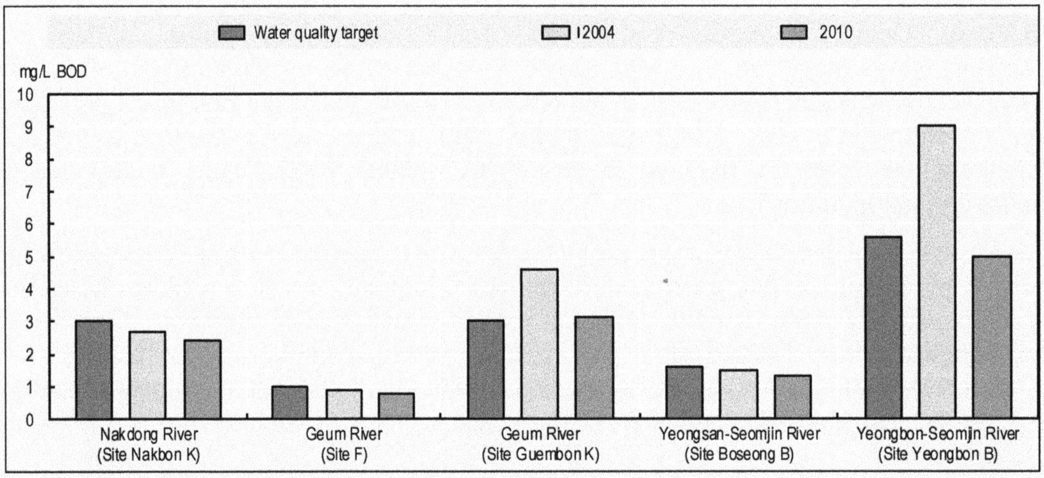

Sources: OECD (2017a), *Diffuse Pollution, Degraded Waters*; National Institute of Environmental Research (NIER) (2014), Technical Guidelines for Korean TMDL Management, Korea.

However, the success of the Korean TMDL is limited for the following reasons:

- The range of pollutants is currently narrow – BOD and TP only.
- It does not consider all inputs of a given pollutant, in particular, diffuse sources of pollution (including from agriculture) are not captured. In recent years, the proportion of diffuse sources in relation to point sources has increased.
- It only applies to the four main river basins, and excludes tributaries and small coastal rivers.
- Compliance monitoring and enforcement is insufficient.
- There is little, if any, relationship with streamflow and ecosystem toxicology.

There are opportunities to expand the Korean TMDL, to include a much broader range of pollutants, polluters and tributary streams so that it reaches its full potential. In addition, it is not clear how, or whether, the limited ecological monitoring programme is used to specify water quality objectives for the protection and improvement of ecosystems. For this to happen, there needs to be an integrated and structured relationship between the parameters specified in pollution discharge permits, the compliance monitoring of those parameters in point source discharges, the breadth of the water quality monitoring regime, and the system used to determine and classify ecosystem health.

Regulations for municipal and industrial wastewater discharges

In 2014, 93% of the population was served by wastewater treatment services, compared with 71% in 2000. In addition, 83% of the population benefits from advanced (tertiary) treatment - a remarkable increase from almost nothing (1%) in 2000 (OECD, 2017b).

Effluent quality standards (discharge limits) from municipal wastewater treatment plants have been set for 49 parameters, including organic substances, suspended solids and phenols. Many standards (e.g. for total nitrogen and total phosphorus discharges) have been made more stringent, representing important progress. Receiving water body characteristics such as the existing water quality grade, are considered in the application of the effluent standards.

Effluent quality standards for industrial wastewater are applied to seven pollutants, including BOD, COD, total nitrogen, total phosphorus and suspended solids. Standards for BOD, COD and suspended solids are more strict for large discharge facilities. Permission or notification for the installation of wastewater discharge facilities is required. Discharge fees are applied, and measures such as instruction, inspection and administrative dispositions are taken to ensure implementation of the regulations (ME, 2015).

To manage the ecosystem impact of hazardous water pollutants, an effluent standard measured in "toxic units" (a composite measure of concentration reflecting the toxicity of individual substances) has been applied to industrial facilities and wastewater treatment plants since 2011. The 2007 National Sewage Master Plan established several targets for 2015, including improvement of influent treatment quality through maintenance, repair of 93% of the sewerage infrastructure, increase of the sewerage connection rate to 92% of the population and 75% of the rural population, and increased reuse rate for sludge (to 70%) and treated wastewater (to 18%).

However, the level of compliance and enforcement of effluent standards is limited and penalties remain rare; in 2013, only 35% of wastewater discharge infringements required corrective measures (ME, 2014b). The majority of polluters often get away with a simple warning (OECD, 2017b). Large plants subject to "Focus" can be inspected up to 4 times per year. The efficiency of inspection depends on continuous monitoring of key parameters and at least daily analysis monitoring of all permitted substances. It also depends on how process failures are reported and dealt with.

Regulations on livestock manure

Currently there are no environmental regulations specifically imposed on agricultural production, with the exception of regulations on livestock manure, stipulated under the Act on the Management and Use of Livestock Excreta. The regulations require each major river basin to establish a 10-year plan of livestock manure management and report it to ME.

Livestock manure is the main agricultural source of water and soil pollution in Korea. As mentioned in Chapter 1. , Korea currently shows the highest nitrogen balance among all OECD countries. Most OECD countries have succeeded in reducing their nitrogen balances over time; Korea has not. The average nitrogen balance in Korea increased from 213.1 kg/ha in 1990-92 to 249 kg/ha by 2012-14 (OECD, 2018). In the Netherlands, the nitrogen balance fell to 148 kg/ha in 2012-14 from the 1990-92 level of 309 kg/ha despite a growth in livestock production. The reason for the nitrogen reduction in the Netherlands was the introduction of a manure quota system and manure land application limits (Annex 2.A).

Since 1991, the ME has provided subsidies for the installation and operation of public manure treatment facilities to reduce small-scale farms' burden of manure treatment. Since 2006, MAFRA has supported R&D in manure treatment technology financially and technically to convert manure into reusable compost and granular and liquefied fertilisers, while reducing chemical fertilisers and dealing with the manure treatment for medium-scaled farms (OECD, 2018). However, because the livestock industry is expanding and the total area of cropland declining, there will be an excess supply of manure composts and liquid fertilisers.

Improving the policy framework to manage livestock manure is a priority considering the future growth potential of the livestock sector. To tackle the growing livestock manure management problem, a more comprehensive policy approach beyond the current regulation is necessary.

Water use charges to improve upstream water quality

Water use charges are based on the volume of water received and used by downstream municipal and industrial users. The revenue raised is collected as River Management Funds (RMFs) to support upstream water quality projects selected by River Basin Committees. A summary of how the charges work and the type of projects the RMF funds are presented in Box 2.2.

Box 2.2. River Management Funds for water quality improvement of Korea's major river basins

To improve the water quality of the four major river basins, the ME set up water use charges to fund projects that would reduce water pollution in upstream areas. Based on the User-Pays Principle, the water use charges collect revenue from downstream users (cities and industries) to offset the losses in opportunity costs to upstream users associated with regulations against various economic activities.

Water use charges apply to downstream households, commercial entities and industry in proportion to the volume of water received and used. Water use charge rates are determined every two years based on forecasted financial resources required to achieve the target level of water quality pursuant to the law. As of 2016, the water use charge rates were KRW 170/ton for the Han, Nakdong and Yeongsan-Seomjin Rivers, and KRW 160/ton for the Geum River.

The revenue from the water use charges enters River Management Funds (RMFs). Water use charges and the RMF were first introduced in 1999 for the Han River, followed by the other major river basins in 2002. In 2015, the RMFs raised a total of KRW 10.14 trillion.

The RMF spend is overseen by the River Basin Committee in each basin, which aims to coordinate the interests of diverse stakeholders on matters relating to water quality improvements. The RMFs supports two main activity areas: i) catchment restoration and protection activities, and ii) wastewater infrastructure. Types of projects include:

- Sewage treatment infrastructure, matching the subsidy funds from national government, and subsidising operational costs (48% of total RMF spend)
- Resident support: income support, low interest rate loans, compensation (18% of total RMF spend)
- Voluntary land purchase and riparian zone projects (transformation and management of acquired land) (18% of total RMF spend). As of 2016, farmers have offered 156 million m^2 of land for purchase, but only 60 million m^2 has been purchased because of funding constraints. The total area of 'designated riparian zones' reached 1197 km^2 as of 2015.
- Total pollutant load control, through subsidies to local government to work on pollution management, monitoring and research (5% of total RMF spend).
- Other water quality improvement projects, including removing litter, monitoring programmes by NGOs, subsidising water treatment from polluted water resources, dredging, public education and ecosystem restoration (8% of total RMF spend).

Source: ME and KEI (2016), River Management Funds for the Four Major River Systems, No. 44, Korea Environmental Policy Bulletin, Vol. XIV, Issue 4, 2016.

There is significant potential to better leverage available funds to improve water quality. In 2015, the RMFs expended KRW 10.05 trillion on water quality improvement projects, the majority of which was spent on wastewater treatment infrastructure (48%), resident support projects (19%) and riparian zone projects (18%) (ME and KEI, 2016). However, little improvement in water quality is evident in the Han, Geum and Yeongsan-Seomjin River basins (Figure 1.6). The following are limitations of the water use charge and RMF:

- Water use charges relate to the volume of water used and not to the amount of pollution generated. Therefore, the water use charge does not incentivise water users to reduce their pollution.
- Water use charges remain low. Because of this, water quality improvement works may be constrained by available funds. For example, requests to sell land far outweigh available funds; as of 2016, upstream farmers have requested the sale of 156 million m^2 of agricultural land, however only 60 million m^2 of land has been purchased.
- Water use charges are similar in each basin despite each basin have different water quality challenges, in particular, the Nakdong River basin.
- It is unclear how policy outcomes are specified, and investment is prioritised and assessed against other (potentially more cost-effective) policy mechanisms. It will be crucial to prioritise investment decisions for policy success in the context of limited funding.
- The budget is set on a two-year basis, which potentially affects the possibility of multi-year commitments, and is based on demand from local governments in previous years (and not future needs).

The following section outlines policy principles to guide decision-making on water quality management that may prove helpful to Korea in reforming their policies and improving water quality and ecosystem functioning.

2.3.2. Policy principles to guide decision-making on water quality management

A set of well-established principles can guide the design and implementation of policy responses to water pollution – namely the Principles of Pollution Prevention, Treatment at Source, Polluter Pays and Beneficiary Pays (Box 2.3). Where there is a lack of scientific knowledge, it is good practice for the Precautionary Principle to be adopted in order to minimise risk. In addition, equity should be considered with regards to fair allocation of pollution rights, costs and benefits of abatement, and the needs of future generations. These set of principles should be considered when designing water pollution control policy instruments in Korea.

Box 2.3. Hierarchy of principles for action on water quality

The following set of OECD principles can usefully guide the development of policy for the management of water quality. They are captured by the 2016 OECD Council Recommendation on Water.

The **Principle of Pollution Prevention** reflects that prevention of pollution is often more cost effective than treatment/restoration options. This means preventing pollutants from reaching water bodies by means such as recovery and re-use of wastewater, product substitution, modification of industrial processes, retirement of land and best land management practices.

The **Principle of Treatment at Source** considers that pollution control measures should be applied as close to the source as possible. In effect, the later the stage of control, the less effective it is likely to be due to wider dispersion of the contaminants. Particularly strict measures of control should be enforced for certain categories of hazardous pollutants with a view to preventing their dispersion into the environment. This applies especially to toxic substances which are persistent in the environment and/or subject to bioaccumulation in living organisms and concentration through the food chain (e.g. heavy metals, DDT). Management measures should aim to prevent uncontrolled pollution transfers to other water resources, or to soil or atmospheric systems.

The **Polluter Pays Principle** creates conditions to make pollution a costly activity and to either influence behaviour to reduce pollution, or generate revenues to alleviate pollution and compensate for social costs. Examples include pollution charges, taxes on inputs (such as fertilisers and pesticides) and sewer user charges. The polluter pays principle should not be accompanied by conflicting subsidies, tax advantages or other measures that encourage polluters to pollute, or assist polluters in bearing the costs of pollution, thereby creating distortions in the market. While there is a case for a public subsidy to address the accumulated damage caused by historical pollution (particularly when the polluters are no longer around to pay), the polluter pays principle should be the first line of defence in securing water quality and incentivising behaviour change.

The **Beneficiary Pays Principle** allows sharing of the financial burden of water quality management. It takes account of the high opportunity cost related to using public funds for the provision of private goods that users can afford. A requisite is that private benefits attached to water resources management are inventoried and valued, beneficiaries are identified, and mechanisms are set to harness them. For example, green infrastructure, such as wetlands and forested catchments, provide water filtration ecosystem services. Benefits and beneficiaries include: improved quality drinking water for city residents; reduced water treatment costs for utilities and health systems, and downstream industrial and agricultural users; improved business for fisheries and tourism operators; and benefits for recreational users, waterfront property owners, the environment, and society at large.

Sources: OECD (2017a), *Diffuse Pollution, Degraded Waters: Emerging Policy Solutions*, OECD Studies on Water, OECD Publishing, Paris. http://dx.doi.org/10.1787/9789264269064-en; OECD (2016b), *OECD Council Recommendation on Water*, [C(2016)174/FINAL], December 2016. https://legalinstruments.oecd.org/en/instruments/349.

Increasingly, OECD member countries are adopting water quality limits that reflect the environmental risk to the receiving watercourse. The initial policy response is usually to implement controls based upon quantitative limits on pollutants, particularly for point sources of pollution. The polluter pays principle is broadly accepted internationally and convenient to apply (e.g. through pollution charges on emissions or taxes on pesticides or fertilisers), so that those responsible for polluting bear the costs of either the damage done to society or of cleaning it up to the required acceptable standard.

However, particular challenges result in diffuse pollution often being under-regulated: difficulties with identifying and targeting polluters, determining reliable estimates of pollution costs, poor enforcement of existing regulations, and strong political opposition. Korea is no exception to these challenges. Table 2.2 lists possible ways to overcome these barriers.

Table 2.2. Barriers and solutions to the control of diffuse source water pollution

Barriers	Solutions
Difficulties with identifying and targeting polluters	Computer modelling as a cost-effective alternative to directly observing individual diffuse pollution emissions Taxes on inputs (e.g. fertilisers, pesticides, cleaning products) or land use (e.g. paved urban surfaces, livestock numbers, intensive land use) Collective accountability at catchment level
Difficulties with determining reliable estimates of pollution costs	Economic modelling and scientific monitoring to inform costs and justify action Market mechanisms to reveal pollution costs and differentiated abilities to cope with them
Poor enforcement of existing regulations	Computer modelling as a cost-effective alternative to directly observing individual diffuse pollution emissions Taxes on inputs (e.g. fertilisers, pesticides, cleaning products) or land use (e.g. paved urban surfaces, livestock numbers, intensive land use) Collective accountability at catchment level Increased financial and technical support for local authorities to enforce regulations
Strong political opposition	Economic modelling and scientific monitoring to inform costs and justify action Stakeholder engagement Collective accountability at catchment level Connecting with higher-level policy priorities

Source: OECD (2017a), *Diffuse Pollution, Degraded Waters: Emerging Policy Solutions*. OECD Studies on Water, OECD Publishing, Paris. http://dx.doi.org/10.1787/9789264269064-en.

Water pollution control mechanisms need to be sufficiently sophisticated to recognise the spatial and temporal complexity of pollution from a range of sources. And because each river catchment is unique, the management controls must be adapted to the natural properties of the river, as well as the nature of the pollution affecting it. Innovative policy responses to control diffuse source pollution are emerging in OECD countries from which Korea may learn. They are based on three options:

1. Managing land use practices (e.g. stormwater, nutrient and erosion control practices) and inputs (e.g. fertilisers, irrigation) as proxies that cause distribution of diffuse emissions;

2. Rewarding or penalising polluters collectively for their jointly determined impacts on ambient pollution levels at particular receptors; or

3. Managing estimated diffuse emissions via computer modelling.

For instance, policy makers and regulators across the EU, USA, Australia and New Zealand manage pollution by modelling the catchment water quality and then using permits with numeric limits which can be monitored and enforced. Even difficulties with monitoring and managing diffuse sources of pollution can be overcome with effective modelling, as demonstrated in the case of New Zealand (Box 2.4).

Box 2.4. Nutrient modelling in New Zealand

OVERSEER®, a national model for farm-scale nutrient budgeting and loss estimation, calculates nutrient flows in a productive farming system and identifies risks of environmental impacts through nutrient loss, including run-off and leaching. The model was originally developed as a tool for farming to create nutrient budgets and has been adapted to overcome barriers that arise from an inability to clearly identify diffuse source polluters. It is recognised as the best tool currently available for estimating nitrate leaching losses from the root zone across the diversity and complexity of farming systems in New Zealand. A summary of the model inputs and outputs are presented Table 2.3.

Table 2.3. OVERSEER® model inputs and outputs

Inputs: Farm level	Inputs: Management block level (i.e. paddock/field scale)	Outputs
Farm location Types of blocks and block areas (e.g. pastoral, fodder crop, house, scrub, wetland, riparian) Types of enterprises (e.g. pastoral, cropping) Stock Stock numbers, breed Production Placement (grazing off, wintering pads) Types of structures Effluent management of structure Stock management on structure Type of effluent management system Supplements imported and where they are fed Wetlands	Topography Climate Soil type Drainage Soil fertility tests Pasture type Supplements made on the block Fertiliser applied Irrigation applied Effluent applied Animals (type, timing) grazing the block Crop rotation; crops grown – yield, fertiliser applied, harvesting method	*Nutrient budget.* N sources: atmospheric, fertiliser, animal transfer, supplements fed on block, irrigation and nutrients out N losses: produce (e.g. milk), animal transfer, supplements (e.g. hay), leaching/runoff, atmospheric (e.g. N_2O). *Farm-level and block-level reports.* e.g. Total N lost to water for blocks and farm; Average N concentration in drainage based on N leached; N surplus per block. *Advisory reports.* e.g. N conversion efficiency (%); total GHG emissions; maintenance fertiliser requirements.

OVERSEER® can, and has, supported water quality policy development, most notably the Lake Taupō nitrogen market and as part of Horizons One Plan to limit nitrogen losses based on the natural capital of the soil in the Manawatū-Wānganui region. New Zealand farmers will increasingly use the model to develop nutrient management plans and budgets, as required by regional councils.

Source: OECD (2017a), Diffuse Pollution, Degraded Waters: Emerging Policy Solutions. OECD Studies on Water, OECD Publishing, Paris.

Korea could benefit from a mix of policy instruments (regulatory, economic, and voluntary) to manage multiple sources of water pollution, hold polluters accountable and improve the cost effectiveness of pollution control Table 2.4). The complexity associated with water pollution from multiple sources and multiple sectors also requires a response which is part of an overarching integrated national water policy framework, rather than sector-specific (OECD, 2017a; 2012). This is discussed in the following section.

Table 2.4. Examples of policy instruments to address water pollution and protect freshwater ecosystems

Water-related risk	Regulatory	Economic	Voluntary or information-based
Water pollution	Water quality standards Pollution discharge permits (with quantity, quality and timing conditions) Mandatory best environmental practices Non-compliance penalties – non-renewal of resource permits or greater restriction on current permits Non-compliance fines Bans or restrictions on the use of harmful substances and land-use practices Registration for low risk activities	Pollution taxes (on inputs, e.g. fertilisers or stock numbers) Pollution charges and sewer surcharges (on pollution outputs) Water quality trading Payment for ecosystem services Subsidies to incentivise uptake of new technologies	Information and awareness campaigns Farm advisory services for improved farming techniques (to minimise negative impacts on water quality) Contracts/bonds (e.g. land retirement contracts) Best environmental practices (or good management practices) Environmental labelling – products that meet certain environmental standards can be marketed and sold at a premium and/or subsidised.
Risk to the resilience of freshwater ecosystems	Minimum environmental flows (also for pollution dilution) Specification obligations relating to return flows and restrictions on discharges in drought conditions	"Buy-backs" of water pollution allowances to ensure adequate water quality for ecosystem functioning	Information and awareness campaigns Voluntary surrender of pollution discharge allowances

Source: OECD (2017a), *Diffuse Pollution, Degraded Waters: Emerging Policy Solutions*, OECD Studies on Water, OECD Publishing, Paris.

2.3.3. The importance of policy coherence for water quality management

Pressures from a range of policies and developments in Korea have affected water quality, including agricultural intensification (in particular the expansion of livestock farming), alterations to the natural morphology of water bodies (including the construction of dams), urban development (including increased stormwater and sewer discharges), historical pollution (including from industry and mining operations) and climate change. Policy coherence is required to ensure initiatives taken by different policy sectors do not have negative impacts on water quality and freshwater ecosystems, or increase the cost of water quality management.

Multiple policy sectors and ministries affect water quality and its management, for example, urban development, agriculture, climate, natural resources, forestry, energy, conservation and human health. This emphasises the need for improved communications and coordination within and between ministries in Korea for sustainable management of water quality and the WELF nexus more broadly. The recent water governance reform through the adoption of the revised Government Organisation Act, June 2018, merges responsibilities of water quantity and quality management under one ministry (ME). This merge is a step in the right direction for improved policy alignment and coherency. However, improved coordination does not come automatically; ME will need to develop and implement a water quality and quantity "coordination" strategy for effective merging of responsibilities at national and sub-national levels.

Korea could improve policy coherence for improved water quality by undertaking the following:

- *Removal of subsidies that encourage land use change or intensification* that can result in diffuse water pollution. For example, producer support, fertiliser or energy subsidies, subsidised irrigation or non-existent pollution charges. Korea remains one of the largest providers of producer support for agriculture in the OECD and consists mostly of market price support, a category of support with potentially environmentally harmful effects (OECD, 2018). Furthermore, the agriculture sector does not pay energy taxes and only partially pays water charges. Such subsidies should be phased out and replaced by targeted payments in exchange to environment best practice and/or targeted subsidies for the poor (unlinked to production) to address social concerns.
- *Looking for win-win solutions*, such as nitrogen oxide reductions to simultaneously improve air and water quality, and reduce greenhouse gas emissions. Such solutions can incentivise uptake of policies by users and reduce transaction costs for regulators. For example, in New Zealand, the Lake Taupo nitrogen market was complemented by the New Zealand Emissions Trading Scheme which incentivised afforestation, and subsequently advanced the achievement of nitrogen reductions to improve water quality and also improved carbon sequestration.
- *Integrating water pollution control (both point and diffuse source) with land use management, and water quantity management*. Water quality and water quantity should be managed in unison as the two are interrelated and interdependent. For example, poor water quality reduces the quantity of useable water and therefore exacerbates the problem of water scarcity; water scarcity reduces the capacity for dilution of point source pollution; and high rainfall events cause diffuse pollution from land runoff (agricultural and urban) and combined sewer overflows into rivers. The unification of water management under ME provides an opportunity to move into this direction. Linking water quality policy with land use planning under MoLIT will be important for reducing flood risks and stormwater pollution in urban areas, and diffuse pollution from agriculture.

The potential synergies and complementarities among the WELF sectors should be used to guide formulation of effective options to maximise gain, optimise co-benefits, and avoid negative impacts. For example, changes in agricultural practice may deliver reductions in nutrient pollution at lower cost (and with less energy consumed) than conventional wastewater treatment solutions at fixed plants. Investment in green infrastructure may provide multiple environmental benefits but may also be less certain in the magnitude and timing of the improvement. Other examples of the potential trade-offs and co-benefits from water quality interventions are provided in Table 2.5. Similarly, there are benefits of factoring water quality into policies that affect water availability, and water and land use.

Table 2.5. Examples of water quality trade-offs and co-benefits between sectoral policies

Water quality intervention	Potential trade-offs and co-benefits
Wastewater reuse to avoid pollution of rivers	*Trade-offs*: reduced environmental flow of rivers, additional energy requirements to process and/or transport manure (including from sewage) from surplus regions to regions with a deficit. *Co-benefits*: utilisation of finite resources, such as phosphate, increased water security, reduced wastewater treatment costs
Higher drinking water quality standards to improve human health	*Trade-offs*: increased energy consumption associated with increased water treatment, and increased carbon footprint *Co-benefits*: reduced health costs
Conversion to decentralised water and wastewater systems	*Co-benefits*: reduced energy consumption from pumping water and wastewater over large distances, reduced carbon footprint
Restoration of wetlands	*Co-benefits*: reduced wastewater treatment and energy consumption, increased biodiversity, carbon capture and storage, reduced flood risks
Sustainable urban drainage systems	*Co-benefits*: reduced stormwater treatment and energy consumption, increased biodiversity, carbon capture and storage, reduced urban flood risks
Soil conservation to prevent erosion and sedimentation	*Co-benefits*: increased land use efficiency, biodiversity, food production, and water and fertiliser efficiency, reduced flood risks

Source: OECD (2017a), *Diffuse Pollution, Degraded Waters: Emerging Policy Solutions*, OECD Studies on Water, OECD Publishing, Paris.

Strengthening valuations of water pollution in environmental impact assessments (EIAs) can assist with the identification of trade-offs and co-benefits. The decision to commit to a new policy can be guided by a benefit-cost analysis that measures whether the potential benefits of water quality protection, adjusted to account for risks, outweigh the potential costs. International experience and lessons from previous policy successes and failures should be applied. Evaluating the impact and effectiveness of new policy after implementation (*ex post*) is equally important.

The links between land use, the underlying soil quality and water quality are particularly critical parts of the WELF nexus. Linking water quality policy to soil characteristics and its ability to retain water and filter pollution will encourage over time a better match between inherent capability and use. In some regions of New Zealand, nitrogen leaching limits have been allocated to individual farmers based on farm soil quality (or the underlying natural capital of the soil) to reduce diffuse pollution and achieve river catchment water quality targets (see OECD, 2017a). The concept of adding ecological boundaries (e.g. a cap on nutrient losses to limit the impact on receiving water bodies), within which land use must operate, moves the analysis from managing land to managing a landscape connected to water. Establishing ecological boundaries, within which resources should be managed, could allow the full economic potential of natural resources to be reached. In Korea, this could be envisioned by ME, MoLIT, MAFRA, RBCs and stakeholder engagement platforms working together to establish nutrient pollution caps to maintain freshwater ecological and human health in each river basin (for various key pollutants identified). These caps could then be linked with the natural characteristics of the land and soil, land use planning and land use management at the farm scale to ensure water quality targets are met.

2.3.4. Water quality management at the basin scale

A collective management approach with stakeholder engagement in setting water quality regulations at the local level (with an overarching national water quality baseline) can create buy-in, increase trust in government processes, and ultimately find effective solutions to achieve desired water quality outcomes. Stakeholder engagement through inclusive basin water governance is increasingly recognised as critical to secure support for reforms, raise awareness about water risks and costs, increase users' willingness to pay, and to handle conflicts (see 0; OECD, 2015c).

The collaborative governance model of the Canterbury Water Management Strategy (CWMS), New Zealand (see OECD, 2017a) may provide inspiration for Korea. In this case, the river basin committee, together with the local community and technical support (with expertise in economics, cultural values, social science, modelling, water quality and ecology), developed a water quality implementation programme comprising of: i) desired community water quality outcomes; ii) recommendations for water quality limits based on maintaining the trophic state of a significant regional lake; iii) catchment nutrient loads for all activities; iv) the method of allocating the nutrient loads; v) methods to incentivise biodiversity protection (e.g. an easier resource permit pathway for development that is accompanied by biodiversity protection); vi) non-statutory actions such as an education campaign for visitors; vii) a rehabilitation programme for degraded water bodies; and viii) an integrated monitoring framework for the committee to track progress and to share data. The Collaborative Governance Model not only resolved how to set water quality (and quantity) limits and other actions to deliver on the CWMS targets, but also facilitated delivering on the National Policy Statement for Freshwater Management. One of the most tangible outcomes was community ownership of solutions. By bringing people together to solve problems, the sum is greater than the total of the parts. The success of the collaborative approach is now spilling over in to other sectors in New Zealand, such as public transport governance.

Based on the experience of the collaborative governance model of the CWMS, requisites to make a collaborative governance process work include:

- *Objective and clarity of the process*. The CWMS set out the principles, targets, and methodology "up-front" and removed any doubt over scope, process, and what was trying to be achieved.
- *Commitment and clarity from governors on the lines of decision making*. The Canterbury Regional Council delegated significant power to the Zone Committees by agreeing to endorse all of the committees' recommendations when consensus was reached with stakeholder and community engagement.
- *Absolute transparency with information and process*, including having difficult conversations in sessions that are open to the public and making all technical information freely available. Traceability is important; the wider community needs to be able to know when, where, why and how, certain decisions were made. It is critical to get right, and be clear about, the scale of operation - hydrological, social, and administrative.
- *Resourcing needs to match the level of ambition for stakeholder engagement and responsibility*. The most substantial expenditure is the resourcing of support staff. Facilitators need to be able to deal with ambiguity, to think and work across disciplines, and be committed to developing resolutions without transposing their

own ideas (i.e. "knowledge brokers"). Other technical support staff who provide science, hydrology, planning, biodiversity, cultural and infrastructure advice need to be able to communicate at various levels, and the facilitators need to be prepared to "hold a space" for stakeholders who may not be well resourced or articulate.

2.3.5. Alternatives to reform of water quality policies in Korea

This final section on water quality management outlines policy recommendations for Korea based on the assessment of Korea's current water quality management regime and the rationale of policy coherence, policy principles and basin governance for improved water quality. The recommendations are divided into two stages:

- *Stage 1:* short-term recommendations that may enhance existing water quality polices in Korea (Table 2.6).
- *Stage 2:* more ambitious, longer-term recommendations that require a departure from the existing water quality regime but may offer greater improvement at least cost to society (Table 2.7).

Table 2.6. Stage 1 - Short-term recommendations for the improvement of existing water quality policy instruments, Korea

Existing policy instrument	Recommendations
Cross-cutting	• Invest in monitoring and water quality assessment. Collect data on key issues at basin and sub-basin levels for both surface and groundwater bodies. Identify pollution hotspots at risk of ecosystem degradation and drinking water contamination. • Adjust water pollution charges to reflect environmental and social costs and to encourage reduced pollution. E.g. raise sewerage charges and the water effluent tax to a level that covers operation, maintenance and replacement of wastewater treatment infrastructure. Bands (upper and lower limits) of charges could be developed at the national level as guidance for basin-specific charges to be developed based on local conditions and financing needs. Where necessary, cross-subsidise between urban and rural areas to reduce inequities in access to sanitation services. • Review existing water, agricultural, energy and land policy instruments to improve their coherence with policy objectives to reduce the conflicting incentives generated by different programmes.
Regulations for the control of wastewater discharges	• Ensure point source pollution is effectively regulated and enforced. • Strengthen the enforcement of water pollution permits, taxes and charges, including the issuance of non-compliance fines and penalties. The very low collection rates on water pollution taxes and charges, suggest imperfect enforcement, which further weakens incentives for pollution reduction and efficient use.
Water use charges, River Management Funds, and the River Basin Committees	• Differentiate water use charges by basin according to the investment needs required to meet water quality objectives. Extend the budget beyond a two-year horizon to accommodate multi-year commitments and projects. • Where the objective is an overall reduction in load of a pollutant, consider reverse auctions for government land purchases to reduce costs.
The total pollution load control programme	• Expand the Korean TMDL to include the whole basin (including small/medium tributary rivers) and other water quality parameters (e.g. nitrogen, heavy metals and pesticides) linked to local ecological limits and social values on water quality.
Regulations on livestock manure	• Increase education campaigns and advisory services in the farming community as a precursor to introducing regulations or general binding rules to set minimum standards of good practice. • Extend the regulations to require good farming practices nationwide. • Use targeted, risk-based measures to reduce pollution, such as livestock units' manure management and farming restrictions on rapid-draining or impermeable soils close to watercourses. Lessons from the EU Nitrate pollution prevention regulations are relevant (see OECD, 2017a). • In high risk areas where restrictions in land use and farming practices go beyond the basic standard, then payment may be justified. For example, land purchase in locally-identified ecologically sensitive areas under the RMF.

Table 2.7. Stage 2 - Longer-term recommendations for the reform of water quality management in Korea

Reform area	Recommendations	Examples of OECD good practices
Cross-cutting	• Establish integrated and collaborative river basin planning – for land and water quantity and quality - to establish objectives and priorities of each of the existing water quality policy instruments in each basin and to assess their cost-effectiveness and sustainability. Linking river flows (volume, residence times/velocity and pollution dilution capacity) and water quality, together with improving connectivity within the river, and the water/land interface (wetlands, marshland, agricultural soil structure etc.) will improve all aspects of the ecosystem and help it function better to provide beneficial services. • Design charges for surface and groundwater abstractions and pollution discharges for all users to fund, on a cost-recovery basis, the cost of monitoring, managing and improving water resources, at basin and aquifer scales (including tributaries). • Issue pollution discharge permits and evaluate environmental impact assessments whilst considering not only the pollution load, but also the river flow regime, the breadth of polluting substances that might adversely affect ecosystem health, and the sensitivity of the ecosystem at different places down the river. Environmental Quality Standards could be used instead or in combination to set permit conditions, to set an upper limit of acceptability to protect human health and freshwater ecosystems. • Phase out any harmful subsidies or reconcile conflicting objectives identified from the review of water, agricultural, energy and land policy instruments and programmes (Stage 1 recommendation). For example, rebalance the portfolio of agricultural support to public investment towards long-term productivity growth and sustainability, such as more targeted support encouraging, or conditional on, provision of good farm management practices that reduce water pollution and improve flood buffering and biodiversity protection.	• A collaborative governance model: The Canterbury Water Management Strategy, New Zealand (OECD, 2017a) • OECD requisites for the design of water pollution charges (OECD, 2017a) • OECD requisites for diffuse pollution allocation and water quality markets (OECD, 2017a) • Taxes to encourage and finance reductions in water pollution and water consumption, France (OECD, 2017a)
Water use charges, River Management Funds, and River Basin Committees	• Phase out the water use charge, which doesn't reflect the amount of pollution nor the polluter-pays principle, and exempts agriculture. • Replace the water use charge with economic instruments to incentivise reductions in water pollution at lowest cost to society. While all polluters should be charged in principle, start with and focus attention on the ones who have the more severe impacts on water quantity and quality. • Apply economic instruments, such as emissions trading schemes, or taxes on fertilisers and pesticides to reduce intensity of agricultural chemical inputs and foster expansion of integrated nutrient management such as nutrient accounting at the farm level. • Provide incentives to develop and disseminate technologies that reduce pollution and improve input efficiencies (e.g. water, pesticides and fertilisers). Technologies may include nitrification inhibitors, cover fertilisers, decentralised wastewater treatment technologies and artificial wetlands.	• OECD requisites for the design of water pollution charges, taxes and water quality trading schemes (OECD, 2017a)
The total pollution load control programme	• In addition to expanding the Korean TMDL to include the whole basin (including small/medium tributary rivers) and other water quality parameters linked to local ecological limits and social values on water quality, include all diffuse source polluters (including agriculture) in the programme. • Allow trading amongst point source polluters and between point source and diffuse source polluters within the Korean TMDL system to cost-effectively meet water quality goals whilst limiting restrictions on future economic development.	• OECD requisites for diffuse pollution allocation and water quality markets (OECD, 2017a) • Water quality trading, Chesapeake Bay, United States (OECD, 2017a)
Reducing diffuse pollution from agriculture	• Use targeted risk-based agri-environmental support payments or payment for ecosystem services in exchange for best farming practices (beyond mandatory good farming practices) in ecologically sensitive areas and drinking water sources. • Take a multi-dimensional approach to manure management beyond regulation to include incentives to invest in developing new technology, capacity-building and building partnerships between stakeholders. Enhance the partnership between livestock and crop farms to recycle and re-use livestock manure through on-farm application, biogas production and composting into organic fertilisers.	• Collaboration with farmers and Payment for Ecosystem Services schemes in England (OECD, 2017a) • Co-operation with farmers for catchment protection in Munich, Germany (OECD, 2017a) • Comprehensive policy framework for livestock manure management in the Netherlands (Annex 2.A)

References

Alliance for Water Efficiency (2017). Transforming Water: Water Efficiency as Infrastructure Investment.

EU Council Directive 98/83/EC (1998). On the quality of water intended for human consumption.

Choi, I-C, et al. (2017), Water Policy Reforms in South Korea: A Historical Review and Ongoing Challenges for Sustainable Water Governance and Management, Water, 9, pp 717.

Mitsubishi Research Institute, Inc. (2001), Evaluation of Multi-functionality associated with Agriculture and Forestry-related with the Global Environment and Human Life (in Japanese), Mitsubishi Research Institute Inc., Tokyo.

Kim, E.J. et al. (2016), The effect of total maximum daily loads (TMDL) program on water quality improvement in the Geum River basin, Korea, Desalination and Water Treatment, 57(2), pp. 597-609.

ME (2015), Ecorea: Environmental Review 2015: Korea, Ministry of Environment, Sejong.

ME (2014a), Introduction to NPS pollution management in Korea. In: Presented at the International Symposium for the 22nd Anniversary of World Water Day. National Institute of Environment Research, Incheon, South Korea.

ME (2014b), Environment Statistics Yearbook, Ministry of Environment, Sejong, http://webbook.me.go.kr/DLi-File/091/020/003/5588561.pdf.

ME and KEI (2016), River Management Funds for the Four Major River Systems, Korea Environmental Policy Bulletin, No. 44, Vol. XIV, Issue 4, 2016.

National Institute of Environmental Research (NIER) (2014), Technical Guidelines for TMDL Management, Korea.

OECD (2018, forthcoming), Innovation, Agricultural Productivity and Sustainability in Korea, OECD Publishing, Paris.

OECD (2017a), Diffuse Pollution, Degraded Waters: Emerging Policy Solutions. OECD Studies on Water, OECD Publishing, Paris. http://dx.doi.org/10.1787/9789264269064-en

OECD (2017b), OECD Environmental Performance Reviews: Korea 2017. OECD Publishing Paris. http://dx.doi.org/10.1787/9789264268265-en

OECD (2017c), Enhancing water use efficiency in Korea. OECD Studies on Water, OECD Publishing, Paris. http://dx.doi.org/10.1787/9789264281707-en

OECD (2016a), Mitigating Droughts and Floods in Agriculture: Policy Lessons and Approaches, OECD Studies on Water, OECD Publishing, Paris. http://dx.doi.org/10.1787/9789264246744-en

OECD (2016b), OECD Council Recommendation on Water, [C(2016)174/FINAL], December 2016. https://legalinstruments.oecd.org/en/instruments/349

OECD (2015a), Drying Wells, Rising Stakes: Towards Sustainable Agricultural Groundwater Use. OECD Studies on Water, OECD Publishing, Paris. http://dx.doi.org/10.1787/9789264238701-en

OECD (2015b), Water Resources Allocation: Sharing Risks and Opportunities. OECD Studies on Water, OECD Publishing, Paris. http://dx.doi.org/10.1787/9789264229631-en

OECD (2015c), Stakeholder Engagement for Inclusive Water Governance, OECD Studies on Water, OECD Publishing, Paris. http://dx.doi.org/10.1787/9789264231122-en

SAI Platform (2012). Water conservation technical briefs: TB15 Drip irrigation and water scarcity.

UN (2017), United Nations General Assembly Human Rights Council (September 2017). Report of the Special Rapporteur on the Human Rights to safe drinking water and sanitation.

US EPA (2016), WaterSense Accomplishments.

Waterwise (2017). Water Efficiency Strategy for the UK.

WHO (2011), Guidelines for drinking water quality, fourth edition. Winarni, W (2009). Infrastructure Leakage Index (ILI) as Water Losses Indicator. Civil Engineering Dimension, Vol. 11, No.2, September 2009.

Annex 2.A. Policy framework for livestock manure management in the Netherlands

The livestock sector in the Netherlands is important to the nation's economy, competitive in international markets and very intensive. The sector produces three to four times more manure than is needed for fertiliser use in the country. A single 500-sow farm producing 20 piglets per sow each year produces the same effluent as a town of 25 000 people, but on a much smaller land area. 80% of manure production (around 70 million tonnes per year) is from cattle, 18% from pigs and 2% from poultry.

The manure management approach adopted in the Netherlands is based on the premise that manure is a valuable product rather than waste and its valorisation can be a key driver of the circular economy. The Dutch manure policy focuses on both the production and the application of manure with the objective to optimise the use of manure through balanced fertilisation and suitable application techniques. The government supports this process through penalising polluters, while rewarding innovators and farmers who find ways to export manure. Their multi-dimensional approach entails: i) regulating the use of manure; ii) market-based instruments to facilitate innovation and investment in new techniques including financing R&D for innovative processing and manure management; subsidies and tax reduction; iii) capacity building for farmers through farmer networks; iv) partnerships between government, industry, NGOs and R&D institution; international co-operation through multi-stakeholder platforms such as the “Global Agenda for Sustainable Livestock”, the “Global Research Alliance on Agricultural Greenhouse Gases” and the “Global Partnership on Nutrient management”.

The cornerstone of the Dutch manure policy is a system of application standards for both nitrogen and phosphate on agricultural land. The legislation for using manure on land requires: i) Application rates: low maximum use of manure per ha land based on minerals phosphate and nitrogen; application in growing season; low emission application techniques, such as obligatory injection of liquid manure; ii) Enforcement: registration of production (livestock, crop and manure); compulsory processing of excess manure into products with high nutrient levels and a low moisture; iii) Obligation to reduce nutrient losses: build low emission housing; emission-free storage. Failing to comply results in an economic offence, which can be investigated and indicted under the criminal law. All farmers with a manure surplus must develop a disposal plan. Farmers who exceed permitted production levels face fines, and there is an escalating level of tax on commercial feed. A “Manure Board” regulates manure flows, provide manure for use in arable areas, and help find new manure users. It also conducts research, assists in the processing of manure and establishes treatment plants.

Another essential element of the Dutch manure management system is manure distribution from livestock farms with a nutrient surplus to arable farms that can use the nutrients in crop production. The most common use of animal manure is its application as fertiliser on agricultural land (90% of all manure). Manure application is only allowed when using low emission technology like manure injection on grassland and immediate covering with soil on arable land. The manure application period is limited to the early growing season of crops. By using animal manure as nutrient source for crops, more than 90% of synthetic phosphate fertilisers and more than 60% of synthetic nitrogen fertilisers have been replaced by phosphate and nitrogen from animal manure.

As of 2014, farmers with a phosphate surplus are obliged to process and export a percentage of this surplus. These percentages increase annually until the desired balance between manure phosphate production and available agricultural land or crop uptake in the Netherlands is reached. The percentages are higher for farms in the livestock concentration areas (south and east) than for farms elsewhere in the Netherlands. Large manure surpluses are produced mainly from pig and poultry farms, as they cover little land, while most dairy farms have land (50 ha per farm on average) and can apply part of the manure to their own land. Transport is expensive because manure consists largely of water. The livestock farmer has to pay approximately EUR 10 to EUR 23 per tonne to the transport company. The transport company will pay approximately EUR 3 to EUR 10 per tonne to the manure receiving arable farmer; the difference must cover the costs of transportation. Cost of manure transport within the Netherlands is around EUR 5 to EUR 20 per tonne. Reducing the water content and manure processing to increase organic matter and nutrient content make distribution more effective.

The evaluation of the Manure and Fertiliser Act 2016 concludes that the current manure and fertiliser policy reduces environmental problems. Agricultural production is economically and ecologically very efficient per unit of product, but because of its volume, environmental pressure remains high: although balanced fertilisation for phosphate reached in 2014 and nitrate surpluses have decreased, in southern sand region nitrate concentration exceeds the target, partly due to manure separation and manure fraud.

Over the coming years the focus of manure management policy in the Netherlands will be on three areas:

- Manure processing: increases export potential for animal manure. In addition, to reduce veterinary health risks, the exported manure must comply with the requirements for animal by-products. Mechanical separation of manure (the initial stage of the processing of liquid manure), manure processing and anaerobic digestion are processing methods to improve export opportunities.
- Animal feed: agreement with farmers and feed industry to: i) decrease the concentration of phosphate in the feed; and ii) develop innovations to create more cost-effective feed
- Fertiliser replacement: upgrading animal manure to products with properties comparable to synthetic fertiliser; more use of renewable resources; fertilisers with high efficiency.

A key lesson from the Dutch approach to manure management is the importance of a coherent system of clear and realistic regulatory standards (e.g. nutrient application standards for agricultural land) which can be adapted as required by local circumstances. An efficient logistics system for manure storage and distribution is also indispensable, as well as accurate records, monitoring, administration and enforcement.

Source: OECD (2018, forthcoming), Innovation, Agricultural Productivity and Sustainability in Korea, OECD Publishing, Paris.

Chapter 3. Towards policy coherence and sustainable management of the Water-Energy-Land-Food nexus in Korea

This chapter focuses on policy coherence and sustainable management of the WELF nexus in Korea. This chapter provides a rationale for improved planning against future water-related risks, and the benefits of independent regulation and other supporting policy instruments (such as permitting, compliance monitoring and enforcement, and environmental impact assessments) to support the sustainable management of the WELF nexus. Good practices in integrated water resource planning, including resilience thinking and scenario planning, and options for delivering independent water regulation are provided.

3.1. Planning as a key instrument to manage the WELF nexus in Korea

3.1.1. How planning combines with regulation and permitting

The basic principles of water management and regulation are summarised in Figure 3.1 below. At the centre of effective regulation are the standards and targets to protect and improve the water (and land) environment, so that it can continue to provide the services on which society depends. The decision on what type of regulatory measures to use will determine whether it should be a conventional permitting approach, an alternative (the right-hand side of the flow chart), or some hybrid. It is essential that as part of the regulatory process, monitoring and reviews are carried out to determine whether the desired outcomes are being achieved. There must then be a policy and knowledge feedback loop to amend (or endorse) the approach to regulation, or potentially to change the standards.

Figure 3.1. The regulatory cycle for sustainable water management

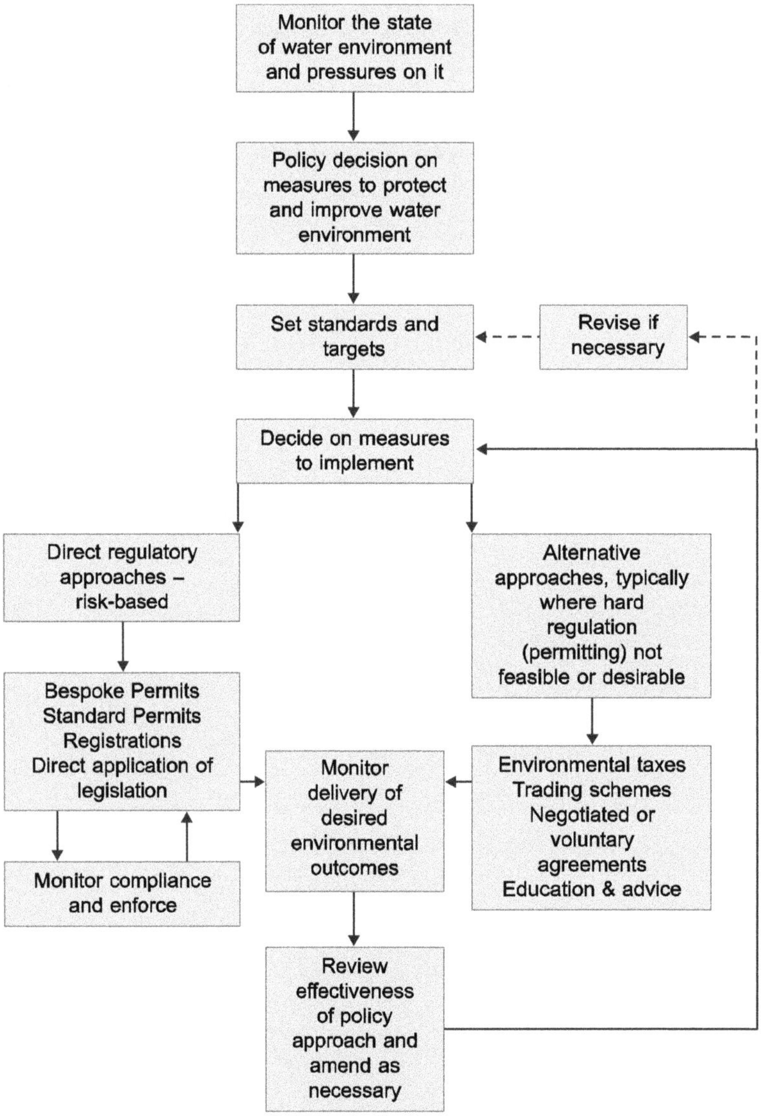

Source: Professor Ian Barker, Water Policy International, *Pers comm.*

There are four key elements to water management and regulation:

1. *Developing plans* to deal with current identified problems of water pollution (e.g. eutrophication), low river flows (scarcity, droughts) and urban flooding.
2. *Setting regulations* (i.e. policy guidance) for the routine management through permitting of water resources and control of pollution, and the financial charging, compliance monitoring and enforcement of those permits. Also, regulations for land use development control and agricultural policy are required so that water and land use management are fully integrated.
3. *Specifying actions during periods of drought and floods* in order to manage diminishing resources, conflicting demands, environmental stress, and flood risk both before and during events.
4. *Considering future pressures and uncertainties*, and what action might be needed to manage the impacts of climate change and increasing development pressures on water and land.

This process is essentially the one followed throughout Europe via the implementation of the Water Framework Directive (see Annex 3.A), which uses costed options appraisal to determine the measures to restore and protect the water environment for the benefit of ecosystems and people.

The four areas listed above all require sound data about the current state of the water environment (quality, resources, hydroecology) and trends over time: how is the water environment changing in response to human pressures and changes in land use? The four work areas should be part of a feedback loop so that where it is clear that more data is required to make sound decisions, those needs are fed back into the monitoring programme. Specific terrestrial sites or water bodies of concern would be subject to detailed investigation as necessary. During periods of drought, additional hydrological and ecological monitoring should be in place to aid the day-to-day management of the drought, planning for the next actions, and to act as a database for future drought management planning so that lessons are learnt (see section 3.1.4). Similarly, every flood event is an opportunity to learn and take action to minimise future risk.

The challenge in Korea is to ensure an integrated approach to planning, regulation and management, with a clear shared and common view on the desired outcomes and success measures. The following points to consider would involve all relevant actors:

- Review the transferability of the EU Water Framework Directive approach and process, and consider which elements might benefit water management in Korea.
- Consider the objectives of the regulatory process in meeting the desired outcomes which emerge from the plans. Be clear about how each permit issued in each water body, including for land development control is contributing to those outcomes, and ensure that all involved in water and land management operate as an integrated whole.
- Ensure that the permitting systems are flexible and dynamic to be able to cope with, and account for, improved understanding and environmental change.
- Monitoring and managing water is expensive, and where water users do not pay a charge they will not value the resource. Consider introducing meaningful charges for abstractions and discharges, as well as for applications for permits, in order to work towards full cost recovery.

The following sections look at how Korea can increase resilience to future water risks through water resource planning, integrated basin planning, and scenario planning and risk management.

3.1.2. Water resource planning for secure water supplies

This section covers the key steps required for water resource planning, including the need for a long-term and holistic view, levels of service and systems resilience, forecasting demand, and options to reduce the supply-demand deficit.

Coordinating water policies

Plans to secure water supplies for people and businesses often focus solely on assessing the resources required to meet demand. However, water demand is not a given: it can be influenced and managed (see Section 2.2).

The challenge in Korea is the lack of inclusive and transparent stakeholder engagement to be able to coordinate and consider viewpoints of various stakeholders in developing a water resources plan. The ME, with other key ministries such as MAFRA, MoLIT, specialised government agencies like KECO and K-water, provinces and municipalities would all need to contribute to a national plan which, as far as possible, aimed to optimise the use of available resources across the country irrespective of hydrological or administrative boundaries. The more that a plan is fragmented, the greater the risk that the solutions to supply challenges will be more expensive, less resilient and less sustainable.

The need for a long-term and holistic view

The intergenerational nature of most water supply investment means that it is essential for planning to take a long-term perspective. A typical minimum planning horizon in water resources is 25 years, but that should not prevent a longer term view where this is appropriate. Given the long lifespan of water infrastructure, it is important that water resources management plans are resilient to a range of potential climate scenarios and are designed with climate risks built in. In addition, in Korea the introduction of environmental flows by ME could introduce uncertainty around the sustainability of existing reservoirs and abstraction licences, which means that the potential reduction in source yield needs to be taken into account.

It is essential to consider how other parts of the nexus can help, or undermine, careful water planning. This is particularly important in Korea, where agricultural water demand and the complex web of dams, reservoirs and weirs need to be optimised across all sectors. The Smart Water Initiative (see OECD, 2017a) is helping to address this need. However, the impact of food and energy policy and land use planning on water availability, demand and quality should be factored in. Planning decisions need to take account of all stakeholder interests, and be in the context of long-term integrated basin management.

Levels of service and systems resilience

A water resources plan should comply with government policy on the sustainable use and management of water, and its efficient use. They should reflect "acceptable levels" of water security (OECD, 2013).

A rigorous options appraisal might be to carry out a probability analysis of drought events not seen in the historic record. This probabilistic approach has been used for London (Borgomeo, 2014) where the potential impacts on levels of service of a non-stationary climate have been modelled, and also an assessment of supply security against a wide range of uncertainties (Borgomeo, 2018). A useful test is to look at the experiences of other nations with unprecedented drought events and to ask 'What would happen if an equivalent drought happened in Korea?'

The appraisal of risk management options (either through demand management or supply augmentation) should consider the costs and benefits of each, recognising that often the benefits might be difficult to monetise. For example, being able to leave more water in a river because of demand management will have a value to other abstractors and to ecosystems. Using different scenarios for demand and supply allows the system to be tested by looking at periods of high demand and low supplies, and uncertainties in planning assumptions, which can be tested against a baseline position to forecast what would happen if no new supply or demand actions were taken.

If, after having been through this baseline exercise it is apparent that there is a supply-demand imbalance, there then needs to be an appraisal of options to manage demand, set alongside options to develop new resources or increase treatment capacity. The options need to be tested against challenging but plausible droughts to understand potential weaknesses to different types of drought, as well as other pressures such as pollution, and against different levels of service, so that it is clear what action needs to be taken at each stage of a developing drought.

Forecasting demand

Understanding the drivers of demand for water, and then translating these into the basis of forecasts, is one of the most challenging elements of any water resource plan.

Forecasts for future water demands from households, energy, agriculture, industry and the environment should be included. Changes in energy policy, for example progressively abandoning coal-fired generation in favour of wind and solar sources (as is the case in Korea), will impact on water availability by reducing water demand for cooling. Industrial and agricultural water demand can be very difficult to forecast, so a scenario approach will help to expose potential risks. Changes in land use, such as afforestation or deforestation, will not only affect overall demand for water in a basin in a way which is difficult to control, but also the runoff characteristics and potentially also water quality.

A further, important consideration is to ensure that there is sufficient water for the environment in the future. In Korea, this is complicated by the potential temperature increases and flow changes as a result of climate change. Such changes are likely to modify ecosystems. This uncertainty needs to be factored into water resources planning and appropriate allocation of water for environmental flows.

All these variables in the forecasts will have a different influence on the location, magnitude and timing of total demand for water. The impact of policy and regulation is critical, particularly for the promotion of measures and behaviours to support water conservation.

Options to reduce the supply-demand deficit

A robust plan will build in headroom to allow for the uncertainties in demand (and supply), and will allow for risk to increase into the future. Over time, the uncertainties will reduce and it will be possible to adapt to changes. Once a series of demand forecasts has been generated it is possible to see whether there is a deficit at any point over the planning period, taking account of the likely impacts of climate change and other pressures on source yields. Where deficits are likely, or headroom is reduced resulting in increased risk of failure, the plan then needs to identify potential options to close the gap.

The aim should be to have a balanced portfolio of options so that the risks are spread, rather than relying solely on one type of option (e.g. supply augmentation). Where there are concerns about the level of confidence in the demand forecasts, a series of incremental developments can ensure a low-regrets approach to investment which can be adjusted as more certainty is available.

A water resources plan should provide a stable basis for decisions, but given the uncertainties about the future it is important to understand the factors which could have the biggest influence on it. Scenario testing can help to show how resilient the plan is to a range of risks, and the timing of critical changes. It can show when the approach needs to be flexible or fixed, and when important decisions need to be made. It can also identify what should be monitored to manage risk, and suggest how the plan may need to change in the future in response to new evidence.

In summary, points to consider for water resource planning include:

- Set levels of service for water supply security, now and in the future. These may be different for different sectors: public supply, energy, industry, agriculture (and within the agriculture sector, they will depend on the types of crops grown), environment
- Take a long term view – at least 25 years – and assess the impact of different climate change and demand scenarios on water availability and demand, for all sectors
- Assess a full suite of options, on both the supply and the demand side, for their risk, cost, sustainability and flexibility in the face of uncertainty.

3.1.3. Integrated basin planning

The value of integrated basin planning and management

The current silo approach to water planning and management in Korea, where water resources, water quality, agriculture and development planning are dealt with separately, is failing to benefit from the synergies and opportunities for multiple benefits which an integrated approach would bring. The benefits of integrated basin planning and management can be summarised as follows:

- The full breadth of the evidence base can be aggregated so that a complete picture is presented of the state of the environment in the basin, together with current and future pressures and how these interact on society and the economy. Where there is uncertainty this can be identified and the consequences of a precautionary approach explored.
- An integrated plan will set the ambition for the basin. This might include: the restoration of the environment to a target state or prevent its further deterioration; to secure more productive agriculture; or to reduce flood risk; or to increase water supply resilience. The important point is that all of these apparently separate ambitions can be viewed together. The outcome from this appraisal may be to use one action – which might be a policy change or an infrastructure development – to deliver wider benefits than just its core purpose.
- An integrated plan provides the basis for understanding the total financial spend requirements, and the relative priorities of different objectives. It can therefore help to shape the type, and to set the level of, charges based on polluter or user

pays as appropriate. At present, spending in each river basin in Korea is largely sectoral or silo driven by the various separate interests.

- The actions within the plan should include the basis for environmental permitting of activities which would otherwise have a detrimental effect. Because the plan has set clear objectives for the basin, these will translate into conditions and restrictions on permits to control abstraction and polluting activities within sustainable limits and reflecting local circumstances. Businesses can then make informed choices about where to locate, using the knowledge of the potential costs at any location.
- Finally, the process of developing and agreeing the plan should be open, inclusive and transparent. All stakeholders should have a voice, and the costs and sharing of actions agreed. Inevitably, this process will result in trade-offs, but these will be understood and arrived at through a negotiated process (see 0).

Integrated basin planning in Korea

The number of national, regional and local actors (OECD, 2017a), each with their own remit, results in the lack of a comprehensive and integrated plan for each major basin. A further omission is that tributaries and small catchments have little monitoring and few controls. Experience from Europe (Annex 3.A) is that the adoption of integrated land and water management plans under the Water Framework Directive helped to identify synergies and multiple benefits from actions to protect and improve the water environment.

Steps to consider for improved river basin planning and management in Korea include:

- Review the potential to adapt and apply the principles of the European Water Framework Directive for integrated water and land planning
- Address the need for a single 'Competent Authority' to own and oversee the planning process and the delivery of actions, both by itself and others, and consider how this approach might work in Korea
- Review monitoring, regulation, permitting, inspection, charging and planning processes in the context of a Water Framework Directive type of approach.

Chapter 4 provides a review of, and recommendations for, water governance and institutions in Korea.

3.1.4. Future-proofing the WELF nexus and planning for uncertainty in Korea

It is unclear from the different climate and hydrological models how water stress in Korea might be affected by climate change, and how the monsoon might behave. Increased precipitation, including from extreme events, seems likely to increase, with consequent implications for the frequency and magnitude of fluvial and pluvial flooding (UK Met Office, 2011). Recent droughts around the world are timely signals that past weather patterns are no guide to the future, and that systems resilience is likely to be tested more harshly. Despite all the uncertainties, there are techniques using scenario planning and resilience modelling which can help in planning for secure supplies and a healthy environment.

This section describes how Korea can anticipate and manage droughts and floods, and use scenarios to test long-term policy options.

Anticipating and managing drought

Although the approach to water supply planning described above takes account of severe drought events, there is always the possibility that a drought of even greater severity could occur. In such unforeseen circumstances, extra measures would be required to respond to an extreme drought. It is prudent therefore to have in place a drought management plan which can be implemented progressively as a drought develops, on a no regrets basis.

Drought can happen anywhere, even in countries perceived as not water stressed. The frequency of drought events can test supply systems and challenge assumptions about their reliability. For example, in northern and western Europe, severe droughts in 2002-03, 2005-07 and 2011-12 all broke meteorological records in some way, and have led to a re-think about drought planning and supply resilience.

In Korea, the recent period of five years with dry springs could be an indication of the potential for more frequent dry spells which would further jeopardise the reliability of reservoir supply systems. The Korea Meteorological Administration forecasts an increase in drought frequency, which will test any inefficiencies in water management and the assumption that droughts are manageable. A prudent approach to planning would be to assess the impact, for example, of two, three and four years in succession with significantly below average rainfall, and what this would mean for reservoir storage and the ability to maintain supplies.

Drought management

Drought impacts are cross-cutting on government departments, regulators, water-using sectors and wider society. It is therefore essential that drought planning and management are integrated across all affected parties, with clarity of roles and accountability. The policy objectives and institutional arrangements should be established as part of the drought planning process, so that where drought management involves trade-offs and compromises, these have been debated and agreed in advance of a drought occurring. Mitigation measures should form part of these conversations. Robust drought risk management will aim to deliver multiple outcomes for people, freshwater ecosystems and the economy within the context of a drought resilient society. This aim is likely to be made more difficult where a society does not value water, or make the link between the water used in cities and ecosystems in the rural areas. When water efficiency is not a priority – as is the case in Korea - effective drought management is compromised because water users are not sensitised to the need to use resources carefully.

The potential actions to secure supplies and protect the environment would ideally have been previously subject to an impact assessment as part of the drought planning process so that the least damaging and best value options can be adopted first. As a drought progresses, the more extreme and expensive options would then be implemented. Early warning systems can be valuable in helping water managers and water users plan ahead. All actions should be associated with triggers such as critical river flows, reservoir stocks, groundwater levels or water demand (e.g. for irrigation). The critical point is that drought management should be part of a planned, proactive process, rather than a reactive one developed during the drought itself.

Korea is potentially vulnerable to droughts (and other shocks), because of the level of water scarcity and nature of the supply systems for drinking water and agriculture. Its rigorous, but reactive approach to disaster management contrasts with the lack of proactive planning and mitigation measures. Recommendations to Korea to improve drought management include:

- For each river basin and drinking water supply area develop plans to set out pre-agreed actions, including compromises and trade-offs, for droughts of different severity and duration
- Carry out Environmental Impact Assessments in order to understand, and be able to mitigate, the impact of planned emergency measures
- Set out pre-agreed triggers for action as a drought progresses, under a range of different scenarios
- Establish communications plans, for participation of key stakeholders as well as the wider public.

Flood risk management

Korea's flood risk index is higher than other countries (OECD, 2017a), at 6.85 casualties per million people exposed, and in recent years there has been significant financial impact and numbers of people affected. Average annual precipitation in 2001-2010 increased by 7.4% compared with the 30 year period to 2010, and flood risk is forecast (Park et al., 2016) to continue to rise, in particular from 2025 to the 2050's. Government ministries are working together to address the risks and to develop comprehensive measures to prevent urban flooding. These include better provision of information and improved flood forecasting and warnings, more use of rainfall radar, and an ambition to increase the capacity of the drainage networks and fully separate foul sewerage where necessary. There is also recognition of the need to promote low impact development and to better manage rainfall runoff in the urban environment, as evidenced by the large number of pilot projects in Korean cities. The challenge is to accelerate progress and innovation on stormwater management; green infrastructure pilots and increases in urban floodwater storage show what can be done, but so far only at a small scale. Box 3.1 presents a case study demonstrating how green infrastructure can be harnessed to manage urban flood risks in New York City, USA.

Box 3.1. Urban Flood Risk Management – Blue-Green Cities Case Study, New York City

Blue-Green Cities help to address modern challenges to quality of life, climate change and inequality. With nearly 70% of the world's population set to live in cities by 2030, keeping up with global urban growth projections for 2030 will mean developing an area the equivalent of 20,000 American Football fields every day up to 2030. Vulnerable water resources and ecosystems will be subjected to the pressures from this growth and urbanisation.

More cities around the world are adopting blue and green infrastructure through retrofit programmes, which use trees, soils and other planting to manage urban water by mimicking the natural hydrological cycle. New York City is aiming to invest US$2.4bn in green infrastructure over the next 20 years. It is planning over 7,000 "kerbside gardens" in the streets to reduce the risk from combined sewer overflows. In Wales, Welsh Water are investing £80 million up to 2020 in their RainScape program, which aims to minimise surface water ingress into the combined sewerage network.

Done well, green infrastructure reduces flooding, improves water quality and replenishes groundwater. The protection of water resources from urban runoff and associated pollutants like sediment, nutrients, metals, pathogens, trash, and hydrocarbons is a constantly growing challenge. It also brings multi-faceted benefits such as beautifying neighbourhoods, increasing property values, reducing the heat island effect and absorbing carbon dioxide.

In an urban context where space is at a premium, blue-green infrastructure is an important integrated design strategy for architects, planners and engineers to consider. For example, in Red Hook Houses in Brooklyn, New York, elevated landscape berms between apartment buildings act to protect the residential buildings from flooding while providing safe and regenerated courtyards for the residents to enjoy. The waterfront park at Hunters Point South in New York City (below) is designed with a significant amount of the park area that is designated to flood intentionally during heavy rainfall events. The challenge until recently was gaining consensus, developing guidelines and finding success in pilot projects; the challenge now for cities is delivering at a scale and pace that protects waterways and combats climate change.

Hunters Point South, New York, under normal conditions (top) and flood conditions (bottom)

Source: Dr. Mark Fletcher, Arup, *Pers. Comm.* Photo credit: Thomas Balsley Associates.

Korea's rapid urbanisation has led to the area of urbanised and paved areas doubling between 1989 and 2009 (OECD, 2017b). Over the same period the area of grasslands decreased by 24% and wetlands by 61%. At both a basin and a local scale, these changes potentially increase flood risk. Land use controls at a basin level appear ineffectual in terms of incorporating flood risk assessment into new developments. Any assessments are carried out at a municipal or regional scale, rather than considering wider (downstream) basin impacts. New factories and other developments are often constructed in flood risk areas, compounding runoff problems rather than seeking a runoff-neutral or positive impact.

Although the techniques and principles of sustainable drainage, such as swales, permeable pavements and green roofs are well understood in Korea, the challenge is in creating the mechanisms for them to be implemented at scale. It requires politicians, developers, architects, planners, engineers and municipal authorities all to be aligned to ensuring not only that new developments are low impact but that there is also a plan to progressively implement such water sensitive schemes in existing towns and cities. It also requires sufficient funds for investment, the governance to ensure that they are constructed to the necessary specification, and ongoing maintenance funding so that they continue to perform as designed. The government has plans to improve rainwater retention and install runoff reduction measures in the 107 areas of greatest risk, and is aiming for a more proactive approach to both pluvial and fluvial flood risk management.

The following are recommendations for Korea to consider in the management of flood risk:

1. Review potential barriers to scaling up LID and green infrastructure, and develop a funded strategy for reducing urban flood risk, taking account of the increased risk from climate change.
2. Design green infrastructure so that it reduces urban diffuse pollution as well as runoff.
3. Establish a campaign for greater public awareness of flood risk, and the need for pollution management.
4. Ensure that land use and development controls consider flood risk at a basin scale, rather than regionally or at a municipal level, so that future land use changes of all types minimise runoff (and do not enhance it).
5. Use integrated river basin planning and management to integrate small and large scale green infrastructure initiatives, and seek to obtain multiple benefits (e.g. water quality, low flow support, flood risk reduction, amenity and recreation).

Resilience thinking

There are a range of threats other than droughts and floods which can lead to failure but which are not routinely considered in planning or operational thinking. The task for water managers is to design and operate systems to overcome them rather than seeking the impossibility of avoiding failure altogether.

This requires a paradigm shift and a holistic approach to addressing water problems. Water systems are designed and operated to deliver to a standard of service; safe drinking water, or clean effluent or reliable supplies. The reliability with which the system does this is the degree to which it minimises level of service failure over its design life when subject to planned loads. Its resilience is the degree to which it minimises level of service failure magnitude and duration when subject to exceptional conditions and threats. The threat can come from anywhere. It might be something which occurs gradually, such as progressive urban expansion (an external threat) or progressive loss of skills, or steady reduction in funding (internal threats), or something which happens quickly such as a natural disaster, cyber-attack or human error (Butler, 2016). The examples given in Figure 3.2 are illustrative and would need to be amended according to the system in question and the operating environment of the user. Similar diagrams can help to show what a threat might mean for different elements of a system, or their impacts and consequences, including wider societal, economic and nexus issues.

Figure 3.2. Threat categorisation and examples

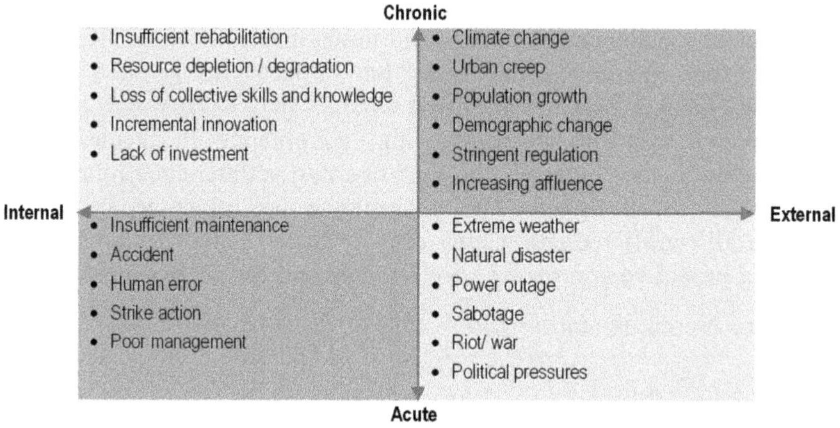

Source: Butler, D. et al. (2016), Reliable, resilient and sustainable water management: The Safe & Sure approach, Global Challenges, 2016.

Failure should not be accepted as an inevitable and uncontrollable state. Once the impact and consequences of failure have been identified, mitigation measures to ameliorate threats can be developed. Where mitigation is not possible, or only to a limited degree, adaptation measures involving targeted actions can be taken to enhance the capability of a system to maintain levels of service. And when failure does occur, coping actions can reduce the frequency, magnitude or duration of the effects of the impacts. All this experience and knowledge should then be embedded in best practice.

Droughts and flooding are just two of many potential threats to a city's resilience, and should not be considered in isolation. The City Resilience Index (Box 3.2) provides a holistic articulation of city resilience, structured around four dimensions, including infrastructure and environment, to measure and test resilience in the round (Rockefeller Foundation, 2016). It would be a useful self-assessment tool for Korea.

Finally, governments and regulators should challenge delivery bodies to consider resilience in their planning and operational activities. This is now happening routinely in England and Wales, where the economic regulator Ofwat has been given a statutory responsibility to promote resilience among the companies it regulates.

Box 3.2. The City Resilience Index

The City Resilience Index (CRI) is a tool intended to help urban populations face the increasing challenges from natural hazards and manmade pressures, and to provide them with a framework to develop effective strategies to create more resilient cities. It is founded on evidence from 16 city case studies, and is now being adopted in 100 resilient cities around the world. Of the more than 1000 applications for the 100 Resilient Cities Network, over 60% indicated challenges with water as critical resilience risks. The CRI provides cities with an accessible, evidence-based definition of urban resilience, and is a mechanism to assess and monitor their present day resilience and their progress towards a more resilient future. The assessment helps cities to develop a deeper understanding of the systems, processes and functions that shape their resilience profile.

The findings from their assessments empowers cities to better identify appropriate actions to strengthen resilience, while allowing them to measure progress over time. It uses qualitative indicators based on specific questions to evaluate and identify the 'qualities' of urban systems, and aggregates scores to build the resilience profile for a city.

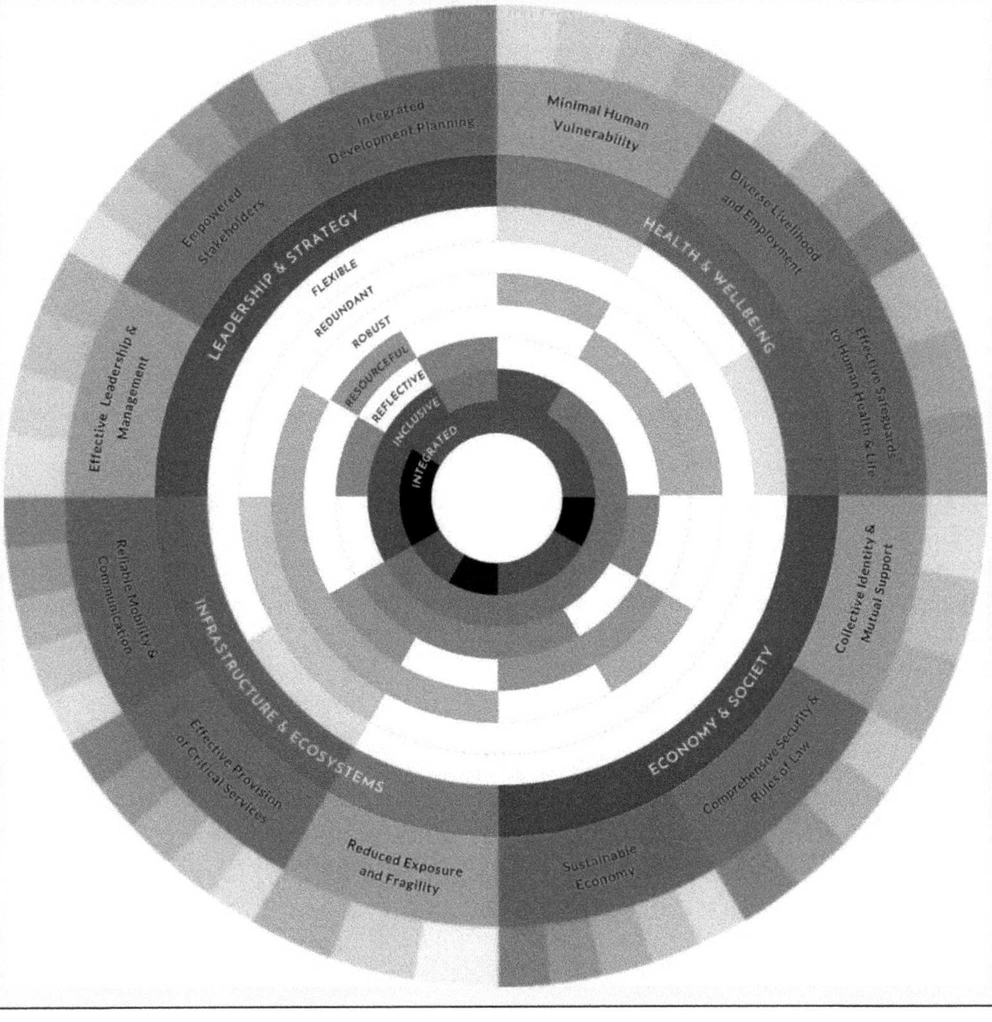

The CRI relates to four key dimensions: People, Organisation, Place and Knowledge; and uses 12 Goals, 52 qualitative and quantitative Indicators, and 156 Metrics, all of which provide a current snapshot of a city's performance and its strengths and weaknesses, its potential to achieve greater resilience, and to assess whether its development trajectory is likely to make the city more or less resilient.

Source: The Rockefeller Foundation/Arup (2016), City Resilience Index – Understanding and Measuring City Resilience.

Using scenarios to test long-term policy options

Background: scenarios and forecasts

Scenarios can inform today's thinking about strategic decisions through exploring different possible futures. They examine a range of internally consistent, plausible futures, not to forecast what they may be like, but to provide a mechanism for thinking through the challenges that might be encountered and the opportunities that might arise. Scenarios are most useful when there is uncertainty about some of the factors that may significantly shape the future and when a range of outcomes may be plausible (even if some are more plausible than others).

Box 3.3. Water demand forecasts will always be wrong: a case study from England and Wales

The dangers of relying upon a single forecast (of water demand) are well illustrated by a review of water demand forecasts for England and Wales. In the 1960's and 1970's growth forecasts made optimistic assumptions (Figure 3.3) about increases in industrial demand for water in north-east England, leading to the construction of the UK's largest reservoir – Kielder Water. Instead, industrial demand collapsed and the reservoir has been significantly under-utilised ever since. Even though household demand for water is likely to increase in the future this will take place in the south-east of England and the reservoir is too far away for an easy transfer of water resources.

Figure 3.3 shows that since the mid-1990s, forecasts appear to have become more accurate, when compared with, in hindsight, actual demand for water. This is because they started to recognise that demand for water did not necessarily have to rise, and that leakage control and promotion of water efficiency could restrict or even reverse demand increases. The forecasts then started to become a self-fulfilling prophecy, in that by demonstrating what might be possible in terms of managing demand, policies were then developed to try and ensure that it did. From 1995, the significant demand reduction arose from a 40 per cent reduction in leakage, followed by increased household metering, promotion of water efficiency in households and industry, and the adoption of more water efficient fixtures, fittings and appliances. If there had been a scenario approach to planning in the 1970's or 1980's it might have identified the potential for demand reduction and led to an earlier policy discussion about the merits of demand management.

Figure 3.3. Water demand forecasts for England and Wales 1949 -2009 (dotted lines), compared with actual demand (solid line)

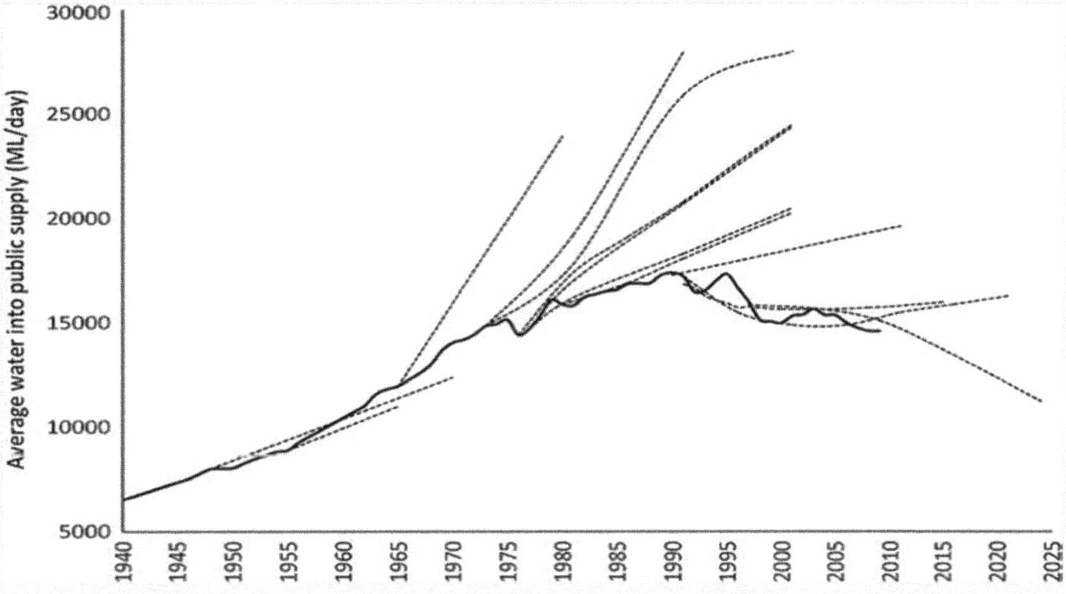

Source: Walker, G. (2013), A critical examination of models and projections of demand in water utility resource planning in England and Wales. International Journal of Water Resources Development, 29:3, 352-372.

Scenarios are not attempts to predict the future: rather, a set of scenarios collectively explores the parameter space in which the future might plausibly sit. This allows decisions to be stress-tested against whether they lock in to trajectories towards less desirable end states, and/or consideration of strategies that are robust to alternative directions. Given the uncertainties about how long land and water systems can be maintained on their current unsustainable trajectories, this avoids strategic lock-in to only "business-as-usual, plus-or-minus" thinking.

Scenario planning in practice

Most forecasts of future water demand project significant and sustained increases with consequent alarming implications for water stress. However, they give little or no recognition to how, for example, better policies and the increased adoption of demand management could lead to a more balanced and equitable allocation of water resources. By 2040 a significant proportion (40%) of the global population will be living in river basins under severe water stress (OECD, 2012). This takes no account that in most of the nations where this might be the case, they are unlikely to sleep walk into a crisis. There will be investment in additional resources, leakage reduction and demand management, and strengthened governance to manage resources more effectively and equitably. However, it does highlight the risk and consequences of complacency.

The scale at which an assessment is undertaken is also important. The same assessment suggests that Brazil will have no water problems in 2040. This is because the assessment uses the total national water availability and a simple ratio of withdrawals to supply. Given that 'supply' includes the Amazon, the national scale of the assessment ignores the fact that some parts of the country are already water stressed and in need of urgent reform to water management; this sort of forecast needs to be treated with caution.

For water, UNESCO (2012) has suggested the use of five possible scenarios (including a business-as-usual scenario), which reflect the potential dominance of key drivers. These are Business-as-usual ('Conventional world'), 'Conflict world', 'Techno-world', 'Global consciousness', and 'Conventional world gone sour'. The storylines or plots of each of scenarios have their merits; bespoke scenarios for the Korean context could include thinking from this approach by UNESCO.

An example of a national-level use of water scenarios is work by the UK Environment Agency (2009, 2017a) to develop a Water Resources Strategy for England and Wales (Box 3.4). This approach would potentially be appropriate for Korea, in that it would build in the range of possible impacts of climate change with uncertainties over future water demand and environmental protection.

Also relevant is the approach taken by Ercin and Hoekstra (2014), who developed scenarios for global water footprints. They constructed four scenarios along two axes, representing two key dimensions of uncertainty: globalisation versus regional self-sufficiency, and economy-driven development versus development driven by social and environmental objectives. Their approach could help to understand the range of possible impacts of different policy decisions and economic futures on agriculture, food production and land use in Korea.

Box 3.4. Scenario planning for the development of a Water Resources Strategy, England and Wales

The UK Environment Agency used a scenario-based approach to develop a Water Resources Strategy for England and Wales. The approach was based on the two key drivers or axes of control for water resources - governance and demand - and overlain with assessments of water availability under climate change projections. The plots for the four scenarios were centred on international governance systems (sustainability led-governance and growth-led governance), and on societal attitudes and behaviour around consumption (dematerialised consumption and materialised consumption). Importantly, the scenarios reflected the breadth of pressures on water systems, from changes in demand across all sectors – municipal, agricultural, industrial and environmental – to different societal attitudes to water use and governance, and under different socio-economic scenarios.

The demand-led scenarios provided an indication of the effects of different socio-economic policies and external evidence. They were then overlain with four climate change scenario assessments of the impact of a changing climate on water availability in each river basin, in order to understand the spatial implications for water availability. Finally, environmental flows were considered; England and Wales uses a sophisticated assessment based upon Environmental Flow Indicators for each water body, which sets e-flows on a variable basis. The concern for future assessments of water availability for human use under climate change is how much water needs to be left in the river for the ecology. Maintaining e-flows at their current level in the face of declining availability would significantly reduce volumes available for abstraction. However, given the uncertainty regarding what environment will need to be protected in a warmer, lower flow hydrology it was appropriate to also use scenarios for e-flows, allowing them to adjust pro rata – or not - with resource availability.

Scenario planning in Korea: a possible approach

Scenario choices for Korea could include:

- *Attitudes to sustainability*: reflect a sustainable future where pollution is controlled, abstraction of water is managed, and ecosystems flourish. Demand for water would be managed, rural land use would ensure that the water environment was protected and diffuse pollution controlled, and cities would be greened so as to limit surface water flooding and treat rainfall as a resource.
- *Innovative future*: how continued growth in GDP is maintained is closely linked to attitudes to innovation. Green growth, the circular economy and innovation can enable ecosystem services to be accessed and the value of natural capital realised more efficiently, even though the general public do not particularly value the environment. There is significant investment in infrastructure, technology and research. High-tech methods are used in agriculture to intensify production. Economic growth coupled with better use of technology results in greater social equity.
- *Making do with less*: a decline in GDP, for whatever reason, could prejudice the ability to make ongoing investment in water supply security, and in maintenance and control systems. Water supply and sewerage networks would continue to deteriorate, with increases in sewer collapses and blockages, and more water lost through leakage. Industry would resist expensive measures to improve effluent standards, and river water quality would deteriorate. Land use controls could be relaxed, and agricultural intensification through aggregating land holdings would become necessary in order to ensure food security, even at the risk of further degradation of the environment. Fossil fuel power stations would continue to be used, and climate change mitigation and adaptation measures would be shelved.
- *Attitudes to self-sufficiency*: global trends in resource availability and demand could lead to the need or desire to take a more insular and local approach, with the aim of national self-sufficiency as far as possible in goods, services and food. Under this type of scenario, water assets would be repaired rather than replaced, and attitudes to water allocation would be geared towards extracting the maximum value from each litre. The environment would be viewed as an asset to exploit, rather than to protect to maximise the breadth of ecosystem services. Water efficiency would become essential to help reduce energy demands and ensure that there were sufficient water resources to maintain production.
- *Uncontrolled consumerism*: economic growth is pursued with little regard for the environment or social equity. Although the country prospers, the gap between the rich and poor widens, and the environment becomes a commodity that only the wealthy can enjoy. Urbanisation spreads, and sustainable land management is abandoned in favour of profiting from intensive agriculture and development.

Increased demand for water means that it becomes more expensive to provide quality and reliability, further disadvantaging vulnerable sections of society.

- *Business as usual*: extrapolating the consequences of current policy approaches to water and land management could result in water supply failures through droughts or increased leakage. The need to abstract more water from rivers already impacted by high demand would cause deterioration in river water quality because of lack of dilution, and further degradation by diffuse pollution, eutrophication and industrial pollution. Groundwater levels would decline because of unconstrained demand and quality would deteriorate.

These brief examples are intended to illustrate the sorts of scenarios which might be developed for Korea, and what they could suggest in terms of risks and policy responses. Scenario development needs to be an inclusive and participatory activity, to ensure that a wide range of stakeholder views are taken into account; this will make the scenarios more robust and realistic.

It is unlikely that any single policy option will be resilient against all possible futures, but some (such as managing demand for water) will be low regrets. Options which are scalable and can be adopted incrementally will be able to respond better as more certainty emerges about the future. Some will be particularly effective in addressing some scenarios, but will fail spectacularly under others; this may not matter too much as long as their weaknesses are understood and other policy options are able to manage the risks created by a particular course of action. In particular, scenarios can be very helpful in managing nexus issues, since they allow for the integrated assessment of different outcomes from policy decisions affecting different elements of the WELF nexus.

Scenarios to support coordinated planning for the WELF nexus in Korea

The incorporation of climate change and socio-economic scenarios into water plans and river basin plans allows decisions for each of these challenges to be tested for potential conflicts and for their robustness in the face of uncertainty. The plan can then drive decisions on day to day operations in a catchment, as well as permitting policy, drought and flood responses, land management, and investment for water supplies or pollution control. Where there is uncertainty, the planning process can specify actions which are incremental or flexible, or can develop a range of options to be implemented as and when necessary depending on the nature of short term events, or longer term trends. By having an integrated and flexible approach to planning, the costs and funding streams can be identified early, and synergies exploited to achieve greater cost efficiency.

3.2. The case for independent regulation

Regulation that is independent of policy-making is important in delivering confidence to consumers, legal services providers, investors and society as a whole. Regulators are key players in the policy arena with an active role in implementing public policies, and overseeing delivery bodies, and are defined “as an entity authorised by statute to use legal tools to achieve policy objectives, imposing obligations or burdens through functions such as licensing, permitting, accrediting, approvals, inspection and enforcement” (OECD, 2016).

There are three core elements of water regulation:

- *Protecting the environment*: ensuring that standards are set and met in order to achieve policy objectives, and that abstractions and discharges operate within safe limits.
- *Protecting customers' interests (economic regulation)*: ensuring that the delivery of water supply and sanitation is efficient, the level of charges fairly reflect and fund the quality of service delivered, and that there are equitable, transparent grievance and remedy mechanisms that allow individuals to complain.
- *Protecting drinking water quality*: providing confidence to customers that water treatment processes are effectively managed and monitored, and that tap water is safe to drink.

3.2.1. Principles and practice of good regulation

For all three aspects of water regulation described above, the following principles should apply:

- *Proportionality*. Solutions must be proportionate to the perceived problem or risk of adverse consequences, and justify the compliance costs imposed. Enforcement should be proportionate to risk. For example, does every type of abstraction or discharge require the same type of permit or level of scrutiny? Or are some a lower risk (e.g. small scale agriculture for household use) and simply require registration, while others (e.g. industrial abstractions from a fully committed river) require more detailed analysis and stringent conditions?
- *Accountability*. Regulators must be able to justify their decisions, and should be open to public scrutiny. They must be able to justify how and why decisions are reached and there should be fair and effective complaints procedures, ideally with independent oversight and the right of appeal.
- *Consistency*. Rules and standards must be joined up and implemented fairly, and regulation must be predictable in order to give stability and certainty to those being regulated. Consistency is about taking a similar approach in similar cases to achieve similar outcomes.
- *Transparency*. Policy objectives must be clearly defined and communicated, and have been subject to consultation and engagement. Those being regulated should be made aware of their obligations and given the time and support to comply. The consequences of non-compliance should be made clear, and there should be public access to compliance information.
- *Targeting*. Regulation should be focused on the problem, and effort should be prioritised on those activities, actions and operators that pose the most risk. Where appropriate, a goals-based approach, with clear, unambiguous targets should be adopted, to allow flexibility in using innovative alternative solutions to be considered as mechanisms for addressing the problem.

If regulation is working well, there will be a culture of trust and openness between the regulator and the regulated body, whether public or private. Service deliverers (for water supply and sanitation), farmers and industrialists will understand what they must do to comply with regulatory standards, and routinely and willingly go beyond the regulatory minimum in looking after the interests of customers and the environment. Ultimately, regulation should become more strict for those who deliberately or significantly break the rules, and penalties should be applied rigorously and fairly. Where there are major breaches in compliance, such as drinking water standard failures, or large scale pollution incidents, there needs to be an agreed and publicly transparent process for applying penalties in an equivalent manner to those levied on the private sector. In view of the general mistrust of tap water quality in Korea, independent oversight could help to restore public confidence. Without this, regulators' credibility and impartiality may be called into question.

Although independence is central to effective and fair regulation, governments may take the view that some decisions, such as on major infrastructure projects, require a wider perspective than a regulator might be able to provide. In these cases, there should be widespread consultation among stakeholders, and a thorough Environmental Impact Assessment should be made available for comment and open debate.

Given the potential impact of water and wastewater service provision on the environment, environmental regulation is also essential to provide a holistic and integrated approach with all other activities, across all sectors, within a river basin. This will ensure that permit standards for abstractions and discharges are defined in accordance with water policy objectives, and are based on robust evidence in terms of the state of the environment and ecosystem needs, and the priorities set out in a river basin plan. Compliance must also be transparently monitored and effectively enforced to ensure equity across all permit holders in all sectors.

3.2.2. *Options for delivering independent water regulation*

Countries regulate the protection of the environment, customers' interests and drinking water quality in different ways. Independent regulation can be achieved by any one, or a combination of, the following four models (OECD, 2015a):

1. *Regulation by government*. The public sector is responsible for the management of the water services and owns the assets. Service provision is delegated to public water operators while regulatory functions are carried out directly by the State at different levels: central, regional or municipal. This is the model adopted in the Netherlands, and to a lesser extent, in Germany. The challenge for this regulatory model is that one public body is regulating another.
2. *Regulation by contract*. The regulatory regimes are specified in legal instruments, and although public authorities are responsible for regulation, water service delivery can be delegated to private operators through contract agreements. These set the rights and obligations for each contracting entity, and service provision is awarded to private companies following public tender. This model is used in France.
3. *Regulation by one or multiple independent regulators*, where independence has three dimensions: independence of decision making, of management and of financing. This is the model used in the United Kingdom, where the regulatory framework is organised around three dedicated agencies with statutory functions relating to pricing and customer service (Ofwat), drinking water quality (Department for Environment, Food and Rural Affairs), and environmental regulation and security of water supply planning (UK Environment Agency).
4. *Outsourcing regulatory functions to third parties*. This model makes use of external contractors to perform activities such as tariff reviews or benchmarking.

In practice, whatever regulatory model is adopted, most regulators will contract out some specialist work such as studies, data analysis, customer surveys etc. Outsourcing all regulatory responsibilities, however, is likely to lead to public concerns about independence, and the potential for corruption or lack of accountability.

The regulatory functions (protection of the environment, customers' interests and drinking water quality) do not necessarily have to be in the hands of a single institution responsible for all of them. Hybrid models are possible, to reflect other institutional, policy and legislative arrangements within a country that the regulators need to take account of or interact with. For example, in England three independent water regulators each have a different organisational relationship with the government, and have clearly defined and separate statutory roles:

- The economic regulator, Ofwat, is a non-ministerial government department, accountable to Parliament rather than a minister. It makes independent decisions, guided by government policy objectives.
- The Drinking Water Inspectorate acts on behalf of the Secretary of State for Environment, Food and Rural Affairs, and is part of his Department (Defra), but the Chief Inspector has vested powers which ensure clear independence in the work of the Inspectorate.
- The UK Environment Agency is a non-departmental public body, which operates as an executive delivery body on behalf of Defra Ministers.

There is no ideal model; regulation should be adapted to local circumstances, and reflect hydrology, culture, legislation, institutional arrangements and challenges. It is essential, however, that regulation is able to operate without being subject to influences that would prejudice its independence and credibility. The actual or perceived level of autonomy will affect the degree of trust and confidence in regulatory decisions. Explicit *de jure* independence through specific legal measures is one way of achieving this; *de facto* independence is ensured through a mixture of governance and operational modalities. Ideally, both would be in place.

The complex and fragmented nature of water governance in Korea means that responsibility for water planning, regulation and management, and water supply and sanitation, is spread across many different policy and delivery bodies. Accountability is equally diluted and unclear, and water and wastewater suppliers, and agriculture and industry are seldom held to account. Independent regulation in Korea (using one, or a combination, of the four models above) may be an effective response to some of the challenges to regulating water services, including the fragmentation of roles and responsibilities in the sector, the public distrust in drinking water services, and the limitations of the tariff setting process.

3.2.3. Regulation to look after customers' interests for water supply and sanitation

Regulators sit between government and its policy making, the bodies responsible for the delivery of water supply and wastewater services, and their customers. This means that they must translate government policy aims into operational standards for those whom they regulate.

How a regulator acquires performance information and sets performance targets is important in bridging any gap between government and customer expectations. An outcome-based approach helps to ensure that the focus is not simply on easily measured outputs, but also considers the longer-term aims for water and sanitation, and the environment. It should expect the delivery body to monitor its service to customers, the operational performance of its assets, and how it is planning for resilient systems operation in the face of shocks, such as drought, process failures or cyber-attacks. The targets, and performance against them, should be published and made available to customers. Suggested performance targets are presented in Box 3.5.

Box 3.5. Performance targets for regulators of water supply and sanitation services

The performance targets for water supply and sanitation services could include:

- Compliance with environmental permits and standards (integrating with and reinforcing the role of the environmental regulator, where this is separate). This can also be an indicator of the quality and state of drinking water and wastewater treatment infrastructure assets.
- Leakage performance and targets for reducing leakage and other unbilled losses, such as illegal connections or treatment process water.
- Reducing per capita consumption for households and demand in other sectors on mains supplies.
- Wastewater pollution incidents, such as from too frequent operation of combined sewer overflows, or major failures at wastewater treatment works.
- Sewer collapses (as a proxy for sewer asset condition).
- Mains bursts (as a proxy for distribution network condition).
- Unplanned outages (loss of supply because of bursts, contamination etc.).
- Risk of demand restrictions in a drought.
- Drinking water quality compliance (integrating with and reinforcing the role of the drinking water regulator, where this is separate).
- Customer experience: how well billing queries are dealt with, information about planned outages and supply interruptions.

The regulator will also want to satisfy itself that the service is being delivered efficiently, and may set incentives and penalties to encourage this. Benchmarking can provide some indication of comparative efficiency, but needs to be treated with caution that like is being compared with like.

Customers should expect to be able to express their views on levels of service, priorities for investment and options for major infrastructure where this is proposed. The extent to which customers participate in the development of business plans can influence both their behaviour – and how much they value water and the service they receive – and that of the delivery body.

The income from water bills should cover not only operational expenditure but also capital and revenue investment to improve resilience and levels of service. In other words, the regulator needs to ensure that the delivery body is funded to deliver efficiently the breadth of its services to the required standard. For household water and sanitation bills, affordability issues are best dealt with through the use of social tariffs or income support measures (outside of the water bill), rather than keeping water bills low and failing to raise adequate revenue and an understanding of the value of water and sanitation services. The United Nations has stated (UN, 2017) that regulatory frameworks must not interfere directly or indirectly with people's existing access to water and sanitation. States must ensure that disconnections due to inability to pay are prohibited. The regulator should seek to moderate bill increases so that it can satisfy itself, and others, that they are necessary and appropriate.

3.2.4. Drinking water regulation

Regular, thorough, comprehensive and accurate testing of water put into supply is crucial to ensuring that customers have confidence in the product they receive at their tap. This is not currently the case in Korea, where past high-profile river pollution incidents have eroded public trust and led to widespread use of bottled water and filters (Um, Kwak and Kim, 2002).

A drinking water regulator's role is to act as an independent auditor of the tests carried out by the water supplier, to enforce drinking water standards and to investigate breaches. The competence of staff and the laboratory facilities and analytical processes would all form part of regulatory scrutiny. Inspectors should have the powers to require the water supplier to make improvements where necessary, and to take enforcement action (including financial penalties) where this is not carried out within a set timescale.

A drinking water regulator, like other regulators, may take a risk-based approach to compliance monitoring. If a water supplier has a positive and consistent record of providing safe drinking water with no failures, and laboratories are well-run and pass routine audits, then the frequency of checks and inspections can be reduced. Conversely, a poor performing supplier can expect much more frequent compliance monitoring and demanding scrutiny. The fundamental aim of the independent regulator should be that the public have confidence in their drinking water and trust in the credibility of the regulatory regime.

It should be the aim of the supplier to minimise the risk to customers by protecting their sources of drinking water supply from contamination. When there is a drinking water quality incident, whether from chemical or microbial contamination, there should be a full investigation and lessons learnt applied and widely disseminated to other suppliers. The strict health-based standards used in Europe are based on expert global opinion documented in World Health Organisation Guidelines for Drinking Water Quality (WHO, 2011).

3.2.5. Water environmental regulation

The role of a water environmental regulator is integral to the delivery of the targets for river flow and quality set out in a River Basin Plan. The limits and conditions on permits to abstract and discharge should be set to ensure a sustainable flow regime, and to improve or protect water quality as appropriate. The regulator's job is then to ensure that the permits are being complied with, and to take enforcement action where they are not.

3.3. Additional instruments necessary to manage the WELF nexus in Korea

3.3.1. Permitting

Water management permitting is a fundamental mechanism by which resources are managed to protect and improve the environment, and to ensure that the needs of societies and economies are met. Effective permitting requires good data on resources and efficient administrative and technical decision making processes, aimed at delivering clear policy objectives. A deficiency in any one of these elements will lead to a poor service to the permit applicant, the environment or society.

Water quality modelling in each basin will inform the discharge permitting process about the safe load for each critical pollutant at different points in the main river and its tributaries. This will be based upon the impact on the ecosystem and the need to protect or improve it from the effects of harmful discharges, both point source and diffuse source, in aggregate with the presence of any toxic substances naturally occurring in the watercourse. For example, a river with a high background concentration of heavy metals as a result of the geology of the catchment would have a lower assimilative capacity for those pollutants where present in effluent downstream. The limits set in permits should take account of the flow regime in the river and the capacity to dilute polluting discharges. There needs to be a close relationship therefore between flow management and abstraction controls, and the approach taken to wastewater management, land use, water quantity and quality are inextricably linked.

The equivalent protection for the river in respect of abstraction impacts comes from the setting of e-flows: environmental or ecological limits on the maximum acceptable divergence from a natural flow regime caused by abstraction. Some countries (OECD, 2015b) simply set a minimum acceptable flow and allow abstraction down to that limit; however, this potentially has the effect of creating drought conditions for most of the year, which many ecosystems would struggle with. It is now generally accepted that to support a healthy aquatic ecology a more sophisticated approach is needed. This recognises that ecosystems in some parts of a river – typically in the fast flowing shallow headwaters and tributaries – are more sensitive to changes in flow and level than elsewhere, such as downstream reaches where flows are more sluggish and the river occupies a U-shaped channel. It also recognises that flow variability is important. Checklists for assessing an application for abstraction and discharge permits are provided in Annex 3.B.

Permitting systems in most countries are set up either to deal with a current challenge, or to try and resolve legacy problems. It is rare for them to be forward looking, which is why most international approaches to the control of pollution and abstraction are subject to ongoing processes of either major or minor reform in an attempt to catch up. With investment in monitoring and assessment, and in planning, Korea could be well placed to make a step change to its permitting processes so that they are fit for purpose for the future and so reduce the need for retrospective reform in the future. The regulatory principles set out above could form the basis of a more risk-based, environmentally sustainable process for managing and protecting water resources for the future, and so reduce the need for retrospective reform.

The current basis for managing groundwater abstraction would benefit from a review. It is not clear how robust is the existing assessment of the available resource in each aquifer unit, both shallow and deep, since groundwater abstractions are neither regulated nor monitored. The key issue is the lack of permitting of groundwater abstraction to prevent excessive abstraction rates becoming a problem. Where there is high hydraulic conductivity and a concentration of wells and boreholes, it is almost inevitable that there will be interference between them, coupled with an overall lowering of the water table and potentially also an impact on surface waters. Measures to protect surface waters from pollution also need to be designed to minimise the risk of groundwater pollution. Long residence times in some aquifers could mean that they become progressively unusable because of contamination. Where 'hotspots' exist there should be increased monitoring of groundwater levels and quality, and compliance with stringent permit conditions. The development of numerical models would help in the assessment of new abstractions, and a requirement for test pumping at critical sites would aid their calibration. Metering abstractions would increase confidence in when and where the resource was being used. The OECD study on sustainable agricultural groundwater use (OECD, 2015c) sets out six general conditions for successful management:

1. Build and maintain sufficient knowledge of groundwater resource and use
2. Manage surface and groundwater conjunctively (together) where relevant
3. Favour instruments that directly target groundwater use over indirect measures (e.g. land use regulation), where possible
4. Prioritise demand–side approaches
5. Enhance the enforcement of regulatory measures (e.g. water entitlements) before moving to other approaches
6. Avoid non-water related price distorting policy measures, such as subsidies towards water intensive crops and energy that could affect groundwater use.

Permitting policy should not be static; it needs to adapt to improved knowledge and changing circumstances. This is more easily achieved if permits are reviewable, without the need for compensation of the permit holder (a major issue with abstraction permits in many countries), and are capable of being strengthened as necessary.

The following are points to consider in order to strengthen the sustainability of water permitting activities in Korea:

- Review current policies and procedures against the five principles of better regulation, and adapt permitting and enforcement accordingly.
- Use risk assessments to determine how decisions are made and the type of permit, and its enforcement.
- Review the water allocation regime in terms of 'how much for the river' and the controls on surface water abstractions, and manage pollution with reference to the environmental capacity of the receiving watercourse. Refer to the OECD Water Allocation Health Check (OECD, 2015b).
- Review the need to commence groundwater permitting on a risk basis, including an assessment of interference between boreholes and their impact on surface waters, and the risk of saline intrusion. Consider the use of test pumping and numerical models as aids to decision making.
- Establish a mechanism to ensure that permitting policy can adapt as rainfall, river flows, groundwater yields and human demands change over time, so that it becomes flexible and adaptive, and able to maintain sustainable exploitation of natural resources.

3.3.2. Compliance monitoring and enforcement

Current enforcement practice in Korea is problematic; permit holders are reluctant to comply with the terms of their permit, and there have been few severe sanctions for breaches of conditions. In 2013, only 1.5% of water pollution cases were referred for criminal investigation (OECD, 2017b). Public prosecutors assign relatively low priority to environmental offences and rarely pursue such cases, and judges generally lack the expertise to consider the merits of environmental breaches. The approach to inspecting discharges is also an issue; during the fact-finding mission in Korea, it was suggested that although permit holders are required to report on their discharge quality, few do so in practice. The routine water quality monitoring regime can sometimes identify problems, but is not designed to be operational monitoring and so many breaches of discharge permits will go undetected and unenforced.

Permitting, inspection and enforcement should operate seamlessly together for the sustainable regulation of water resources quantity and quality. Ineffective enforcement means that the permit has failed to deliver the intended outcome - to allocate and protect water resources sustainably, for the common good. Failure to enforce undermines the purpose of the permit and the underlying legislation.

Any inspection regime will have to balance the need to ensure compliance with permits where and when it is most important, against the available staff resource and budget. This might mean that some lower risk permits would be inspected very infrequently, but they would still be part of the programme of visits. Where resources are limited, action should be targeted on the basis of risk (Box 3.6).

Box 3.6. Risk-based compliance monitoring and enforcement checklist for water abstraction and discharge permits

Target resources and action according to:

- Risk to the environment from failure to comply with permit conditions
- Risk to other water users, including the environment
- The likelihood of the operator not complying (i.e. some permit holders will be more inclined to cheat; their track record is an important consideration)
- During periods of stress from drought, when exceptional measures are in place and need to be complied with
- Where there is a concentration of permit holders and there is a need to demonstrate that compliance is important, and breaches will be enforced
- Where complaints demonstrate concern from the local community.

For water abstraction permits, the measurement condition is perhaps the most important in terms of compliance, and one of the most straightforward to enforce. Either a water meter is in place or it is not. And if it is installed, is it working and is the calibration up to date? For discharge permits, the critical issue is the polluting load into the watercourse and whether it is in accordance with the permit conditions. Routine sampling and reporting by the operator, with periodic independent checks, are essential.

To track compliance monitoring performance, an important metric is the percentage compliance according to the risk category of the permit. The effort should be to ensure that the highest risk permits (or permit holders) have a high compliance ratio. For very low risk permits, a lower proportion of compliance might be acceptable, because the impact would be limited. The outcome from effective inspection and enforcement should be to ensure that, if compliance is maintained, the environment and water users are protected. Where monitoring suggests that environmental problems exist, these can then be dealt with by tightening permit conditions or tackling the causes by using different policy mechanisms where they are not able to be dealt with through conventional permitting, such as diffuse pollution from agriculture (see section 2.3).

If enforcement is weak, then there is no way of knowing whether the permitting regime is also too lax. A robust permitting and compliance monitoring regime is essential to provide public confidence in water management, and to ensure fair treatment for all water users. Poor performers are often minimising their operating costs whilst imposing higher costs on other water users because they are polluting or reducing water availability. Points to consider when assessing inspection and enforcement activities of permits are as follows:

- Review the inspection programme according to risk criteria appropriate to each basin or catchment.
- Ensure that the inspection visit raises awareness of the consequences of non-compliance.
- Follow up permit breaches with enforcement. Depending on the severity of the breach, and the attitude of the permit holder, this could range from a verbal warning, to a written warning, to sanctions or a fine, or criminal prosecution.
- If necessary, use enforcement mechanisms to set an example of persistent poor compliance, and publicise the action taken as a warning to others.

Environmental regulation should be applied fairly and consistently to all those that use and abuse the water and land environments. The EU Water Framework Directive calls on Member States to 'determine penalties applicable to breaches' which should be 'effective, proportionate and dissuasive' (EU WFD Article 10). Most European countries use operator self-monitoring, where the permit-holder is responsible for monitoring and reporting on compliance with permit conditions for abstraction and discharges. This brings risks if quality assurance methodologies and risk-based compliance monitoring are not in place, or are ineffective. The penalties for non-compliance, especially in the most severe cases of failure, can act as deterrents.

3.3.3. Environmental Impact Assessment

Environmental Impact Assessments (EIAs) have been in use in Korea since the 1980's, and are required as a precondition for a construction permit in 17 activity sectors, mostly covering infrastructure development (OECD, 2017b). Industrial sites less than 150 000m^2 are subject to a "strategic" EIA based on the project concept, and sites greater than 150 000m^2 are subject to a comprehensive EIA. The required scoping report is reviewed by a locally relevant committee of public officials, experts and residents' representatives. The authorities consider the public's comments upon review of EIA reports. The ME must be consulted before approval. The operator is responsible for monitoring the project's impacts, and reporting to the ME and the approving authority. The ME has developed extensive guidelines and regulations, and an online support system helps to ensure transparency.

The challenge for any major development which has the potential to impact the water cycle is to ensure that there is a comprehensive assessment which considers it from the perspective of the entire river basin. For land-based development, this means considering (mainly) the downstream impacts on flood risk and water quality, as well as its water demand. For water developments, such as a dam or weir that causes an obstruction to flow, the concerns might also include the effect on the passage of fish, or the potential for increased eutrophication. If the baseline data are poor, then the assessment will also not be able to identify the full range of impacts, leading to unforeseen and usually adverse consequences. The objectives set out in an integrated river basin plan also provide a benchmark against which to test the potential impact of any proposed development, whether for water supply, flood risk management, urban expansion or other major land use change. The European Union has published guidance (EU, 2017) which describes in a practical way the steps to be followed in an EIA and the preparation of the report.

The application of the above reasoning and EU guidance to EIA processes in Korea would help to address concerns about the quality and independence of such assessments, and the impact of new developments. Extensive consultation is a key element of the EU's legal requirement for EIA; this can help to reassure affected stakeholders and also be a way of using their local knowledge to support the assessment.

References

Borgomeo, E. et al, (2018).”Risk, Robustness and Water Resources Planning Under Uncertainty”. *Earth's Future*, 6.

Borgomeo, E. et al (2014). “Risk-based water resource planning: incorporating probabilistic nonstationary climate uncertainties.” *Water Resources Research* 50 (8), p 6850-6873.

Butler, D. et al. (2016), *Reliable, resilient and sustainable water management: The Safe & Sure approach*, Global Challenges, 2016.

Defra (2011). *Water for Life*, Department for Environment, Food and Rural Affairs, December 2011.

Ercin, A.E. & Hoekstra, A.Y. (2014) “Water footprint scenarios for 2050: A global analysis. Environment International”, Vol 64, p 71-82.

European Union (2017). *Environmental Impact Assessment of Projects: guidance on the preparation of the environmental impact assessment report.*

UK Met Office (2011), Climate: Observations, projections and impact – South Korea. https://www.metoffice.gov.uk/binaries/content/assets/mohippo/pdf/f/b/republic_of_korea.pdf.

OECD (2017a), *Enhancing water use efficiency in Korea*. OECD Studies on Water, OECD Publishing, Paris. http://dx.doi.org/10.1787/9789264281707-en.

OECD (2017b), *OECD Environmental Performance Reviews: Korea 2017.* OECD Publishing Paris. http://dx.doi.org/10.1787/9789264268265-en.

OECD (2016), *Being an Independent Regulator, The Governance of Regulators*, OECD Publishing, Paris. http://dx.doi.org/10.1787/9789264255401-en.

OECD (2015a). *The Governance of Water Regulators.* OECD Studies on Water, OECD Publishing, Paris. http://dx.doi.org/10.1787/9789264231092-en.

OECD (2015b), *Water Resources Allocation: Sharing Risks and Opportunities.* OECD Studies on Water, OECD Publishing, Paris. http://dx.doi.org/10.1787/9789264229631-en.

OECD (2015c), *Drying Wells, Rising Stakes: Towards Sustainable Agricultural Groundwater Use.* OECD Studies on Water, OECD Publishing, Paris. http://dx.doi.org/10.1787/9789264238701-en.

OECD (2013), *Water Security for Better Lives*, OECD Studies on Water, OECD Publishing. http://dx.doi.org/10.1787/9789264202405-en.

OECD (2012), OECD Environmental Outlook to 2050: The Consequences of Inaction, OECD Publishing. http://dx.doi.org/10.1787/9789264122246-en.

Park, J. et al. (2016), "Probabilistic Risk Assessment of Flood Disaster in South Korea Under the Impact of Climate Change", *Irrigation & Drainage,* Vol. 65 (52), p 16-25.

The Economist (2016), *Liquidity crisis*, Water scarcity, Nov 5th 2016.

The Rockefeller Foundation/Arup (2016), City Resilience Index – Understanding and Measuring City Resilience.

UK Environment Agency (2017a). *Delivering sustainable river basin management: plausible future scenarios for the water environment to 2030 and 2050.* Environment Agency (England), 2017.

UK Environment Agency (2009), *Water resources strategy - water for people and the environment,* http://webarchive.nationalarchives.gov.uk/20140328091448/http://www.environment-agency.gov.uk/research/library/publications/40731.aspx.

Um, M.J., Kwak, S.J. and T.Y. Kim (2002), "Estimating willingness to pay for improved drinking water quality using averting behaviour method with perception measure", *Environmental and Resource Economics*, Vol. 21, 287–302.

UN (2017), United Nations General Assembly Human Rights Council (September 2017). *Report of the Special Rapporteur on the Human Rights to safe drinking water and sanitation.*

UNESCO (2012), *Five stylised scenarios*, Global Water Futures 2050.

Walker, G. (2013), "A critical examination of models and projections of demand in water utility resource planning in England and Wales". *International Journal of Water Resources Development,* Vol 29:3, p 352-372.

WHO (2011), *Guidelines for drinking water quality, fourth edition.*

Annex 3.A. Integrated river basin planning: The European Water Framework Directive

Most countries now aspire to use integrated river basin management as the basis for managing water resources and the associated land environment, and their interactions. The European Union has established a process for Member States to follow, which is one of the most structured in the world: the Water Framework Directive.

The purpose of the Directive is to establish a framework for the protection of inland surface waters (rivers and lakes), transitional waters (estuaries), coastal waters and groundwater. It aimed to ensure that all aquatic ecosystems and, with regard to their water needs, terrestrial ecosystems and wetlands, met 'good status' by 2015. Where this was not possible, longer timescales are permitted subject to justification. The Directive requires Member States to establish river basin districts and for each of these to prepare a river basin management plan. The Directive sets out a cyclical process where river basin management plans are prepared, implemented and reviewed every six years. There are four distinct elements to the river basin planning cycle: 1) characterisation and assessment of impacts on river basin districts; 2) environmental monitoring; 3) the setting of environmental objectives; and 4) the design and implementation of the programme of measures needed to achieve them.

There are a number of objectives in respect of which the quality of water is protected. The key ones at European level are general protection of the aquatic ecology, specific protection of unique and valuable habitats, protection of drinking water resources, and protection of bathing water. All these objectives must be integrated for each river basin. The central requirement of the Directive is that the environment be protected to a high level in its entirety.

For this reason, a general requirement for ecological protection, and a general minimum chemical standard, was introduced to cover all surface waters. These are the two elements "good ecological status" and "good chemical status". Good ecological status is defined in terms of the quality of the biological community, the hydrological characteristics and the chemical characteristics. As no absolute standards for biological quality can be set which apply across the Community, because of ecological variability, the controls are specified as allowing only a slight departure from the biological community which would be expected in conditions of minimal anthropogenic impact. A set of procedures is provided for identifying that point for a given body of water, and establishing particular chemical or hydromorphological standards to achieve it, together with a system for ensuring that each Member State interprets the procedure in a consistent way (to ensure comparability).

Good chemical status is defined in terms of compliance with all the quality standards established for chemical substances at European level. The Directive also provides a mechanism for renewing these standards and establishing new ones by means of a prioritisation mechanism for hazardous chemicals. This will ensure at least a minimum chemical quality, particularly in relation to very toxic substances, everywhere in the

Community. The list of chemicals is kept under review, and priority substances added to the monitoring and reporting schedules as new ones become of concern.

Some of these uses impact not only on flow or quality, but also on the hydromorphology: the physical characteristics of the shape, boundaries and content of a water body. Increasingly, this is recognised as fundamental to the classification and health of a river. Put simply, even if the river sustains a healthy flow of clean water, it will never support the ecosystem it should if the flow is constrained within a trapezoidal concrete channel, or interrupted by dams and weirs. Hydropower, water supply and agricultural reservoirs, and flood risk management structures can, if poorly designed and operated, have a major adverse impact on river ecosystems.

Once the objectives have been established for the river basin an analysis of human impact is conducted so as to determine how far from the objective each body of water is. The Member State must identify the causes of failure and design whatever additional measures are needed to satisfy all the objectives established. These might include stricter controls on polluting emissions from industry and agriculture, or urban waste water sources. Agricultural diffuse pollution is one of the greatest challenges across much of Europe. Improved monitoring is also showing the presence of metals, pharmaceuticals, hydrocarbons, biocides and industrial pollutants, derived from both point source and diffuse sources, and at levels which are raising concerns.

All the elements of this analysis must be set out in a plan for the river basin. The plan is produced by the 'Competent Authority' and is a detailed account of how the objectives set for the river basin (ecological status, quantitative status, chemical status and protected area objectives) are to be reached within the timescale required. One additional component is that an economic analysis of water use within the river basin must be carried out. This is to enable there to be a rational discussion on the cost-effectiveness of the various possible measures. It is essential that all interested parties are fully involved in this discussion, and in the preparation of the river basin management plan as a whole. This is the final major element of the proposal: the public participation requirements, since the decisions on the most appropriate measures to achieve the objectives in the river basin management plan will involve balancing the interests of various groups. The economic analysis requirement is intended to provide a rational basis for this, but it is essential that the process is open to the scrutiny of those who will be affected.

The river basin management plan must first be issued in draft, and the background documentation on which the decisions are based must be made accessible. After this consultation the plan is modified as necessary, and is then published. Each action will have been costed as part of the options appraisal process, and the organisation responsible for its delivery is identified. Progress is monitored and reported on, both locally and to the Commission.

The need to conserve adequate supplies of a resource for which demand is continuously increasing is also one of the drivers behind what is arguably one of the Directive's most important innovations - the introduction of water pricing. Adequate pricing acts as an incentive for the sustainable use of water resources and helps to achieve the environmental objectives under the Directive. Member States are required to ensure that the price charged to water consumers - such as for the abstraction and distribution of fresh water and the collection and treatment of waste water - reflects the true costs. Although this principle has a long tradition in some countries, this is currently not the case in others, who are having to introduce meaningful charges.

The Water Framework Directive has been instrumental in providing a focus on water resources based on the most rational unit – the river basin or catchment – and in reinforcing the relationship between land management and the water environment. It has also ensured that Member States' monitoring programmes are comprehensive (typically around 40 separate criteria) and able to provide, for the first time, a more realistic assessment of the state of the environment and the extent of the human influences on it. It has also been a catalyst for wider engagement and discussion on water and, critically, providing a mechanism to apportion ownership of the necessary actions to deliver improvements.

Annex 3.B. Checklists for assessing applications for water abstraction and pollution discharge permits

Checklist for assessing an application for a water abstraction permit

The basic questions to be addressed in determining any application for an abstraction permit include:

- Is it a valid application: does it comply with the relevant legal and administrative requirements?
- Are the volumes of water applied for reasonable for the required purpose? It is poor management to permit more water than is needed, since this ties up a resource which others could use. Equally, someone might apply for less than they need in order to reduce charges, and then breach the terms of the permit.
- Is the resource available for permitting in the surface water body or aquifer?
- What will be the impact of the abstraction on other, existing abstractors and water users? If it is a borehole, will it lower the water table unacceptably for nearby existing boreholes?
- What will be the impact of the abstraction on the water environment of the river? Or if it is a groundwater abstraction, on wetlands and river flows?
- What conditions need to be applied to protect low flows in dry years, or other water users? Are they enforceable?
- How must the abstraction be measured, and at what frequency? If a meter is to be used, how often should it be calibrated?
- How will change be dealt with; for example, following improved flow monitoring and assessment of resources, or of ecological need? Should the permit be time-limited or subject to periodic review as necessary?
- What information about volumes abstracted is required for water management purposes, and at what frequency?

Source: Professor Ian Barker, Water Policy International, *Pers. Comm.*

Checklist for assessing an application for a pollution discharge permit

The basic questions to be addressed in determining an application for a discharge permit include:

1. Is it a valid application?
2. Do the volumes seem reasonable for the type of process involved?
3. What pollutants are likely to be present in the effluent, in what concentration?
4. What is the current water quality of the receiving water, and what are its target water quality objectives?
5. Is there sufficient flow to absorb and dilute the additional load from the permit and still meet the objectives?
6. What standards need to be applied to the range of pollutants likely to be present in the effluent?
7. What additional conditions are required, for example, in relation to sample frequency and analysis by the permit holder and submission of information? Or for monitoring of the effluent flow volumes?
8. If the effluent is important in maintaining low flows in the receiving river, and so acting as a resource for others to use, does there need to be a requirement to maintain the discharge at that location?
9. How will change be dealt with; for example, in the objectives for the river or improved understanding of the toxicity of the pollutants in the effluent?
10. Should the permit be time-limited, or subject to periodic review as necessary?

Source: Professor Ian Barker, Water Policy International, *Pers. Comm.*

Chapter 4. Towards effective water governance for the sustainable management of the Water-Energy-Land-Food nexus in Korea

This chapter examines Korea's water governance framework, including mechanisms for horizontal and vertical co-ordination in relation to the WELF nexus. The chapter explores options for improved river basin management and stakeholder engagement. Lessons learnt and best practices from OECD countries are provided.

4.1. Introduction

The previous chapters have argued that managing the WELF nexus requires: i) coordinated policies and plans; ii) the capacity to reflect local situations and to make decisions at basin level; and iii) stakeholder engagement, preferably at basin level. Governance is a *means to an end* and water policies and institutional fit need to be tailored to different water, socio-economic and political contexts. While it is well recognised that there are no one-size-fits-all solution to water challenges, this chapter proposes a menu of options fit for the Korean context, inspired by best institutional practices and findings based on the OECD Principles on Water Governance (OECD 2015a; 2016; 2018).

Previous responses to water challenges in Korea were, to a large degree, based on technology and infrastructure development to augment water supply. Current and future responses will increasingly have to be about moving towards decentralised, coordinated and inclusive decision-making for efficient water use, where water users and other stakeholders are part of decision-making processes.

Much international experience of water reform has clearly moved towards polycentric governance. In a simplified way, this means shifting away from top-down mono-centric government approaches, to new modes of water governance that blend top-down and bottom-up approaches, including changing roles for government and increased engagements from civil society (NGOs, farmers' associations, consumer associations, community based organisations, etc.) and the private sector (see for example OECD, 2015b; Pahl-Wostl and Knieper, 2014; and Tropp, 2007).

The government of Korea has demonstrated clear intentions of moving towards more polycentric, integrated and multilevel governance regimes through proposals of increased stakeholder engagement, integrating water quality and quantity under one ministry, and strengthening basin governance as an important scale for managing the WELF nexus. Some of these reforms are now starting to be implemented. But coping with existing and future water challenges raises not only the question of what should be done, but also who does what, at which level of government and how? Policy responses will only be viable if they are coherent, if stakeholders are properly engaged, if well-designed regulatory frameworks are in place, if there is adequate and accessible information, and if there is sufficient capacity, integrity and transparency.

4.2. Identifying water policy gaps

Korea faces a range of water policy and governance related gaps or challenges (Table 4.1).

Table 4.1. Water policy gaps and some possible causes in Korea

Policy-implementation gaps	Possible causes
Gaps in the policy-formulation process	Political disagreements and different interests among key government stakeholders leading to no consensus on policy reform
Gaps in the operationalisation of policy	Institutional fragmentation, including misaligned decision-making and policy implementation Siloed and piecemeal reactive "project-oriented" approaches to respond to water challenges, leading to policy misalignments and ineffectiveness Lax enforcement of and compliance with existing policies, rules and regulations (see Chapter 3.) Unclear separations between administrative functions of policy development, regulation, project development and implementation, and day-to-day operations
Gaps related to the characteristics and behaviour of stakeholders	Different vested interests among stakeholders Lack of capacities among NGOs and "local level" stakeholders Lack of water information, or limited access to existing information
Gaps related to the overarching country governance situation	Centralised style of decision-making Limited tradition and space for multi-stakeholder dialogues, especially with non-state stakeholders

Source: Based on OECD (2017a), *Enhancing Water Use Efficiency in Korea: Policy issues and recommendations,* OECD Studies on Water, OECD Publishing, Paris. See OECD (2011) for framework on water governance gaps analysis.

Institutional reform in Korea needs to take into account water policy and governance gaps. Differences in policy formulations call for consensus building activities. The operationalisation of policies and their alignment calls for strengthened horizontal and vertical coordination mechanisms. Improved stakeholder engagement would for example require transparency and access to information and inclusive platforms where stakeholders can make their voices heard. Greater clarity on mandates of policy making, regulation and project implementation can go a long way to hold government agencies to account with regard to policy implementation. The following sections of this chapter describe the ways forward to overcome these challenges.

4.2.1. The new water policy and institutional reform

There are considerable efforts in Korea to enable water policy and institutional reform to improve policy alignment and coordination between water resources and water quality issues, and across sectors and stakeholders. The most recent water policy institutional reform was adopted by the National Assembly in June 2018. The act - called the Government Organisation Act - provides the basis for transferring responsibilities of water resources management from MoLIT to ME. As a consequence, it led to the adoption of two new acts – The Framework Act on Water Management (to be enacted June 2019) and The Water Management Technology and Industry Act (to be enacted December 2018) under ME[1]. In essence, transferred responsibilities and functions from MoLIT to ME include: Conservation, utilisation and development of water resources, including water allocation (permits), flood control, and the operation and conservation of water resources. MoLIT maintains responsibility for river maintenance, including the maintenance and construction of river banks for flood protection. See Table 1.2 and Table 1.3 for the full list of water acts, plans and responsibilities related to water management in Korea.

In addition, five acts have moved from the responsibility of MoLIT to ME: Act on Investigation, Planning and Management of Water Resource; Groundwater Act; Act on Construction of Dams and Assistance, etc. to their Environs; Special Act on the utilisation of Waterfronts; and Korea Water Resources Corporation Act, as well as parts of the River Act. MoLIT remains responsible for parts of the River Act and the Special Act on the Compensation of Land Incorporated into River. The General Directorate for Water Resources, three Directorates, four Flood Control Offices (at basin level) and K-water are all transferred to ME. It is expected that the interim organisational set up will be re-arranged by ME.

The transfer of water quantity management to ME holds promise of improved coordination of policies and plans at both national and basin scales. However, to keep the River Act under MoLIT may risk creating unnecessary coordination gaps or "grey zones" in relation to responsibilities of long-term planning and implementation. This can fuel further misalignments when it comes to water policy development and implementation, and missed opportunities of the WELF nexus management at both national and basin level. As part of water reform in Korea there is also a strong emphasis on the river basin level as an appropriate scale of planning. Considering that also the Flood Control Offices are moved to ME makes a strong case that the long-term planning at basin scale should be under ME (through the RBCs).

The ongoing water reform puts emphasis on basic water management principles, such as:

- Water should be increasingly managed at the basin level
- Integrated and coordinated approaches are key to improved water management
- Water management should be based on economic efficiency and social equity
- Stakeholder engagement is seen as important for improved water management development and implementation
- The user pays principle should apply.

ME has proposed to develop (building on the existing Water Management Committee) a National Water Committee under the Prime Minister's Office to promote national coordination, policy alignment across ministries and regions, and conflict mediation. It is envisaged that the committee would consist of 30-40 members from ME, experts and non-governmental organisations. The representation of non-governmental stakeholders is a new feature and reflects the government's intention to strengthen multi-stakeholder engagement for informed and outcome-oriented contributions to water policy and planning development and implementation. The committee would set the long term national priorities in a national master plan for water.

ME has proposed to set the 10-year plan on the supply and use of water resources (ME is already setting the long-term plan for water quality, but under the new set-up also water quantity will be included). ME has also suggested to strengthen the coordination role and mandate of the existing four River Management Committees (RMCs), and propose to merge them the River Basin Committees (RBCs) under the new Framework Act on Water Management. RBCs will set the basin management work plans on the supply and use of water based on the 10-year plans set by ME. The RBCs are also suggested to have responsibilities to mediate conflicts and continue to charge water user fees and manage the river management fund.

Even though many details are still to be worked out by ME, the implementation of the new Water Act entails many potential benefits for enhanced consistency and coordination across existing legal provisions, as well as across relevant ministries, to cope with future water challenges. In financial terms, it is estimated that the integration of water quality and water quantity management can provide financial benefits in the range of KRW 15.7 trillion (KECO, *Pers. Comm.*). Similar studies should be undertaken to assess potential financial gains of improved water management as part of WELF nexus. It can provide guidance for coordination priorities and identify where the "low-hanging fruits" may be for financial efficiency gains.

The reform steps taken are seen as very positive but should be perceived as an iterative process. Even though water quantity and quality is put under one ministry "unification" of water management will not be an easy task and would require structural organisational changes within ME, capacity development of, and motivation by, staff, and strengthening of coordination mechanisms at all levels within ME as well as between ME and other relevant ministries, water users, water and environmental NGOs and private sector.

The biggest water user and polluter in the country - agriculture, and the responsible ministry, MAFRA - are driven by distinct policy objectives to: pursue rural development; undertake cooperation in international trade of agricultural products; and improve the income, stability and welfare of agricultural households. Still, there are policy coordination challenges between ME and MAFRA, namely due to three policy misalignments: i) agriculture water is managed more or less independently from the rest of water resources through a distinct and disjointed network of infrastructure and institutions; ii) there is little incentive to promote water use efficiency in agriculture and to make more water available for other purposes, where water is scarce; and iii) there is little incentive to reduce diffuse water pollution and create synergies within the WELF nexus.

An expanded re-organisation to manage the agricultural water of MAFRA and the river management responsibilities for disaster prevention of the Ministry of Public Safety and Security can reduce duplication of policies and budget, and solve the problems caused by lack of communication. In addition, rapid water policy decision-making and planning will be facilitated, and policy consistency and responsible administration can be expected. Furthermore, reorganisation could enable a shift from a development-oriented water management approach (i.e. reservoir constriction) to water cycle recovery.

4.3. Managing water at basin level

4.3.1. Rationale for managing water at the basin scale

Water management at the basin scale emphasises coordination of water, land and related resources, and social and economic activities in a river basin to achieve certain water-related objectives. For Korea, managing water at the basin scale has been identified as an option to better achieve water policies, as well as to more effectively manage the WELF nexus and ensure ecosystem protection in the long-term. The coordination of policies, decisions and costs are necessary across a multitude of sectors and stakeholders are necessary to achieve this.

Managing water quality and quantity at the basin scale can have certain benefits in Korea, such as:

- Stakeholder engagement. Managing and cooperating on water at the natural hydrological scale can more easily bring together all upstream and downstream water users and interests for improved policy and planning coordination and implementation to reach common objectives of sustainable water and environmental development, and to mediate differences between upstream and downstream water uses.

- Cross-sector coordination. Increasing competition for water across economic sectors – for food and energy security, protection against floods and droughts and to maintain ecosystem services through securing environmental flows – makes river basins the appropriate planning unit to apply water quantity and quality measures.
- Communications. Collecting, managing and communicating data at the basin scale regarding water availability, water demand (including environmental requirements), and water quality can support different basin functions.
- Environmental and socio-economic analysis. Water modelling and socio-economic analysis at the basin scale can provide essential information for policymakers and managers to, for example, estimate the social and economic benefits of water user efficiencies and re-allocations.

River basin management in many countries marks a policy shift from more technocratic planning and water management implementation, to increasing the role of decision-making and operations through social and political processes. River basin organisations are perceived as important fora in which stakeholder interests can be reflected and mediated, as well as providing a platform to meet the requirements of national water priorities, local realities, and base decisions and actions on robust science and engineering.

4.3.2. Korea: Managing water at the basin scale

An awareness of the unique hydrological, ecological, social and economic characteristics of each river basin is important, especially when formulating policies and plans, and for explaining and analysing the outcomes of different river basin plans and projects.

For water management purposes, Korea is divided into four major river basin areas: Han River; Nakdong River; Geum River; and Youngsan-Seomjin rivers. The characteristics of the river basins vary considerably (see Section 1.2) and the overarching priorities to be addressed in one basin differ from those in another. In addition, 30 percent of the surface water resources (medium and smaller scale rivers) fall outside the responsibility of the four basin areas, but are supposed to be managed by local government.

Each of the four major river basins display different traits of conflictive issues and needs for conflict mediation. There are a number of conflicts and tensions between upstream and downstream stakeholders within the river basins (see section 1.1.4).

Several policy instruments do not reflect basin features or local conditions in Korea. For instance, neither the river water use fee nor the multi-regional water tariff signal water-related risk (scarcity) as they reflect neither local water conditions nor shifts in water availability (OECD, 2017a). Instead, nationwide unitary rates are set for each tariff and fee, and revisions are infrequent and minor. Similarly, the water use charge for Han River is KWN 170/m^3 (EUR 0.13/m^3), and for the other three basins it is set to KWN 160/m^3 (EUR 0.12/m^3). In principle, water abstraction fees could be differentiated by basin but there is a strong perception in Korea that the cost of water should be the same for everyone (principle of water equity).

Managing water at the basin scale is a new feature in Korean water management. There are some basic institutional structures in place at the basin level that can be built on for more effective management of water and the WELF nexus. The text below outlines the current institutional structure for water governance in Korea, which is essentially consists of: i) National Water Management Committee; ii) National Water Resource Management Committee; and iii) various sub-national committees, offices and councils.

In 2015, a Water Management Committee was set up at the central level (re-established in 2017 as the National Water Resource Management Committee). It is an inter-ministerial co-ordinating and advisory body gathering water-related stakeholders across levels of government. It cannot exceed 15 members who currently are the vice-ministers that play a role in water resources management, under the chairmanship of the Minister for Government Policy Coordination. Depending on the Committee's agenda, directors of state-owned corporations and agencies, as well as representatives of provinces and metropolitan cities, are invited to participate. The Committee is supported by a working-level committee with director-level public officials from central, provincial and metropolitan agencies involved in water management (OECD, 2017a).

The National Water Resource Management Committee deliberates on river management issues and mediate disputes over the use of river water. The Committee can have up to 50 members. The Chair and the members are appointed by ME; the Chair is a staff of ME and members can be academics, lawyers, or experts.

At the basin / sub-national level there is the following institutional set up under the jurisdiction of ME:

- Four River Basin Committees, one for each major river basin, have been established. They involve multiple stakeholders from government and expert community: they are chaired by the Vice-Minister of Environment and include MoLIT's Assistant Minister, vice-governors in each river basin and the CEO of K-water. River Basin Committees manage the river management funds, raised from the water use charges. Under the new Framework Act on Water Management, local River Management Committees, which were formerly under the responsibility of MoLIT, will be transferred to ME and merged with the River Basin Committees (to collectively become River Basin Committees). The River Management Committees, one for each major river basin, were mandated to deliberate on matters of river management and disputes. They were set up by provinces and metropolitan cities with the Chair and the members of the committee appointed by the City Mayor or Do (administrative unit) Governor. Members represented MoLIT, cities, academia and law.
- Four River Basin Environmental Offices, one for each major river basin, are in charge of river basin management, waste management, regional environmental impact assessments and pollution sources management. They are also responsible for the approval of the Basic Plans for Sewerage Improvement, the maintenance of the drinking water protection areas and the water treatment facilities.
- Three Regional Environmental Offices are tasked with developing and implementing environmental management plans in their areas of jurisdiction, providing formal ME opinions on environmental impact assessment (EIA) and SEA reports, and providing oversight and control of compliance by local governments (OECD, 2017b). The Regional Environmental Offices manage drinking water protection areas and the status of water purification facilities and review, approve and evaluate the "Total Water Pollution Load" management system.

- Four Flood Control Offices (previously under MoLIT), one for each major river basin, have two basic functions; 1) issue water permits, and 2) provide flood forecasting, hydrological observation, and hydrological data collection and management for their respective basin. Basically they are in charge of opening and closing the dam gates.
- Four River Adjustment Councils are hosted by each of the Flood Control Offices and mandated to mediate over water allocation issues. They were established in 2015 and 2016 as an emergency response to the 2015 drought, requiring negotiation and mediation across water users and other stakeholders. Each council is composed of water users, stakeholders, experts from the private sector and NGOs. River Adjustment Councils are in charge of co-ordinating river water allocation and deliberation over allocation conflicts when needed. However, since 2015 drought, these Councils have been dormant.

Under the jurisdiction of MoLIT, five Regional Construction Management Offices will remain in operation at the sub-national level to cater for the needs of five large cities (i.e. Seoul, Wonju, Daejeon, Iksan and Busan). They act as policy implementing bodies in charge of safety facilities, flood damage prevention, waterfront zoning and management, river development in relation to construction, and land use policies and practices.

In addition, as part of transferring water resources responsibilities, the Korea Water Resources Corporation (K-water) has been moved from MoLIT to ME. K-water operates at multiple scales and develops and manages water resources and water supply facilities, including for example multi-regional waterworks and multi-purpose dams.

The basin level cannot and should not replace typical central government functions of policy making and over-arching long term planning, as well as local water resources and spatial planning and implementation of rules and regulations. Managing water along hydrological borders can facilitate more effective upward and downward coordination and accountability of water decision-making. Towns and cities are also part and parcel of catchments, and need to be considered in the context of upstream and downstream dynamics in terms of water quantity and quality.

The current water reform and governance changes provide the ME an opportunity to strengthen basin coordination of the WELF nexus. But coordination benefits will not be automatic; it is critical that ME puts in place proper institutional change and staff incentive programmes that can effectively increase water quality and quantity coordination, including with MAFRA and MoTIE.

4.3.3. Managing water at the basin scale: Examples of water management cases

There are no blue prints for effective water governance. This section documents water governance systems at the basin scale in France, England/Wales and the Netherlands. Despite that water reform in the three cases started well before the adoption of the EU Water Framework Directive (WFD), they have all had to adapt basin governance to meet the WFD requirements to its requirements. Importantly, the WFD is a *framework* that can be implemented in different ways (see Annex 3.A). The cases show that even though they are adhering to the same framework, countries find their own unique pathway on how to implement basic water management principles.

The purpose of the case studies is to provide useful examples of water governance that can serve as inspiration for Korea. It is important to acknowledge that the hydrological, socio-economic and political contexts are diverse, and that any new system that Korea chooses to implement will be different. Based on its geophysical conditions, socio-economics and history Korea will have to find its own water management model that can meet both current and future water challenges. It is important to keep in mind that water governance is considered as path dependent, meaning that bigger changes may not come into fruition easily since they may lack support from existing institutional frameworks and may face resistance from some or many water users and other stakeholders. In this regard, it would make good sense for Korean policy makers to think in terms of iterative and step-by-step approaches towards reforming water governance.

Governing water in France

Summary: The characteristics of the river basin management in France are: (1) financial independence of river basin authorities (RBAs – Agence de l'eau) and loans/subsidies to local governments; (2) stakeholder engagement through river basin committees (RBCs) and (3) active roles of local governments in policy making and basin planning. Coordination between water management and land use are positively incentivised through RBAs loans to local governments.

France is divided into six major river basin areas as water management administrative districts. Each district has a decision-making authority in the form of a basin committee, as well as a water management secretariat to support the committee. The basin committee sets "basic guidelines for water development and management". The basin plans include general action plans for conserving surface water, groundwater, water-related ecosystems and wetlands. The French Water Act, 1992, stipulates that local entities are required to form water-related local alliances with the basin agencies, which enables local water management groups to participate in consultative processes.

River basin management in France has been regarded as a successful system because of the roles of the RBAs, RBCs and local government.

At central government level, and as a response to implement the EU-WFD, the French National Agency for Water and Aquatic Environments (ONEMA) was created in 2006 under the authority of the Ministry of Environment (now the French Biodiversity Agency). ONEMA is mandated to improve the links between the water cycle and water services management. It also works to better align European guidelines with decentralised implementation at basin scale (Colon et al., 2018).

A most significant feature of the French water management system was to transfer political, administrative and financial power from the centre to river basin levels. It is somewhat of a paradox, that France - with a long tradition of strong central government powers - took a pathway on strong decentralisation of water management at river basin and local scales since the 1960s. The complex and dynamic political situations of the time paved the way for the central government to allow river basin organisations to levy and collect water taxes within the river basins (Barraqué, 2003).

Another distinctive feature of RBAs in France is that they have served as a mutual bank to provide loans to local governments in case local governments need to implement water projects. Such a system has produced favourable a relationship between RBAs and local governments, and has achieved effective water management as well as land development (Barraqué, 2003).

Stakeholder engagement has been a critical factor for the establishment and functioning of the RBCs in France. Each of the six basin committees is chaired by an elected local official and made up of representatives from: local authorities (40% of seats); users and associations, including industries, regional developers, farmers, fishermen, tourism and nautical activities, electricity producers and water suppliers (40%); and central government (20%). As members of the basin committee, these stakeholders orientate the water policy priorities in their respective river basin. See Box 4.2 for an example of stakeholder participation in the Loire-Bretagne basin.

A core feature of the RBAs is to prepare a mandatory master basin plan for water development and management, which is then approved by central government. The RBCs are responsible for monitoring implementation of the master plan. They also formulate the priorities of each RBA, in particular regarding tax levies. The RBC votes on the water agency's multi-year action programme, which sets the priorities and methods for financial assistance to fund the implementation of the river basin master plan. At the sub-basin level, local water commissions are set up in certain cases to develop a water development and management plan that aims to adapt the basin master plan to local specificities. These commissions are composed of representatives of local authorities (50%), water users (25%) and central government (25%) (Colon, et al., 2018; OECD, 2015b).

Governing water in England and Wales

Summary: Privatised water supply and sewerage services, and strong independent regulators are what stands out in England and Wales. Stakeholder engagement has played an increasingly important role in both water services and river basin management. The development of a catchment-based approach is a more recent development where stakeholder oriented catchment partnerships are established across England and Wales.

Water management in England and Wales has three independent regulatory authorities: the Environment Agency (EA), Drinking Water Inspectorate (DWI) and Water Services Regulation Authority (OFWAT), the economic regulator. The regulators were established at the time of privatisation of water services in 1989, in order to protect the interests of customers and the environment. Integrated water management in river basins is primarily overseen by the EA, working under policy guidance from the Department for Environment, Food and Rural Affairs (DEFRA). Other distinctive traits are the limited roles of local government which, apart from assistance with the management of urban flooding risks, have little involvement in water management. In the past, stakeholder engagement was less of a priority, but is now integral to shaping and prioritising investment by the water companies, and also in river basin management.

The EA is the lead entity for the implementation of river basin management in England (in Wales the role has passed to the devolved regulator Natural Resources Wales). Ten water supply and sewage treatment companies operate broadly at a river basin scale. The EA is the competent agency to deal with regulation of water supply, water abstractions and pollution, flood risk management and environmental protection. The Agency, however, does not have any mandate to make a final decision on land use and planning; this was the responsibility of the Deputy Prime Minister's Office and is now with the Ministry of Housing, Communities and Local Government. This is a situation that resembles the case in Korea and where there is a need for reform to strengthen the coordination between water management and land use (Lee and Kim, 2009).

A less well developed feature of the water management system in England and Wales set up at the time of privatisation (1989) was stakeholder engagement. Subsequently, the Consumer Council for Water (CCWater) was set up in 2005. CCWater is independent of both the water industry and OFWAT. Since its creation, the Council has become much better known and its influence in support of customers' interests is now an integral and respected part of the water governance regime.

In its mandate to protect and represent customer needs and to encourage customer engagement, OFWAT, the water and sewage companies and CCWater carry out customer surveys in order to gain a detailed understanding of customers' needs and priorities. This also includes customer's willingness to pay for company specific improvements and can lead to improved standards of service where a company demonstrates that particular priorities are of concern. Since 2009, increased operational efficiency by the companies has meant that in real terms, customers' bills have remained static or have reduced.

The water companies in England and Wales are required to develop a business plan every five years, and their customers are given the opportunity to influence water prices and investment priorities for each planning period. Water companies work to create opportunities for improved local ownership and leadership in water price setting to engage with stakeholders through extensive consultation, and use Customer Challenge Groups to create an informed network of stakeholders able to advise on priorities and preferred standards of service.

The implementation of the EU WFD meant that from 2009, the UK government, the EA and a variety of other organisations have developed a catchment-based approach for integrated basin management. It aims to better engage river catchment stakeholders; establish common ownership of problems and their solutions; build partnerships that balance environmental, economic and social demands; and align funding and actions within river catchments to bring about long-term improvements. The purpose of the new approach is three-fold: i) to generate more coordinated "on the ground" local action; ii) to generate more evidence to better understand and obtain buy-in to problems; and iii) to look for innovative, more cost-effective solutions.

Following a 12-month pilot phase in 2012, a formal independent evaluation of the 25 catchment scale trials across England was carried out to assess how catchment-level planning and collaboration could better inform planning and delivery of the EU WFD. The UK government formally announced the launch of the catchment-based approach in June 2013. Since then, the EA has worked with public, private and not-for-profit sectors to set up over 100 collaborative "catchment partnerships" in the 87 management catchments across England (plus 6 cross-border catchments with Scotland and Wales). The EA now employs over 60 dedicated "catchment co-ordinators" to support these independently-led groups and enhance engagement and partnerships for effective catchment governance across England. A Guide for Catchment Management has also been developed as a "how to" handbook to translate lessons learnt from the pilot phase into useful guidance and reference materials (UK Environment Agency et al., 2018). A national support group was also established to help transition and mainstream the approach in England (OECD, 2015c).

Governing water quality in the Netherlands

Summary: River basin management in the Netherlands puts strong emphasis on the integration of policies and plans as a means to overcome fragmentation. A particular focus of river basin management in the Netherlands is on improving water quality. Basin water quality plans coordinate with the plans of other government agencies also responsible for water quality. The planning of water quality at basin level also coordinates with the Dutch Delta approach – a national programme that aims to protect the Netherlands against flooding and to ensure freshwater supply, now and in the future. Stakeholder engagement is considered key for effective coordination.

In the Netherlands a number of key plans for water management are based on a river-basin approach. Managing water at the basin scale is considered a joint task where the government, water boards, provinces, municipal councils, the governing body of protected sites (Rijkswaterstaat), non-governmental organisations and companies are working together with similar ambitions in mind to improve water management.

A key milestone was the adoption of the river basin management plans 2016-2021 for the Rhine, Meuse, Scheldt and Ems in December 2015. These plans are about water quality and form part of the requirements to meet good water quality status under the EU-WFD. They provide direction on how to reduce water pollution, with the specific objective to improve the quality of the water in both a chemical and an ecological sense.

The case in the Netherlands illustrates a strong requirement for coordination between plans and policies. The river basin management plans provide an overview of the condition, problems, objectives and measures related to the improvement of water quality. Importantly, the river basin management plans are not isolated plans, but are interconnected with the plans and measures of water managers, and other water-related plans and regulations. Many government agencies in the Netherlands work on water quality, providing an imperative to coordinate the river basin management plans with the water plans of other government bodies.

The characteristics of the river basin management plans in the Netherlands are summarised as follows (Ministry of Infrastructure and the Environment, 2016):

- Integrated approach: the plans comprise all aspects of water quality
- Applies to surface water, groundwater and protected areas
- River basin approach: plans are drafted for each river basin (Rhine, Meuse, Scheldt, Ems) with both an international/transboundary part (part A) and a national part (part B)
- Member states within a river basin hold each other accountable for objectives and measures
- Describes objectives, loads, condition, measures and costs
- Starting point: attainable and affordable measures
- Detailed programme of measures: progress of implementation in past period (2010-2015), measures for the next period (2016-2021) and tasks remaining after 2021
- Where possible, measures must be linked to measures from the Dutch Delta Programme and other policy challenges
- Coordination with other bodies by means of a bottom-up approach with own role for the regions. Key role for Regional Administrative Consultation Committees, and
- International coordination: all EU member states draft river basin management plans and report on progress to the EU.

4.3.4. Possible approaches to river basin management in Korea

The WELF nexus approach (see Introduction to the report for a summary) is a new concept in Korea and under development. Its increased use and meaningfulness would require that there is a common understanding of the concept among key stakeholders, especially ME, MoLIT, MoTIE and MAFRA, but also by local governments, water users, NGOs and other stakeholders. A common understanding of the nexus approach and its potential benefits, limitations and priorities in the Korean context is required for the concept to take a firm root and be perceived as making a contribution to improved coordinated water management. Considering that ministries such as MAFRA and MoTIE seem to be less interested in adapting their work to nexus approach is a particular concern.

In the context of WELF nexus approach, and as part of strengthening basin level management, it is proposed that ME and MoLIT focus on water and land use interactions, including different economic water and land uses such as food and energy production (under the remit of MAFRA and MoTIE). An opportunity for ME is to build a strong case for making environmental flows part of the nexus approach. Considering ME's agenda to secure environmental flows in the four river basins and new a prototype of low impact development, environmental sustainability needs to be made a significant part of the nexus approach. Therefore, from the ME perspective, the nexus should put strong focus on water, land and ecosystems. Various economic uses of water and land can be integrated into this framework.

Addressing nexus and governance challenges at the basin scale cannot be the responsibility of a single ministry. The improved coordination between sectors related to the WELF nexus will require a broader set of policy options found in a mix of water governance, infrastructure and technology, and investment and funding. It will require a whole-of-government approach to take co-ordinated action at central, basin and local levels. As such, further assessment to address the aforementioned institutional challenges would justify a more systematic and in-depth analysis that would bring together all ministries involved in water management – particularly MoLIT, ME, MAFRA, MoI and MoTIE – in a coordinated approach.

For improved coordination, it is required that ME assesses the institutional mandates to identify overlaps, and management and economic efficiency opportunities at the basin scale for improved coordination among the River Basin Management Committees; River Basin Environmental Offices; Regional Environmental Offices; and the newly acquired Flood Control Offices and River Adjustment Councils in each of the four major river basins. Similarly, MoLIT should undertake a similar type of nexus coordination assessment to identify weaknesses and opportunities for improved coordination of land and water management related to the five regional Construction Management Offices. A basin level assessment can provide a basis for a dialogue between ME, MoLIT, MAFRA and other government and non-government stakeholders (including NGOs, private sector, academia, regional and local governments, etc.) to put in place a coordination platform between water and land management.

An important required policy change, and that cuts straight to the functionality of river basin organisations, is to acknowledge the basin management principle of: *Each water basin is different* and comes with their own hydrological and socio-economic characteristics and challenges. The very essence of basin management is that such unique characteristics need to be taken into account in the planning and implementation of river basin management plans. Consequently, a successful set up of river basin organisation requires that they can make their own independent decisions (albeit in line with national water priorities) on: long- and short-term plans, levying of water user fees, investment priorities, mechanisms for stakeholder consultation, and dialogue and conflict mediation.

The OECD recommends that the RBCs, under ME, gradually take on typical features of river basin organisation roles and responsibilities related to: planning, data collection, conflict mediation, setting water user fees, and provide mechanisms for stakeholder engagement. It would be beneficial to merge the River Management Committees (RMCs) with RBCs for a combined basin organisation for water management. See Box 4.1 for requirements for successful water management at basin level. The steps below outline a longer-term iterative approach. ME should retain ongoing oversight and delivery of RBCs Globalcilitate learning from experience. ME should also provide process guidance to RBCs to ensure alignment with national policy priorities, and to ensure that basin plans are implemented consistently across the different basins and the people are being treated fairly.

1. **Start reflecting basin issues in national policies**, even before ME sets the institutional framework to shift towards river basin management. This requires data collection and information on basin features, the capacity to reflect these features in national policies, and stakeholder engagement to signal local priorities and strengthen political buy in.
2. **Mandate RBCs to develop river basin management plans**. Based on the national long-term water plan and national water management principles, the RBCs in Korea should be mandated to develop river basin management plans (RBMPs). Considering that there is a big vertical coordination gap between central and local levels in Korea, RBMPs are one important step, as an intermediary institution, towards operationalising water policies, basic water management principles, and new concepts such as the WELF nexus approach. The RBMP can for example include: an appraisal and evaluation of water resources and their condition and trends; an analysis of community needs; alignment with broad policy objectives for the basin or catchment (typically in terms of economic development); coordination with land use, agriculture, food and energy supply policy; setting sub-catchment goals and implementation guidelines; details of cost-sharing programs for on-ground works and other actions; details of a monitoring program; and description and analysis of special catchment management issues, areas and management techniques. All other plans at the basin level (e.g. land use and spatial plans, transport plans and energy plans) should take heed to the RBMP; the RBMP in each basin should drive smart investments that contribute to the delivery of water objectives and minimise exposure to water-related risks. ME should ensure that updates of plans are done in consultation with relevant government and non-government stakeholders, and lessons learned are incorporated into future plans.
3. **Empower RBCs to mediate conflicts**. The RBCs would be one appropriate level for mediating conflicts along the basin (see section 1.1.4 for example of basin conflicts), with potential impacts to set precedence and to better support local governments to mediate conflicts at local scales. Currently, many water conflicts end up with the central government, creating inefficiencies and unnecessary transaction costs. Conflict mediation is better done at the basin or sub-basin scale. The central government should only deal with conflict mediation in case it is of national importance and in terms of developing appropriate policies.

4. **Gradually devolve decisions on water use charges to RBCs**. RMCs and RBCs are currently not independent entities, and water user charges are decided by central government through the RMCs. Considering Korea's strong policy on "water equity", initial reform change can be to allow fee variation in between a band-width of fixed lower and upper rates set by ME. The lower rate could be set at today's level (more out of simplicity than anything else) and the upper level should clearly allow for a significant shift towards the promotion of more efficient use and management of water, differentiated by local water risks and the accepted level of risk. In case required, measures can be put in place to support poor water users and to compensate upstream users affected by economic restrictions due to water quality protection or water conservation.
5. **Give RBCs responsibility for the planning of water supply, water quality and flood protection**. The OECD recommends that ME, MoLIT, MAFRA and other relevant ministries explore an initial joint coordination mechanism at the basin level for coordinated decision-making in water quality and quantity projects (currently a lot of overlaps). Such a mechanism should also allow for stakeholder engagement. The current Integrated Water Management Forum (under ME) could serve as an initial step to strengthen water management at the basin scale. Some of the required steps that need to be taken include:
   i. Establish a common vision for integrated water management and WELF nexus at basin scale based on policy directions (basin management core values of integration, and basic principles and systems, such as a mandate to develop basin plans, and stakeholder engagement);
   ii. Establish clear objectives and strategies for achieving the established vision on managing water at the basin scale; and
   iii. Develop and propose an institutional design at the basin level (such as through RBCs), including stakeholder engagement platform, roles and responsibilities, along with investment priorities and policy directions to advance on managing water at the basin scale.
6. **Establish a stakeholder engagement platform for each river basin.** Government and non-government engagement will be a critical element as part of operationalising an expanded role of RBCs. Stakeholder engagement will be key to developing RBMPs, but also in terms of having a voice in matters pertaining to conflict mediation, the setting of user fees and data collection. The OECD recommends that ME continue to develop stakeholder approaches in relation to its nexus work and under the existing institutional set up. A starting point is to assess and analyse the role and current mandate of the four RBCs, vertical and horizontal policy linkages, and use the assessment as a basis for how to move forward. Such a review should at least include and analysis of water and land use linkages with local governments, MoLIT and MAFRA. For example, the French case suggests that a financial link between local governments and basin organisation is key for improved coordination of water and land use decisions. If RBCs are mandated to independently use revenue generated from water use charges, they could potentially use part of the revenue to incentivise (through locally driven water investment demands) better coordination between basin and local levels.

Box 4.1. Some requirements for successful river basin management

- Research and data collection at the basin scale to better understand the hydrology, environmental, climatological and the socio-economic dynamics for informed decision-making.
- Clear division of roles and responsibilities at all levels of management and that various government and non-government actors can be held to account. A river basin entity needs to be endowed with a very clear mandate and a certain level of independence is required from central government.
- Stakeholder buy-in and inclusiveness in the development of water policies and basin plans for enhanced policy relevance and better implementation efficiency.
- Transparency in planning and policy processes and access to information. All stakeholders should be able to access similar data and information for informed decision-making.
- Establishment of a long-term river basin management plan that is the outcome of diverse stakeholder engagement around the basin. The plan should cover the entire river basin, including medium and small scale watersheds. In addition, river basin management needs a clear purpose and a systematic approach.
- Consideration of the needs and demands from different sectors (such as agriculture, energy, urban development, environmental flow, industry, etc.) and the costs involved.
- Financial viability and adequate staff capacities to fulfil the mandate of the river basin organisation. Entirely new capacities may be required to cater for multi-stakeholder engagement and to improve coordination at the basin scale. Financing should be based on economic principles such as appropriate water tariffs, taxes and/or transfers. River basin organisations may levy water charges as a means to secure their own financial viability.

Sources: OECD (2015a), *OECD Principles on Water Governance*, OECD, Paris. http://www.oecd.org/cfe/regional-policy/OECD-Principles-on-Water-Governance.pdf; Pegram, G. et al. (2013), *River Basin Planning: Principles, procedures and approaches for strategic basin planning*. Paris, UNESCO.

The gradual development of RBCs will require some initial investment from ME to enhance certain capacities, for example, skills related to water planning and stakeholder engagement, investments and fee systems. However, it is envisaged that in the long-term, RBCs will be funded through water user fees and build their own sustainable financing base to be able to deliver on those roles and responsibilities mandated to the RBCs. This increased independence can favour RBCs devolution of responsibilities and capacitate RBCs to deliver on new proposed mandates of river basin planning, data collection, conflict mediation and establishing and implementing stakeholder platforms. Increasing financial self-sufficiency can also lead to improved accountability of new responsibilities. However, it is important to be aware of that this type of funding modality also can lead to economic distortions and inefficiencies; earmarking can be an inefficient use of public money for several reasons (OECD, 2017c). Hence, it is critical that financial viability and efficiencies are assessed and monitored on regular basis by ME, and expenditures should be commensurate with the revenue collected so stakeholders see the benefit.

4.4. Stakeholder engagement

A stakeholder refers to an individual, group, or organisation that has a direct or indirect interest or stake in a particular organisation. These may be governments, private or public sectors, research institutions, and civil society such as Non-Government Organisations (NGOs). In Korea, stakeholder engagement platforms could prove helpful networks for communication on, and management of, competing demands for water, managing coordination problems and conflicts, coalition-building, and planning and visioning.

Stakeholder engagement in water management is a means to an end. Various stakeholders' participation in policy development and implementation, and access to relevant water information are essential preconditions for successful water resources management and water policy reform. Stakeholder engagement is conducive to improved water management because it enables water management to be better balanced among water users, and that water management policies and plans better reflect various interests and knowledge of society and be tailored according to local needs and demands. There are several mechanisms through which stakeholder needs, demands and knowledge can be made known to decision-makers. For example, stakeholders being part of various water committees and boards, and public hearings. For any engagement mechanism chosen, it is critical that it is inclusive and transparent, and provide a space where stakeholders can be heard in constructive ways.

The water sector in many OECD and non-OECD countries is experiencing a movement towards more formalised and structured forms of stakeholder engagement, going beyond reactive *ad hoc* approaches. New legislations, guidelines and standards at various levels related to public participation and stakeholder involvement have spurred the emergence of more formalised versions of stakeholder engagement. Organisations are referring to such engagement in their overarching principles and policy. Increasingly, either because of legal requirements or on a voluntary basis, public authorities, service providers, regulators, basin organisations and donors have included requirements for co-operation, consultation or awareness-raising in their operational rules and procedures (OECD, 2015b).

Some of the benefits of a formalised and structured form of stakeholder engagement are reflected in the Dutch Delta programme, created in 2010. Stakeholder engagement within this programme has, for example, led to a new working method in three areas: flood risk management, the availability of freshwater and water-robust spatial planning. The Delta Commissioner is required by law to submit a yearly proposal for action to the Cabinet, in consultation with the relevant authorities, social organisations and the business community (OECD, 2015b). This case can be illustrative for Korea in the sense that it shows that stakeholders can be involved in different water management issues and that there are many potential benefits of engaging long term with stakeholders. In fact, the establishment of stakeholder engagement may take time since stakeholders may lack experience and capacity, and there may also be distrust between some stakeholders that will require dialogue and trust-building. Some of the benefits of stakeholder engagement may not be immediately visible, but may pay off at later stage.

Stakeholders contribute to water governance in different ways and can pursue different objectives. The OECD Survey on Stakeholder Engagement for Effective Water

Governance (OECD, 2015b) indicates that stakeholders' contribution to better governance covers a variety of activities (Figure 4.1). The most common are that stakeholder engagement: contributes to information sharing (88% of respondents surveyed); raises awareness on water availability, risks, quality and costs (86%); and supports the effective implementation of water policy, reform or projects (84%).

Figure 4.1. How stakeholders contribute to better water governance

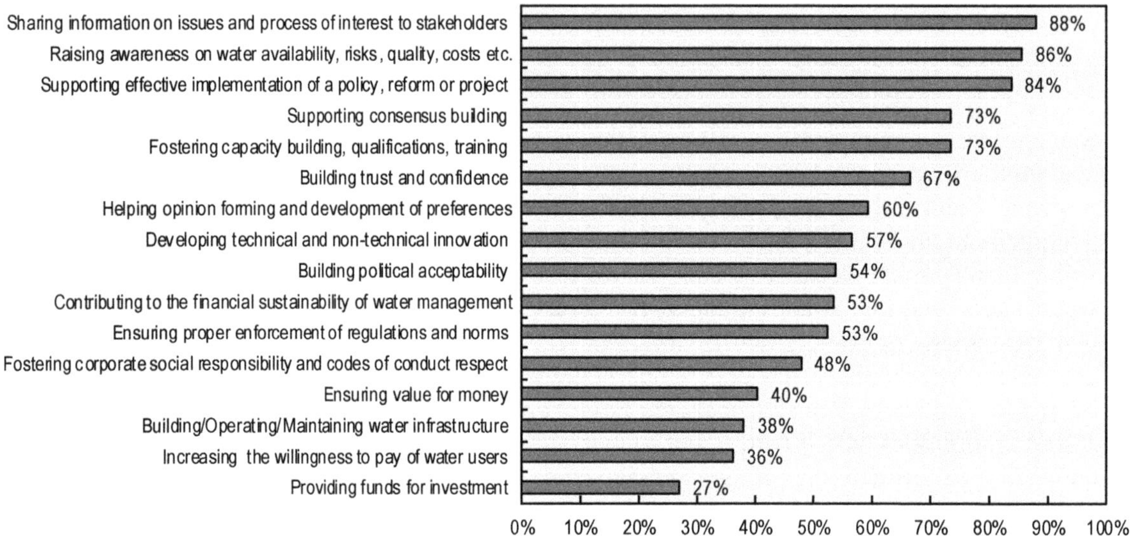

Source: OECD (2015b), *Stakeholder Engagement for Inclusive Water Governance*, OECD Studies on Water, OECD Publishing, Paris. http://dx.doi.org/10.1787/9789264231122-en.

In most water reforms in OECD and non-OECD countries, stakeholder engagement has been, and is considered to be, one important reform element. The EU WFD integrates engagement by relevant water stakeholders. The current development of EU Drinking Water Directive views communication with the public and engagement by relevant stakeholders as a key reform element.

Shifting from an *ad-hoc* based to a structured form (i.e. as stipulated by legislation, rules and regulations) of stakeholder engagement raises some challenges for decision makers. Formalising, or even institutionalising, collective decision-making related to water issues – such as for example as the French river basin management system - requires strong political leadership, with clear objectives and strategies (such as to prevent capture of engagement processes). It also implies investments to secure financial and human resources at the appropriate levels to sustain the engagement process. Appropriate skills are necessary to set up and facilitate the process for formal stakeholder engagement and to ensure its expected outcomes. This requires dedicated staff trained in mediation, communication, use of information and communication technologies (OECD, 2015b).

The Loire-Bretagne Basin Agency in France illustrates how stakeholders can be engaged in the development of a river basin management plan (Box 4.2). It is worth noting that in the French case, stakeholders can be engaged in two main ways: i) through being a member of the basin committee; and/or ii) through taking part in particular stakeholder consultation processes. It shows how stakeholder engagement can benefit the content and relevance of river basin planning, as well as its implementation.

Box 4.2. Stakeholder involvement in the development of a river basin master plan: The example of the Loire-Bretagne basin in France

In France, as required by the EU WFD (see Annex 3.A), a master basin plan is developed in each of the six river basins. Each plan defines water quality and quantity objectives, and actions to be carried out for achieving them. The basin master plans are updated every six years.

The relevant stakeholders are involved in the development of the basin master plans in two main ways: first, as being part of the basin committee; and second, during a consultation process organised within the basin.

Each river basin in France has a committee which is responsible for the development of the basin master plan. The committee is the pivotal place for discussing and collectively defining the keys points of the water policy within the river basin. A basin committee functions as a multi-stakeholder assembly that represents and mediates different interests along the basin. For instance, the Loire-Bretagne basin committee (one of the six French basin committees) is made up of 190 members appointed for six years. Out of these, 40% are elected representatives, mainly from local governments, and also from regional and county governments. Another 40% of the members are water user representatives, such as industries, farming, angling and environmental NGO's. The last 20% is made up of state representatives (public and administrative central state bodies at decentralised levels).

The development of the master basin plan can, at times, be a hard process. For instance, in the Loire-Bretagne basin, the basin master plan in force was developed over a two-year period. The process itself required many meetings and debates, and sometimes even in the form of conflicts between stakeholders. More than 20 meetings of the thematic commissions ("planning", "seashore" and "communication") of the basin committee were necessary for reaching a compromise, and at the end getting an approval from the committee.

Stakeholders are also involved through a consultation process that takes place a few months before the final approval of a river basin plan. The basin committee makes a formal notice to local stakeholders to get their inputs on a draft of the basin master plan. The objectives are to strengthen the technical content of the plan, and to foster their buy-in and their future engagement in the implementation phase. During a four-month period, various local stakeholders can contribute to the consultation process, such as regional councils, county councils, chambers of agriculture (regional and county levels), chambers of commerce and industry (regional and county levels), management bodies of natural parks, sub-basin commissions, etc. During the consultation process, any relevant publications and other materials are made accessible to involved stakeholders. Moreover, they can also get technical support from state and basin agency services through local meeting participation.

In the Loire-Bretagne basin, about 260 local stakeholder bodies were consulted in the drafting phase the current basin master plan, and 3000 comments were made on its content. Every comment was analysed and their potential inclusion arbitrated by the thematic commissions of the basin committee. Some comments were taken into account, such as requests for clarifications, the need for greater relevance of stakeholder data, and suggestions of financial and technical feasibility issues that were not initially identified. Other comments did not lead to a change, specifically when comments were not precise enough and/or justified.

Examples of comments from the stakeholder consultation process on the master river basin plan of the Loire-Bretagne basin include:

- Request that some high-priority areas be extended, reduced or suppressed. This can, for example, be relevant for lakes subject to eutrophication, erosion sensitive areas and abstraction sensitive areas.
- Request to change some of the proposed technical standards, for example value of pluvial network flow, filling period of irrigation reserves, and yield of drinking water networks in rural area, and
- Request for additional clarifications and details on technical terms, such as biological minimum flow and water economic values to avoid misinterpretation.

Source: Hervé Gilliard, *Pers. Comm.*, Peer Reviewer, Loire-Bretagne Water Agency.

4.4.1. Non-government stakeholder engagement in Korea

During the 1990s and 2000s, Korea witnessed a changing civil society. The challenge of civil society is to increasingly become a key part of "co-governance" as an engaged and informed partner to the government. It is reported that civil society has become a stronger social force with increasing abilities of getting involved in, and influencing, government decision-making processes (Kim, 2013).

A number of environmentally oriented NGOs in Korea work to influence government and/or monitor environmental situations, including water, and to inform and educate the public. Large NGOs such as the Korean Federation for Environmental Movement have built up considerable competencies in the field of environmental policy, while smaller NGOs have focused on water service provision. Consumer associations (e.g. Korea Consumer Agency, Green Consumer Agency) are also important actors with a voice in consultative platforms such as the Water Tariff Committee, River Water Adjustment Councils, as well as local price committees. Academia also plays an important role to produce and share technical and scientific information and evidence to build a sound knowledge-base in support of the formulation of policies and practices (OECD, 2017b). Water and environmental NGOs work, among other things, includes monitoring of water quantity and quality issues, restoring wetlands and initiating river restoration projects, and informing and educating the public. They do their best to feed into policy processes by sending reports and other documents to government agencies, and by trying to draw public attention to harmful practices.

A water reform ambition in Korea is to engage more with stakeholder groups in water. Stakeholder engagement processes in Korea have been *ad hoc* and reactive, rather than being aimed at prevention and long-term resilience. They tend to be a response to a particular water need, crisis or emergency (droughts, floods, economic crisis, river restoration etc.), rather than a process carried out on a voluntary basis. Efforts are required to develop more systematic stakeholder engagement in decision making, including clear objectives for the engagement process, in order to more systematically integrate stakeholder interests and knowledge into water management.

One objective is to integrate stakeholder engagement under the RBCs in Korea. For this reason, a one-year project was recently set up in the Han River to test and promote stakeholder engagement. The River Basin Participation Centre is meant to promote improved water management, including principles for fund management. The Centre is mainly meant to improve planning at the sub-basin level and to seek alignment with the Han River Basin long-term management plan. Planning is not mandatory for medium and small scale rivers, resulting in only 10 % of them having water management plans.

In the follow-up of the pilot Han River Basin Participation Centre, it is critical the ME undertakes an assessment. It should assess experiences and lessons learned, through a survey with the various engaged stakeholders on their experiences, and explore ways in how they can and are willing to participate. It is important that these types of pilots are properly assessed so that stakeholder engagement mechanisms can evolve.

Despite trends of a more vivid and influential civil society, progress is at a slow pace in relation to the water sector. Challenges faced by water related NGOs and other non- state stakeholders in Korea include:

- The lack of institutionalised stakeholder platforms and process whereby they can dialogue directly with the relevant decision-makers. This is considered as a major hindrance that leave many NGOs frustrated and without any clear channels for their voices. The experience so far with stakeholder engagement is to consult stakeholders in some specific projects, often related to river restoration.
- Limited experiences within NGOs as well as the government system of working with water management at the basin scale. The RBCs under ME are mandated to manage the river management funds raised through the water user charges. The RBCs are currently not mandated to making planning and decision-making on water management.
- There is overall an awareness and information gap among the Korean population about water management, which is mainly due to lack of information. The country has made efforts to open up public data, most recently with its "Government 3.0., which is an e-platform for government operation to deliver customised public services by opening and sharing government-owned data to the public and encouraging communication and collaboration between government departments. Government 3.0 aims to make the government more service-oriented, competent, and transparent (http://www.mois.go.kr/eng/sub/a03/Government30/screen.do). However, such tools may take time to implement, and information on water is for the time being limited, making water users and consumers less aware of the costs of water management and water pricing, sources of supply, and water quality and flood risks. Better informed water users and consumers should be seen as an important asset, since it makes them more aware to reduce their own water footprint, and to improve their willingness to comply with legislation or to pay for certain water services.
- Efforts by NGOs tend to be fragmented and piece-meal partly due to the lack of plans for medium and smaller scale basins (only 10% of them have plans). NGOs base their work on the water plans, but the long term plans by MoLIT and ME need to be operationalised to a higher degree.

4.4.2. Moving forward: Towards increased non-state stakeholder engagement

Relevant ministries, such as ME, MoLIT and MAFRA, should start to build longer-term stakeholder engagement platforms as part of strengthening water management, including basin level management. While most water and environmental related NGOs in Korea are currently operating at a basic level, such platforms will help the NGOs to gradually build their capacities and experiences. Table 4.2 on OECD Principles on Stakeholder Engagement suggests a number of steps that would be important to apply for more effective stakeholder engagement.

Table 4.2. OECD Principles on stakeholder engagement in water governance

Principle	Description
Inclusiveness and equity	Map all stakeholders who have a stake in the outcome or that are likely to be affected, as well as their responsibility, core motivations and interactions
Clarity of goals, transparency and accountability	Define the ultimate line of decision making, the objectives of stakeholder engagement and the expected use of inputs
Capacity and information	Allocate proper financial and human resources and share needed information for results-oriented stakeholder engagement
Efficiency and effectiveness	Regularly assess the process and outcomes of stakeholder engagement to learn, adjust and improve accordingly
Institutionalisation, structuring and integration	Embed engagement processes in clear legal and policy frameworks, organisational structures/principles and responsible authorities
Adaptiveness	Customise the type and level of engagement as needed and keep the process flexible to changing circumstances

Source: OECD (2015b), *Stakeholder Engagement for Inclusive Water Governance*, OECD Studies on Water, OECD Publishing, Paris.

Six levels of stakeholder engagement have been distinguished depending on the processes and purpose of engagement (OECD, 2015b) (Figure 4.2). As a start, ME, MoLIT and MAFRA need to strategically assess the type of engagement required. For ME, one question to be posed is how stakeholders can be better engaged to advance on water quality and quantity management and to improve compliance with existing water rules and regulations.

The first level is communication, which intends primarily to share information and raise awareness, but implies that engagement is mostly passive, i.e. stakeholders are provided with information related to water quality and quantity policy and projects, but not necessarily with the opportunity to influence final decisions. The typology incrementally progresses up to the level of co-production and co-decision, which correspond to deepened decision-making where stakeholders exercise direct authority over the decisions taken. Stakeholder engagement is a multi-faceted exercise with various progressive levels that imply different forms and intensity of stakeholder engagement.

Figure 4.2. Levels of stakeholder engagement

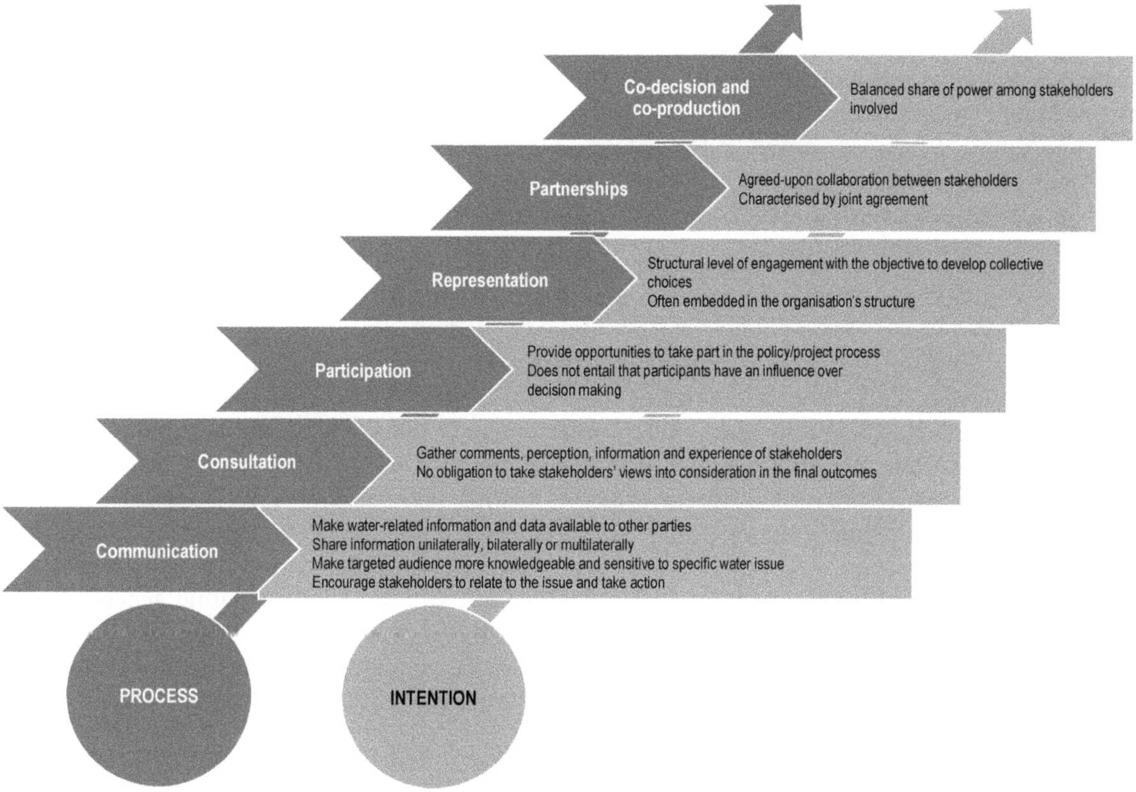

Source: OECD (2015b), *Stakeholder Engagement for Inclusive Water Governance*, OECD Studies on Water, OECD Publishing, Paris. http://dx.doi.org/10.1787/9789264231122-en.

Below follows examples of stakeholder engagement that illustrate different ways on engagement. The cases are meant to provide examples of strategies and methods used to provide inspiration to ME and other ministries. The full case studies are presented as Annex 4.A. It is important that ME assesses and sets stakeholder engagement objectives in relation to river basin management and the management of the WELF nexus.

In the Netherlands, many citizens were perceived to lack capacity and interest to engage in water issues. A survey was carried out specifically targeting citizens to assess their knowledge on water, their positions regarding certain water issues and their willingness to participate further in decision-making. In Portugal the "Water Heroes" programme increased water awareness and spurred students to do research to encourage innovation, originality and applicability.

These cases illustrate that the assessment of stakeholders' willingness and capacity to participate at the basin level could be a useful starting point for ME. Since most environmental NGOs in Korea operate with capacity limitations, it is important that ME surveys the stakeholders and their interests and capacities. As a first step, it is recommended that ME (and MoLIT and MAFRA) provide some incentives in the form of small grants (travel grants, grants for holding local stakeholder meetings, trainings etc.) for which NGOs can apply to improve their abilities and capacities to take part in stakeholder processes. Trainings and capacity development on stakeholder engagement will be required for ME staff and stakeholder groups. Engaging with non-conventional stakeholders, such as with youth, can be a useful means to spur innovation and interest for water.

Stakeholder engagement processes under the EU-WFD provides clear guidance on important elements Korea can apply in a stakeholder engagement process, including how to engage with stakeholders, for what purpose, avoidance of too technical information, time-bound processes, drawing the attention of all interested groups and individuals, being open-minded in analysing the results, and providing clear rationale for why and how a certain decision is made.

In Spain, stakeholder engagement was a strong element in reaching consensus on key water decisions and achieving good water quality status in the Mancha Oriental water body, Júcar Basin. Stakeholder engagement also led to the adoption of a new water management plan. In Germany, the state of Baden-Württemberg took measures to involve the key stakeholders through a series of over 70 different local events to produce a water plan. These cases show how stakeholders were engaged in the development of river basin management plans, and that engagement can be both *ad hoc* and by law. It also shows that sometimes a series of different types of events (consultations, workshops, public hearings, public exhibitions, etc.) may be required as a strategy to engage with different types of stakeholders. In Korea, it is important that long-term plans are properly consulted with the stakeholders. As mentioned in the German case, the level of public acceptance was high and something that most likely made the implementation of the plan more effective. ME can consult with stakeholders on existing long-term plans to check their viability from stakeholder perspectives as part of their renewal.

In the Durance Valley, France, the objective of stakeholder engagement was to optimise water allocation between energy generation and irrigation, and to develop appropriate incentives for water savings to restore financial margins and to answer future water demands. This case illustrates two important items which may also benefit Korea. First, stakeholder engagement was beneficial for coordinating complex nexus issues on water, energy and agriculture. The solution in this case was with the private electricity company and the farmers, and was not something that the government could have designed alone; it was enabled through a river basin management collaboration platform. Second, it illustrates a non-uniform and iterative river basin management approach. Diversified management based on river basin conditions can in fact be a very good way of stimulating innovation that can spread along a basin or even between basins.

In the South Saskatchewan River Basin, Canada, stakeholder engagement assisted with addressing adaptation to climate change, also an increasing challenge in Korea. Stakeholder engagement was conducted on a voluntary basis, and was supported by mechanisms such as collaborative modelling processes, and using sophisticated simulation for modelling water systems.

The case studies show that there can be multiple ways to engage with stakeholders depending on the objectives and type of stakeholders. For example, processes can range from being voluntary and *ad hoc*, to systematically structured and required by law such as under the EU-WFD, or under the French river basin agencies (see Box 4.2). Importantly, one modality does not exclude another, and it is important to design stakeholder processes according to their purposes. A viable engagement strategy can also be to work with different types of stakeholder engagement methodologies for different types of stakeholders, such as consultations, workshops, public hearings and public exhibitions.

For ME, it is important to develop a clear strategic long-term stakeholder engagement strategy, particularly with regard to non-government stakeholders and other key WELF nexus-related ministries (MoLIT, MAFRA and MoTIE). While stakeholder engagement is yet to be better structured in Korea, the ME can start by assessing the options for a multi-stakeholder, inter-ministerial mechanism for the WELF nexus at national level. Simultaneously, various stakeholder platform options should be assessed for the RBCs, with a clear purpose to advance on planning at the basin scale. To support this endeavour, it is recommended that ME organise a set of national and basin level workshops on the WELF nexus to collect views and ideas from various stakeholder groups as guidance for moving forward.

Notes

[1] Please note that the new Framework Act on Water Management and the new Water Management Technology and Industry Act are yet to receive official names in English.

References

Barraqué, B. (2003), Past and future sustainability of water policies in Europe, *in Natural Resources Forum,* 27: pp 200–211.

Colon, M., S. Richard and P.A. Roche (2018), The evolution of water governance in France from the 1960's: Disputes as major drivers for radical changes within a consensual framework, *Water International*, 43/1, pp. 109-132 https://doi.org/10.1080/02508060.2018.1403013.

European Commission (2003), Common Implementation Strategy for the Water Framework Directive (2000/60/EC), Guidance Document No 8, Public Participation in Relation to the Water Framework Directive, Working Group 2.9 – Public Participation, European Communities, Luxembourg.

Kim, H-R (2013), State-centric to Contested Social Governance in Korea: Shifting Power, Routledge Studies on Modern Korea, Routledge, New York.

Lee S. and S. Kim (2009), A new mode of river basin management in South Korea, Water and Environment Journal 23 (2009) p. 91-99.

Ministry of Infrastructure and the Environment (2016), River basin management plans 2016-2021 of the Netherlands, The Hague, The Netherlands.

OECD (2018), *Implementing the OECD Principles on Water Governance: Indicator framework and evolving practices*, OECD Studies on Water, OECD Publishing, Paris. https://doi.org/10.1787/9789264292659-en.

OECD (2017a), *Enhancing water use efficiency in Korea*. OECD Studies on Water, OECD Publishing, Paris. http://dx.doi.org/10.1787/9789264281707-en.

OECD (2017b), *OECD Environmental Performance Reviews: Korea 2017.* OECD Publishing Paris. http://dx.doi.org/10.1787/9789264268265-en.

OECD (2017c), *Water Charges in Brazil: The Ways Forward*, OECD Studies on Water, OECD Publishing, Paris. http://dx.doi.org/10.1787/9789264285712-en.

OECD (2016), *OECD Council Recommendation on Water*, [C(2016)174/FINAL], December 2016. https://legalinstruments.oecd.org/en/instruments/349.

OECD (2015a), *OECD Principles on Water Governance,* OECD, Paris. http://www.oecd.org/cfe/regional-policy/OECD-Principles-on-Water-Governance.pdf.

OECD (2015b), *Stakeholder Engagement for Inclusive Water Governance*, OECD Studies on Water, OECD Publishing, Paris. http://dx.doi.org/10.1787/9789264231122-en.

OECD (2015c) *The Governance of Water Regulators*. OECD Studies on Water, OECD Publishing, Paris. http://dx.doi.org/10.1787/9789264231092-en.

OECD (2011), *Water Governance in OECD Countries: A Multi-level Approach*, OECD Studies on Water, OECD Publishing, Paris, https://doi.org/10.1787/9789264119284-en.

Pahl-Wostl, C. and Knieper, C. (2014), "The capacity of water governance to deal with the climate change adaptation challenge: using fuzzy set Qualitative Comparative Analysis to distinguish between polycentric, fragmented and centralized regimes". *Global Environmental Change*, Vol 29: p 139-154.

Pegram, G. et al. (2013), *River Basin Planning: Principles, procedures and approaches for strategic basin planning*. Paris, UNESCO.

Tropp, H. (2007), Water governance: trends and needs for new capacity development, *Water Policy* 9 Supplement 2, pp 19–30.

UK Environment Agency et al. (2018), Working together to manage our catchments: Opportunities for catchment partnerships and water companies to work together for the benefit of people, the environment and local economies, https://catchmentbasedapproach.org/images/2018/02/Working-together-to-manage-our-catchments-water-companies-and-catchment-partnerships---final.pdf.

Annex 4.A. Case studies: Managing water at the basin scale

Stakeholder engagement for awareness-raising in the Netherlands and Portugal

In **the Netherlands**, Dutch citizens face a critical awareness gap whereby they take current levels of water security for granted. This is explained by a high degree of trust in public authorities and the absence of a major flood disaster in the last 60 years (in a country that has 60% of its territory in floodable areas, of which a considerable part is below sea level). A symptom of this is the low voting turnout for the elections of Dutch water authorities every four years. Citizens have to elect officials of regional water authorities in charge of managing water, including for flood defence, while being unaware of their practical duties and roles. The resulting low participation levels during elections calls into question the legitimacy of elected officials. In order to get a better sense of how much the public knew about water issues, to fill-in existing gaps and to motivate a cultural shift across stakeholders, particularly the public, the regional water authority of Rijnland decided to design its new working programme and Policy Plan for 2015-21 jointly with stakeholders, including citizens, in the area. A survey was carried out specifically targeting citizens to assess their knowledge on water, their positions regarding certain water issues and their willingness to participate further in decision making. Results were used to set up an online participation platform to familiarise people with the roles and responsibilities of the regional water authorities, facilitate discussion on important issues and encourage new ideas. A large congress took place in June 2014 and gathered citizens as well as other stakeholders (e.g. environmental organisations, municipalities, etc.); the outcomes are currently being considered for inclusion in the draft policy plan.

In **Portugal**, the "Water Heroes" project aimed at raising awareness on efficient water use, in particular among students. The project started in 2012 in the Beja region and was led by the municipal water and sanitation service provider (EMAS). It aimed to foster environmental awareness through teaching materials tackling the description of the water cycle, information on water contaminants, consumption of treated water, tips for saving water, as well as the presentation of the environmental and economic value of water. To stimulate research among students, the project also launched two contests inviting new ideas and a pilot project on efficient water use to be submitted to encourage innovation, originality and applicability. Twenty-nine schools were targeted in the first year of implementation, reaching over 2 300 students. As the project enters its third year, the service provider continues to receive invitations to organise visits within and outside the school community.

Source: OECD (2015b), *Stakeholder Engagement for Inclusive Water Governance*, OECD Studies on Water, OECD Publishing, Paris. http://dx.doi.org/10.1787/9789264231122-en.

Code of practice on written consultation for the EU WFD

According to Article 14 of the EU Water Framework Directive (WFD), consultations with the public should be carried out throughout the different steps of development of the river basin management plans (e.g. timetable and work programme for the production of the plan, interim review of significant water management issues, draft plan, etc.).

The WFD specifies that documents, analyses and measures should be made available for written comments from the public (e.g. in paper form, by mail or via e-mail). Additionally, other ways of consultation can be considered such as interviews, workshops or conferences. During these meetings, major issues are presented and the invited stakeholders are asked to give their perception, knowledge and ideas on the specific issues. Codes of practice on written consultation were developed as part of the WFD Common Implementation Strategy:

1. Timing for the organisation of consultation, apart from the dates mentioned by Article 14, should be built into the planning process for a policy or service from the start.
2. It should be clear who is being consulted, what is being asked, the timescale and the purpose.
3. The documents which are subject to consultation (timetable, work programme, draft copy of river basin management plan) should be as simple and concise as possible (including a two-page summary of the main questions being asked). Summaries for a broader audience should be prepared.
4. The documents should be made widely available, using electronic means to the fullest extent possible, targeting and drawing the attention of all interested groups and individuals.
5. Anyone with an interest has six months respond to the documents.
6. Responses should be carefully and open-mindedly analysed, and the results made widely available, with an account of the views expressed and reasons for final decisions taken.
7. Departments should monitor and evaluate consultations, designating a consultation co-ordinator who will ensure the lessons are disseminated.

Source: European Commission (2003), Common Implementation Strategy for the Water Framework Directive (2000/60/EC), Guidance Document No 8, Public Participation in Relation to the Water Framework Directive, Working Group 2.9 – Public Participation, European Communities, Luxembourg.

Spain has a long history of multi-stakeholder decision making for water resources management, which has been reinforced by the requirements of the WFD. The Júcar river basin authority promotes information, consultation and public participation in the process leading to the establishment of the river basin management plan, and supports the involvement of interested parties in achieving good status of the Mancha Oriental water body to build multi-stakeholder consensus on key water decisions. This led to the adoption by Royal Decree of the new Water Management Plan for the Júcar River Basin in July 2014, as required by the EU WFD, with monitoring and control tools for water bodies' quality and quantity; resource-saving actions; and measures to substitute water pumping practices. In addition, the revised Water Law (approved by Royal Decree in

2001) also set up formal participation bodies to ensure that decisions taken by the river basin authority are in accordance with water users in the basin, for example the Central Board of Irrigation in the Eastern Channel, which is represented in the governing board of the Júcar basin authority.

In **Germany**, the implementation of the WFD mandated river basin authorities to develop river basin management in consultation with the public and interested parties. The state of Baden-Württemberg took further measures to involve the public during the development of the first river basin management plans published in 2009. In the framework of an advisory board, information was shared with NGOs, institutions and the industrial sector, and overarching concepts and strategies were discussed. Over 70 local events were organised prior to the production of the plans where participants were actively involved in formulating concrete measures. The process helped to identify significant problems, find appropriate solutions and secure high levels of public acceptance.

Source: OECD (2015b), *Stakeholder Engagement for Inclusive Water Governance*, OECD Studies on Water, OECD Publishing, Paris. http://dx.doi.org/10.1787/9789264231122-en.

Optimising the water-energy nexus in the Durance valley, France

In 2003, a Water Saving Convention was signed between Électricité de France (EDF) and the two main irrigators in the Durance valley, France, to improve water efficiency and allocation through better local stakeholder engagement.

The objective was to optimise water allocation between energy generation and irrigation, and to develop appropriate incentives for water savings to restore financial margins and to answer future water demands. The Durance valley is host to a major dam and reservoir comprising 32 hydropower plants producing over 6 billion kWh of renewable energy, supplying drinking water and water for industrial purposes to the entire region, and irrigating 150 000 hectares of farmland.

As part of the process, EDF carried out an assessment of the monetary value of water savings from reduced abstraction for agricultural irrigation in the valley. The main business argument for the valuation study was to demonstrate the benefits of optimising water uses for each party (farmers, water institutions and energy producers). The two parties entered a win-win agreement whereby EDF was to optimise hydro-generation and benefit from further flexibility to generate electricity during daily peak periods when energy prices are higher, while irrigators were to benefit from remuneration by EDF based on the water savings they were able to make, and having more water stored in the reservoir to cope with drought periods. This agreement led to a reduction of agricultural water consumption from 325 million to 235 million cubic metres.

The convention was renewed in 2014 and plans to save a further 20-25 million cubic metres through an annual remuneration based on defined objectives. It allows irrigators to revise their objectives each year while knowing the economic consequences of their water consumption choices. The new convention also includes the Rhône-Méditerranée-Corse water agency, which expects to benefit from additional saved volumes of water for the environment in order to reduce water deficit in the river basin.

Source: OECD (2015b), *Stakeholder Engagement for Inclusive Water Governance*, OECD Studies on Water, OECD Publishing, Paris. http://dx.doi.org/10.1787/9789264231122-en.

Stakeholder engagement for river basin adaptation to climate change, Canada

Between 2012 and 2014 the South Saskatchewan River Basin Adaptation to Climate Variability Project brought together regional water systems experts looking for opportunities to enhance the resiliency of the Bow and Oldman-South Saskatchewan river basins in Southern Alberta, Canada.

The project supports the notion that adaptation to future climate uncertainties and other environmental changes is key to ensuring environmental, economic and social prosperity, growth and sustainability. It builds on, and integrates, existing data, tools, and water use and decision-maker expertise to improve the knowledge base and to explore options to manage the range of potential impacts of climate variability in the river basin.

Stakeholder engagement was conducted on a voluntary basis and was supported by mechanisms such as collaborative modelling processes, using sophisticated simulation for modelling water systems. The modelling sessions integrated computer techniques and included over 80 years of historic data on water management structures and demands. Together with developing performance measures, they allowed parties to set common objectives and collaborate effectively to identify practical and implementable solutions to improve resilience and to adapt to current and future water challenges. Stakeholders involved in the project included governments and regulators, water institutions, civil society, business and farmers who were interested in the reliability and quality of raw water supply. It also comprised scientists and researchers that ensured scientific rigor and made the best information available for the project, as well as parliamentarians and municipalities that ensured that municipal water needs were properly taken into account. Since the completion of the project, stakeholder groups have been able to use the same model to discuss a series of flood mitigation options in the Bow river basin and the interactions between them with respect to water management in the basins.

Source: OECD (2015b), *Stakeholder Engagement for Inclusive Water Governance*, OECD Studies on Water, OECD Publishing, Paris. http://dx.doi.org/10.1787/9789264231122-en.

ORGANISATION FOR ECONOMIC CO-OPERATION AND DEVELOPMENT

The OECD is a unique forum where governments work together to address the economic, social and environmental challenges of globalisation. The OECD is also at the forefront of efforts to understand and to help governments respond to new developments and concerns, such as corporate governance, the information economy and the challenges of an ageing population. The Organisation provides a setting where governments can compare policy experiences, seek answers to common problems, identify good practice and work to co-ordinate domestic and international policies.

The OECD member countries are: Australia, Austria, Belgium, Canada, Chile, the Czech Republic, Denmark, Estonia, Finland, France, Germany, Greece, Hungary, Iceland, Ireland, Israel, Italy, Japan, Korea, Latvia, Lithuania, Luxembourg, Mexico, the Netherlands, New Zealand, Norway, Poland, Portugal, the Slovak Republic, Slovenia, Spain, Sweden, Switzerland, Turkey, the United Kingdom and the United States. The European Union takes part in the work of the OECD.

OECD Publishing disseminates widely the results of the Organisation's statistics gathering and research on economic, social and environmental issues, as well as the conventions, guidelines and standards agreed by its members.

OECD PUBLISHING, 2, rue André-Pascal, 75775 PARIS CEDEX 16
(97 2018 42 1 P) ISBN 978-92-64-30651-6 – 2018

www.ingramcontent.com/pod-product-compliance
Ingram Content Group UK Ltd.
Pitfield, Milton Keynes, MK11 3LW, UK
UKHW051503290926
15471UKWH00008B/1390

9 789264 306516